SHELVING DETAILS

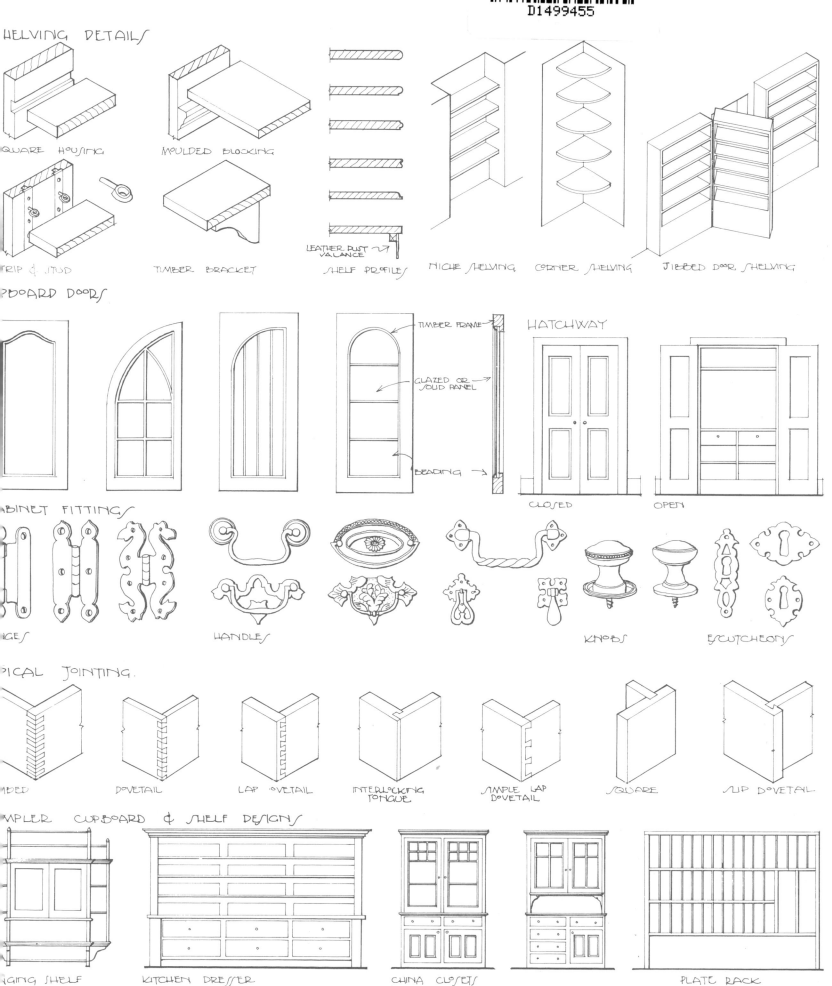

SQUARE HOUSING   MOULDED BLOCKING

STRIP & STUD   TIMBER BRACKET

LEATHER DUST VALANCE

SHELF PROFILES   NICHE SHELVING   CORNER SHELVING   JIBBED DOOR SHELVING

CUPBOARD DOORS

TIMBER FRAME

GLAZED OR SOLID PANEL

BEADING

HATCHWAY

CLOSED   OPEN

CABINET FITTINGS

HINGES   HANDLES   KNOBS   ESCUTCHEONS

TYPICAL JOINTING.

COMBED   DOVETAIL   LAP DOVETAIL   INTERLOCKING TONGUE   SIMPLE LAP DOVETAIL   SQUARE   SLIP DOVETAIL

SIMPLER CUPBOARD & SHELF DESIGNS

HANGING SHELF   KITCHEN DRESSER   CHINA CLOSETS   PLATE RACK

THE VICTORIAN HOUSE BOOK

The

VICTORIAN
HOUSE BOOK

A PRACTICAL GUIDE TO HOME REPAIR AND DECORATION

Robin Guild

FIREFLY BOOKS

A FIREFLY BOOK

Published by Firefly Books Ltd. 2008

First printing

Publisher Cataloging-in-Publication Data (U.S.)

Guild, Robin.
    The Victorian house book : a practical guide to home repair and decoration / Robin Guild.
Originally published: New York : Rizzoli, 1989.
[320] p. : ill., photos. (some col.) ;   cm.
Includes bibliographical references and index.
ISBN-13: 978-1-55407-371-9
ISBN-10: 1-55407-371-5
Summary: Comprehensive source book and guide to home repair and decoration during the Victorian period. Recreates the social history; describes the building methods; explains the original function of the fixtures and fittings; gives references for fireplaces, windows, doors, tiles, ironwork and plaster moldings; and charts the changing tastes in decoration and furnishings.
1. Architecture, Victorian—Themes, motives.
2. Architecture, Domestic—Themes, motives.
3. Decoration and ornament—Victorian style—Themes, motives. I. Title.
728/.09/034 dc22   NA7125.G853 2008

Library and Archives Canada Cataloguing in Publication

Guild, Robin
    The Victorian house book : a practical guide to home repair and decoration / Robin Guild ; editor: Simon Rigge ; US contributor: Virginia McAlester.
Includes bibliographical references and index.
ISBN-13: 978-1-55407-371-9
ISBN-10: 1-55407-371-5
    1. Architecture, Victorian–Conservation and restoration. 2. Architecture, Domestic—Conservation and restoration. 3. Decoration and ornament—Victorian style. 4. Historic buildings—Maintenance and repair. 5. Architecture—Details.
I. Rigge, Simon II. McAlester, Virginia, 1943–
III. Title.
NA7125.G85 2008   728'.370288   C2007-905190-1

Published in the United States by
Firefly Books (U.S.) Inc.
P.O. Box 1338, Ellicott Station
Buffalo, New York 14205

Published in Canada by
Firefly Books Ltd.
66 Leek Crescent
Richmond Hill, Ontario L4B 1H1

Printed in Singapore

For Sheldrake Press
Editor: Simon Rigge
Commissioning Editor: Diana Dubens
Deputy Editor: Antony Mason
Managing Editor: Susan Mitchell
General Consultant: Charles McKean
Contributing Editors: Francis Graham, Adam Hopkins
Assistant Editors: Chris Schler, Frances Kennett, Peter Brooke-Ball, Wendy Lee
Special Contributors: Gail Cotton, Stephen Hoare, Annie Sloan, Charles Brooking, Ian Hedley, Angela Burgin
Sub-Editors: Helen Ridge, Amanda Ronan, Marianne Ryan, Sue Midgley, Judith Hart, Linda Lambert, Valerie Bingham, Eric Smith, Ruth Burns
Editorial Assistants: Selina Akhtar, Eleanor Blatchley, Julia Churchill, Kathryn Cureton, Alessandra Falcone, Sophie Glass, Astrid Joublanc, Lalya Lloyd, Matthew McCann, Vera Pirri, Emma Rigge, Amelia Rowland, Tracey Stead
Researcher: Kieran Costello
Indexer: Valerie Chandler
Picture Editor: Eleanor Lines
Picture Co-ordinator: Anna Smith
Picture Researchers: Jane Lewis, Philippa Lewis, Irene Lynch
Picture Assistants: Linda Bassett, Harriet Peel, Sarah Tudge
Art Direction: Bob Hook, Ivor Claydon
Designers: Caroline Helfer, Nic Bellenberg
Photographers: James Mortimer, Ken Kirkwood, Derry Moore, Peter Woloszynski, George Ong, Robin McCartney
Illustrators: Black and white line drawings in Chapters 1-7 by Nigel Husband and Stephen Carpenter, Chapter 8 by Ian Sime, color illustrations by Ann Winterbotham
Production Manager: Hugh Allan
Production Controllers: Rebecca Bone, Helen Seccombe

CONSULTANTS

Virginia and Lee McAlester are the authors of the award-winning book, *A Field Guide to American Houses* (Alfred A. Knopf, 1984), as well as *Great American Houses and their Architectural Styles* (Abbeville, 1994), *Home in the Park Cities* (University of Texas Press, 2008) and other books and articles on American architectural and urban history.
    Virginia is an Advisor Emeritus for the National Trust for Historic Preservation and is an ardent advocate of architectural conservation and historically sensitive restoration. Her husband Lee, a geologist with an avocational interest in the built environment, joins in many of her undertakings.

Front cover This elaborate Gothic marble fireplace is one of the newly installed period fixtures that embellish a small Victorian country house decorated by Robin Guild.
End-Papers The line drawings which are reproduced here and complement the text and photographs in Chapters 1 to 7 are by the architects Nigel Husband and Stephen Carpenter.
Half-title page The main bathroom in a Victorian Gothic country house has the benefit of space, which allows it to be used as a comfortable family room. Medicine cabinets have been created by recessing a pair of Gothic-shaped cupboards into the wall on either side of the main window.
Frontispiece Built-in cabinets with mirrors have been added to match the original detailing of this Gothic house and increase the sense of space in an upstairs passageway. The walls have been decorated with a faded stencil effect.

NOTICE

This book has been written for all who own Victorian houses or are interested in them. Some homeowners who are skilled in do-it-yourself techniques may use the information in the book to carry out their own projects, but we have assumed that most will use the professional services of architects, engineers, surveyors and builders. The author, editors and publishers have gone to great pains to ensure that the information given in the book is accurate and reliable. We cannot accept liability for damage, mishap or injury caused by anyone attempting to carry out projects described in the book without professional advice, nor can we be held responsible for any contravention of building regulations, which must be checked by the homeowner before alterations are made to the fabric of a house.

CONTENTS

PREFACE

Architecture is a vulnerable art; like the landscape, it is subject to meddling by succeeding generations. In this respect, music and literature are more fortunate, for however much abuse or neglect they may receive, the essential integrity of the original will probably survive. This is not at all the case with buildings, and very few houses over a hundred years old have survived unaltered. In many cases, the effects of weather and pollution – together with the additions, alterations and repairs made by several generations of inhabitants – have changed them to such an extent that their builders would have difficulty in recognizing them.

The United States still affords little protection to historic buildings, even those landmarks that are listed on the National Register of Historic Places. Ownership normally confers the right to pull down anything considered obsolete or which stands in the way of future development. In contrast, Britain began serious preservation many decades ago. Starting with Scotland in 1933 and followed by England, Wales and Northern Ireland in 1947, buildings of architectural importance began to be surveyed and actively protected from unsympathetic changes or demolition. For this preservation attitude the British must thank William Morris, the instigator in 1877 of the Society for the Protection of Ancient Buildings. True, Morris would probably not have cared much if all the houses of the 18th century had been pulled down, but at least he brought to public attention the state of many medieval buildings which were then suffering serious neglect or were threatened with demolition.

Although we think of ourselves as more enlightened today, our aesthetic vandalism is more insidious. If a roof needed retiling in the 19th century, the chances are that the replacements would have been made of the same clay – or even in the same kiln – as the originals. The brick and stone, and even the mortar used for pointing, may all have come from local clay beds, kilns and quarries; the building materials quite literally arose from the surrounding landscape, and blended naturally with those of neighboring buildings.

Nowadays there are countless substitutes on the market, and nearly all of them are visually inferior to the originals. A glance down any Victorian street will illustrate this sad decline. The roofline will probably have suffered most, with slates replaced by asbestos shingles and cast-iron gutters by plastic ones. Nor will the façades have survived unscathed; good brickwork may have been painted over or repointed in coarse cement, and wood sashes may have given way to aluminum-framed or plastic-coated windows.

Opposite: The rich glow of stained glass in this very British Victorian doorway offers a warm welcome and the promise of comfort, security and good cheer – qualities which are leading more and more home buyers to turn to period housing.

PREFACE

Opposite: A new conservatory has been built onto a Victorian detatched house. It is an assured and confident construction, while remaining entirely in keeping with the rest of the building. The geometric tiles and the cast-iron brackets bear witness to the upsurge of small firms willing to make authentic reproductions of 19th-century fittings.

Each age works within the cost limits and technology of its time. The industrial components of the suppliers – concrete tiles, plastic rain-water goods, mass-produced bricks and blocks, metal windows, flush doors and building boards – can be seen as the only architectural currency capable of satisfying present housing demands. Houses built of these new materials are truly houses of today, and for better or worse, homes throughout the country reflect their dubious standards. Unfortunately these same materials are quite unsuitable for repairing and restoring the older housing stock in which a large proportion of us still have to live, or choose to live.

The building heritage of the United States may be divided into four periods: pre-1830; the loosely categorized Victorian period, extending from the 1830's to the outbreak of World War I (1914-18); "between-the-wars;" and the post-war period from 1945 to the present day. Pre-Victorian buildings represent a very small percentage of the private housing stock. A look at properties in Cambridge, Massachusetts or Alexandria, Virginia will confirm that in urban areas Georgian and Federal houses are highly sought-after and well beyond the reach of most buyers. In smaller towns, however, they may still be found at more realistic prices.

The housing of the inter-war period continued the themes of the turn of the century; it drew on the aesthetics of the Garden Suburb Movement and drew from newly published books of photographs and details of European houses to build handsome adaptations. The location of many of these houses, in well planned, close-in suburbs, makes them attractive to those who prefer contact with city life. In much post-war housing, these standards have been reduced to the absolute minimum. With the aesthetics of the Modern Movement, they house people; they keep them warm and dry, and as such they have a respectable function.

For many people, however, this is not enough. More and more of us are coming to appreciate the character and craftsmanship of older houses, to value the special atmosphere of a place that has been lived in for generations and to take pleasure in the wealth of architectural detail so lacking in more modern homes. And of the earlier housing stock, a large and accessible proportion will have been built in the 19th century. In the United States alone, it is estimated that more than five million houses were built during Queen Victoria's reign.

"Victorian" – the very word that was shunned for years by real-estate agents – has now become a positive selling adjective. This has its ironic and even absurd aspects, but it is also an accurate gauge of public opinion. Real-estate agents may like to believe that they lead trends, but in reality they merely reflect the changes in public taste. In the United States, in Britain and on the Continent,

Above: In an exciting combination of modern spatial planning and period detail, a light well has been artfully created in a second-floor landing and fenced with a reproduction Victorian balustrade to create a feeling of space; metal balusters, such as those seen here, were much more common in Britain than in the United States.

the real trendsetters have been artists, followed by architects and craftsmen. Greenwich Village, Chelsea and the Left Bank were all infiltrated by artists and poorer professionals such as architects, who wanted homes with some character and were able and willing to renovate a run-down property. They created a pleasant and lively atmosphere which attracted the richer professionals and pseudo-artists – lawyers, bankers, advertisers and public relations people. In due course, the new arrivals pushed up the prices, forcing the artists to look elsewhere; in London the move was northwards to Islington, in New York to SoHo, and in both these districts the pattern is now repeating itself.

Nostalgia may be an element of the charm which Victorian buildings hold for us, but it can be a misleading quality. We can only see Victorian houses through 21st-century eyes, and cannot transport ourselves back to the aesthetic, moral and social climate of more than a hundred years ago, any more than the Victorians could feel empathy with the Georgian era. Their dislike of 18th-century architecture was echoed in our own age by the condemnation of Victorian taste by many "enlightened" people until quite recently.

This was a natural enough reaction. The generation which knew at first hand the darker side of 19th-century life – the grinding drudgery of factory life or the suffocating respectability of a middle-class Sunday – felt little nostalgia for the period. After World War I, the blueprint for the Modern Movement in architecture – often called the International Style – was drawn up. Its basic tenets – austerity, the absence of ornament and the simple lines created by the machine tool – were the antithesis of everything Victorian architecture stood for. The widespread building after World War II allowed the architects of the International Style to put their ideas into practice on a large scale, and the urban renewal that followed saw many old buildings swept away as the impractical, squalid survivors of a recent, unloved past.

With the passage of time, however, the art and architecture of the Victorian age can be reviewed in a more sympathetic light. The new theories, case studies and aesthetic polemics have failed to solve the problems of society, and are actually felt by many to have aggravated them. High-rise building has come to be seen by some as a blight on the landscape, a hostile and impersonal environment that does little to foster human values or community spirit. Victorian houses, in contrast, no longer strike us as gloomy and forbidding but as cozy and cheerful.

The appeal of 19th-century housing is based on much more than bricks and mortar, but a house must, first and foremost, provide a sound and practical place in which to live. There are people in England who have turned the restoration of their Victorian house into a rigorously purist exercise, creating something akin to a museum-piece, but in the end they are left in a period cocoon. Their gaslight, coal boilers, tub baths and belfast sinks may be irreproachable, but nothing will stop the world going on its way outside. Cars will pass in the street, not carriages, and their children will come in wearing jeans, not pinafores.

What is important today is not so much the pursuit of total authenticity as finding a balance which reconciles our own way of living with what is valuable in Victorian style and decoration. Gaslight, with its gentle hiss and mellow tone, is most attractive, but electricity is more convenient; Victorians would not have used a coffee table, but having one may suit the way we live. The degree to which we shape a period house to modern requirements is a highly individual matter; to accomplish this with tact and sensitivity does not require textbook knowledge so much as a feel for Victoriana that can be acquired through familiarity.

This book is intended to give the reader just such an acquaintance with the developments of Victorian style. Our aim has been to show what Victorian houses were like, and why, and to show

how they may be adapted to modern living without loss of character. The photographs illustrate houses that have been decorated in a wide variety of Victorian fashions and complementary modern styles. The black and white line illustrations give accurate details of a huge range of Victorian hardware, woodwork, plaster moldings, door furniture and other fittings and furnishings.

The chapters lead you through the house, from its foundations to the decorative details of each room. The information is organized in approximately the order that a homeowner contemplating a plan of repair and decoration will find useful – background history in Chapter 1, structural and building information in Chapter 2, interior architectural detailing in Chapter 3, followed by decoration of the public and private rooms in Chapters 4, 5 and 6. Finally, Chapter 7 takes you out into the garden. Technical advice is given in Chapter 8 for those who want to undertake restoration work themselves, or want to be able to talk to architects, surveyors and builders on something like equal terms. A list of suppliers provides information on where to find period fittings and decorations, both genuine antiques and authentic reproductions. Nothing demonstrates better the renewed interest in Victorian domestic architecture than the resurgence of manufacturers, craft studios and designers covering virtually every aspect of period restoration.

This book is itself an expression of that renewed interest, and is addressed to all those who, disillusioned by sterile modernism, are seeking to make their home into a haven; not a precious or purist re-creation of the past, but a shelter in the best sense of the word, comfortable and welcoming.

Above: This ceramic fireplace – a stunning example of French Art Nouveau at its most luxuriant – would probably have shocked the original owners of the English Victorian house in which it has now been installed.

Below: Part of a modern addition to a Victorian house, this lancet-shaped doorway with its two flanking niches adeptly revives the Gothic Revival – a clever *jeu d'esprit* in the spirit of postmodernism.

Left: The columns and capitals of this beautiful drawing room fireplace, executed in three different types of marble, show the Victorian love of Early English Gothic.

Chapter One

THE VICTORIAN
INSPIRATION

All generations see themselves as modern. Our local geography bears witness to this harmless vanity in such now venerable names as New York, New Mexico, New Orleans, or New Jersey as well as in Britain's countless Newports, Newtowns, New Streets or Newchurches, most of them christened in the Middle Ages. Nevertheless, in looking back over the Victorian age it is impossible not to be struck by a truly new kind of modernism, one born out of the Industrial Revolution that created changes so profound and irrevocable that it was soon clear that the world would never be quite the same again. Some of the liveliest and most brilliant minds of the time celebrated and reveled in the possibilities of new technology while others, equally gifted, found its prospects frightening. This divergence of intelligent opinion has persisted, and even deepened, in our own times as the full effects of man's superiority over the natural world unravel.

The most profound social effect of the Industrial Revolution was to draw workers from the countryside into the towns where new industries – textile mills, coal mines, iron foundries, and so on – were being established. Coal, iron machinery and steam power, in turn, made possible an expanding network of railroads which completed the cycle by bringing coal, the essential fuel, into regions where it was scarce to provide power for still more new industry.

Before this time the outskirts of most towns had been subordinate to the nucleus itself, or else were strung in chains of villages like those that surrounded Boston or London in the 18th century. Now towns began to grow by accretion around their perimeter, particularly along connecting roads and railroads. The suburb had arrived and with it a new middle class whose mobility linked the city's fringes with the commerce and government of the central core.

As urban land acquired new value for building sites the developer made his appearance. Architects, surveyors and engineers formed professional associations to consolidate and protect their interests. The days of the amateur building designer working with a skilled master carpenter or mason were numbered. Building regulations inevitably followed; rules to improve drainage and water supply and to make buildings structurally sounder and more healthy were introduced.

Opposite: "The Hall and Staircase of a Country House" by Jonathan Pratt, 1882, depicts the vitality of the High Victorian era. With its Gothic arches, stained-glass windows, elaborate iron balusters, and the clutter of interesting objects from a wide variety of sources, this hall in its day would have seemed the epitome of modern taste.

Above: Transitional well-to-do British town housing from the middle of the century continues the stucco Italianate tradition, a style about to give way to the more severe all-brick treatment glimpsed further down the street.

Above: Built for mill workers, rows like this raw brick housing in Oldham covered miles of the industrial heartlands of Britain. The façades are functional, for financial reasons. The sole concession to decoration can be seen in chamfered reveals to windows and lintels.

The industrial age also led to a profound change in the nature of architectural fashions. In the 18th century and before, building design changed very slowly and a single favored style, Georgian for example, remained the dominant fashion for many decades. During the 19th century, mass-production of building materials, particularly factory-made doors, windows and other architectural details, first made it possible for designers to choose from a range of historical building styles. Equally importantly, components from different periods could now be combined to create new eclectic fashions, and these were encouraged by improved printing techniques which produced illustrated books and a growing flood of magazines showing fashionable new designs. As a result, Victoria's long reign was not dominated by a more or less unified building style, as with the several Kings George who preceded her, but by a competing plethora of historical revivals and newly designed "modern" styles.

For simplicity, these 19th-century styles may be divided into three large and sometimes overlapping categories based on the architectural traditions that inspired them – classical, medieval or modern. The classical styles derived from the architecture of ancient Greece and Rome, and from the re-interpretation of those forms in the Renaissance; the medieval were based upon Gothic church architecture and early manor house building; and the modern styles variously redefined or abandoned these historical precedents in order to create something distinctively new. Each category had its outspoken proponents – critics and designers who marshaled their troops for an artistic "Battle of Styles," that raged throughout the Victorian era. In spite of periodic major victories and long intervals of armed truce, this bloodless war still continues today with no armistice in sight.

Through much of the Victorian period, architectural fashion leaders in the United States drew their battle plans from across the Atlantic, particularly from Britain. American stylistic trends thus generally parallel those of Britain through the 19th century, but with each new fashion typically beginning somewhat later and sometimes diverging in directions that differed sharply from contemporary British practice.

These transatlantic similarities and differences are further obscured by somewhat different systems of nomenclature in the two regions. The British, quite naturally, use their ruling monarchs as a kind of historical shorthand, a system that rapidly fell from favor in her former colonies after 1776. British Late Georgian and Regency fashions, for example, are known in America as the "Federal" style. This trend continued until the last decades of the century when Queen Victoria, by then much beloved everywhere, again captured the hearts of her former subjects.

In both countries it is convenient to divide the 19th century into 25-year segments which broadly define four great periods of changing architectural fashion. The first quarter of the century was effectively the final phase of the Renaissance, those rigidly balanced and symmetrical designs of classical inspiration that had dominated Europe for hundreds of years. In Britain this interval is known as the "Regency" period, after young George IV who served as Prince Regent for his incapacitated father before ascending to the throne in 1820. In the United States this is the last phase of the Federal period of architectural fashion.

Federal architecture drew heavily on the formal, balanced

Below: This 1860-ish home in Washington D.C. owes much to the Second Empire style which was transforming Paris. Popular with Americans, it also borrowed details from the contemporaneous Italianate style.

Below: The low-pitched roof and simple upper windows of this middle-class house in South London could be almost Regency – the bay windows and chunky porch below indicate that the building is later, if only by a decade.

Right: This cheerful Italianate house in Savannah, Georgia, has some Gothic influence in the quatrefoils (four-leafed clover shapes) in its porch decoration. The dark paint against a light background is unexpected but effective.

Above: Sunlight is an essential ingredient for this generous American verandah. The mixture of wood and cast iron combine to create a deck like an ocean cruiser's, with complementary furniture. The deep overhang is only practicable for hot summers.

Right: As a contrast, this High Victorian interior in Castell Coch, Cardiff, is completely inward-looking. Designed by the extraordinary architect William Burges for Lord Bute, this bedroom for Lady Bute was never actually used. Understandably perhaps, for while the conception is dazzling, the end result is hardly cozy. It is an interior which represents the very peak of medieval fantasy, all paid for out of the profits from the Cardiff docks.

designs of the preceding Georgian style but differed in scale and subtlety of architectural detail. Windows were larger while doorways had smaller and more delicate decorative surrounds than did Georgian entryways. The most dramatic decorative changes, however, came in Federal interiors. Formerly sedate mantels, ceilings and cornices sprouted light-hearted swags, garlands and friezes, loosely based on Greek and Roman prototypes, which had become the popular rage in Britain. The principal advocates of this new fashion were two Scottish architects, the brothers Robert and James Adam, who reached the pinnacle of their profession in 1761 when Robert was appointed "Architect of the King's Works." Because of its similar roots, the American Federal style is generally considered to be merely the New World phase of the British "Adam" style which slightly preceded it.

Adam-based designs dominated the United States from the 1780's through the 1820's but in Britain they were supplanted after 1800 by a related fashion that has no direct American counterpart. This is the delightful "Regency" style which dominated British housing during the period from about 1810 to 1830.

Regency designs grew from an important technological advance that first made its appearance in the late 18th century. This invention was Coade Stone, a complicated formula devised to make an artificial stone which could be applied outside and would last without damage from the weather. In other words, it served outside as plaster had done for many years inside.

Smaller Georgian houses had, for the most part, been simple boxes, decorations being limited to carved doorcases and cornices. Only grand houses could afford the luxury of extensive carving in wood or stone. Now mass-produced decorative features could be incorporated at low cost, and these were eagerly seized upon by developers and architects. Stucco followed close upon Coade Stone. Since Roman times, walls had been rendered, that is coated, with layers of a mixture of lime and sand, the ingredients of brickwork mortar. In about 1800 a new "Roman cement," much stronger than the traditional lime, was introduced followed shortly by Portland cement, a still stronger material (later used in concrete), developed in 1825. These new materials made possible stucco rendering, a finish which could be painted, and which was taken up enthusiastically by British Regency architects, including John Nash, famous for his grand terraces round Regent's Park in London. A contemporary jingle ran: "John Nash, that very great master, who found us all brick and who left us all plaster."

In the years between 1800 and 1830 some of the simplest and most beautiful houses in Britain were built with stucco rendering, to provide a masterful synthesis of flat painted surfaces set against simple rectangular or round-headed openings, exquisitely balanced in proportion and in terms of light and shade. Elegant ironwork created a decorative tracery against these painted walls, whose charm and simplicity are particularly appealing to the modern eye. Today these Regency houses are among Britain's most esteemed designs from the 19th century.

In summary, then, during the first decades of the 19th century housing designs on both sides of the Atlantic – "Federal" in the United States and "Regency" in Britain – were final refinements of the Renaissance-inspired Georgian fashions of the 1700's. This was changing by 1830 as revolutionary new architectural trends began to spread on both sides of the Atlantic. In Britain, a revolt against the formal classicism of Renaissance design, which had been simmering in the background for many decades, burst into full flame as informal "Picturesque" designs, loosely based on rambling medieval manors or quaint Italian farmhouses, suddenly became the fashion rage. By 1845 the Queen herself had begun a new seaside residence, Osborne House on the Isle of Wight, in the new "Italian Villa" style. Most of her contemporaries, however, preferred more familiar examples from medieval England and it was these informal "Gothick" designs, as they came to be called, that dominated English domestic building during the Early Victorian period.

During this same period, from about 1825 to 1850, American domestic design took a sharp divergence from British practice. Instead of becoming less classical after the Renaissance-inspired Georgian fashions of the 1700's, American housing turned back to Greece, the original font of all classicism; Greek revival houses, many with colonnaded façades that closely mimicked Greek temples, became the dominant national style. At about the same time a related movement in Britain and on the Continent led to numerous Greek-inspired public buildings and row house terraces, but only in the United States did mock classical temples, mostly built of wood, dominate the design of single family dwellings.

British and American housing fashions again converged in the third quarter of the century. By the 1840's the Picturesque movement – previously popularized in Britain through the prolific writings of John C. Loudon (1783–1843), a landscape designer turned architect and fashion arbiter – was similarly being spread in the United States, here largely through the efforts of Andrew Jackson Downing (1815–52) who leaned heavily on Loudon's ideas and shared with him a background in landscape design.

Downing's father was a Newburgh, New York nurseryman whose trade served many wealthy clients with estates bordering the scenic Hudson River valley. From an early age Andrew's interests grew beyond the mere supply of plant materials and as a very young man he became a sought-after local expert on landscape design, a profession that was then in its infancy in this country. Inspired by Loudon's example, Downing wrote a less comprehensive work

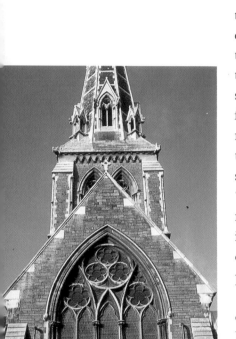

Saint Giles, Camberwell, in London, built in 1844, is one of the first and most muscular Gothic revival churches by the young Gilbert Scott. This serious and committed return to Gothic form (here Early English) coincides with two decades of religious turmoil and renewal among the English middle classes.

Above: As early as 1750 Horace Walpole was contemplating ideas for one of the first Gothick houses (as opposed to garden buildings or follies) in England. Strawberry Hill, Twickenham, was the result. The vaulting, based on Henry VII's chapel at Westminster (but translated into plaster), is enchanting; indeed the early 16th-century masons might have found its flamboyance nearer their taste than Gilbert Scott's severe exercise opposite.

Top: Unraveling the details of this wooden confection in Georgia, one discovers elements of classical, Gothic, Saracenic and oriental precedents.

Above: John Rylands Library, Manchester, built by Basil Champneys in 1890–1900, is a superb high-style example of the Victorian Gothic tradition.

Left: Heywood, Wiltshire, dates from 1869, an assured neo-Jacobean house with intricate gables and chimneys which create a lively skyline.

21

entitled *Treatise on the Theory and Practice of Landscape Gardening Adapted to North America* in which he advocated naturalistic planning. This first appeared in 1841, when he was 26. In a concluding chapter he illustrated several picturesque Gothic revival or Italianate villas that he felt made appropriate centerpieces for his landscape designs.

The following year Downing published a second work, *Cottage Residences*, which reversed the emphasis by giving plans, renderings and discussions of fifteen picturesque dwellings with only an abbreviated discussion of landscaping. These works captured the popular fancy and were reprinted in many editions over the next decades. In 1850 Downing published a longer and more mature treatise, *The Architecture of Country Houses,* in which he expanded the coverage to 31 house plans and also included chapters on interior design, furnishings and other aspects of domestic art.

This book was to reach a still larger audience over the next decades, partly as a result of the author's heroic early death in 1852. While traveling with his wife and baby along their beloved Hudson River, the steamboat captain indulged in the popular but dangerous sport of racing a passing rival. Fire quickly spread from the overheated boiler and, as a result, the vessel sank. Mrs Downing was saved, but her unfortunate husband was last seen throwing wooden chairs from the burning decks in an attempt to save drowning passengers in the water below.

Above: The Egyptian House in Penzance, by the Plymouth-based architect, George Wightwick, is a Regency excursion into one of the exotic styles which so entertained both architects and patrons in the early part of the century. By contrast the fantasies of the Victorians tended to more traditional influences.

Right: The Gothic revival style is given a thoroughly ecclesiastical treatment at Holly Lodge in Highgate, London.

Above: One of the most charming manifestations of early 19th-century romanticism resulted in these estate cottages at Blaise Hamlet, near Bristol, designed by John Nash for a local landowner. Some are thatched, others – like the example here – tiled in stone. Many of these vernacular features were rediscovered later in the century by architects on both sides of the Atlantic.

Left: This neo-Norman castle was built by Sir Robert Smirke at Eastnor, Herefordshire, in 1812. Although picturesque in outline, a classical discipline is evident beneath: not surprising from the hand that designed the British Museum, although Smirke seems to have retained a special fondness for the romantic in country commissions.

Above: The door to a kitchen garden, heavily embellished with Gothick detail, provides an unexpected sense of romance and history to intrigue the visitor on a tour of the grounds.

A later colonial mansion in South Africa with both Italianate and Gothic revival elements, uses mass-produced ornaments from the builder's catalog to decorate the wide verandah. The design is intended to provide an interior coolness and shaded sitting areas.

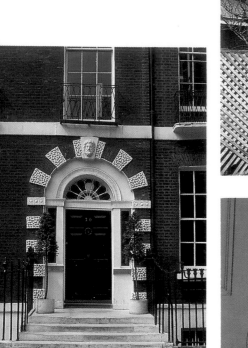

Above: Bedford Square, London, built in 1775, may be described as high-quality developer's Georgian. The vermiculated quoins and voussoirs round the door are in Coade Stone. With the invention of Portland cement, cheap stucco decorations similar to these proliferated in the 19th century. The 18th-century squares and terraces of London's Bloomsbury were admired by British Victorians for their construction and interior detailing.

This typical Victorian embellishment was made of stucco or artificial stone, and painted. Precedents for these features are obscure, but they probably derive from plates taken from one of the many mid-century pattern books.

Osborne House on the Isle of Wight was designed by Prince Albert and built in 1850 by Thomas Cubitt, the London builder. The Prince Consort chose to employ the famous builder rather than an architect in order that he himself should have a free hand in the design and decoration of the royal home. The Italianate style remained popular in Britain and the United States for both houses and public buildings.

At the time of his death, Downing's writings had made him a national celebrity; he was then engaged in designing both New York's Central Park and a revised Capitol Mall in Washington, D.C. Both projects were finished by others but his lasting monument was to be his influence on domestic architecture. By 1850 Downing-inspired Gothic revival and Italianate designs were rapidly replacing Greek revival houses as the dominant American housing fashions, a trend that persisted into the 1880's. This is known as the "Romantic" phase of 19th-century American architecture.

In the United States, Italianate designs were to become far more common than Gothic, whose pointed windows, complex shapes and elaborate decorative detailing were difficult to execute in wood which was then, as today, the dominant American house-building material. In Britain, on the other hand, the third quarter of the century is known as the "High Victorian" era and was the apex of Gothic-inspired design. Earlier "Gothick" houses had been rather loosely based on their medieval precursors but beginning about 1847, when the first phase of London's new Houses of Parliament was completed in formal Gothic style, more authentic medieval designs, drawing on both English and continental precedents, became the dominant theme of British architecture. Chief among the protagonists of this British movement were A.W.N. Pugin (1812–52) who as a young architect helped with the design of the new Houses of Parliament, and John Ruskin (1819–1900), writer and critic whose popular books romanticized the medieval past as the ideal model for contemporary living.

Pugin first worked as an assistant in the firm of the distinguished architect Charles Barry, whose Gothic designs had won an international competition for the new Houses of Parliament. The exact contribution Pugin made to the competition designs has been debated; what is certain is that he had almost complete control over the interior furnishings. To Pugin, Gothic represented the culmination of craftsman and builder working together for the glory of God. The Renaissance, based on pagan forms and heartless geometry, was anathema. Pugin himself had assisted his father in the production of books of measured drawings, *Specimens* and *Examples of Gothic Architecture*, and followed this up with fanciful cityscapes depicting classical forms opposed to Gothic ones, the former miserable, ugly and debased, the latter beautiful and flourishing, with men free to work together for the common good. It was all, of course, a delightful fraud, a sentimental misinterpretation of building in the Middle Ages. There was, in reality, little real freedom of craftsmanship for the men quarrying and carrying stone, or for the masons shaping standard shafts for cathedral columns. In all architecture there is much repetitive work and even more sheer hard labor, the drudgery of which is overlooked in the glory of the completed statement.

Above: Carlton House Terrace, London, was built in the 1830's and 1840's by John Nash. The use he made of stucco was bold and individual. Many of his contemporaries frowned on the material, yet his skill in creating dramatic monuments out of brick and plaster bequeathed to London row housing of lasting value.

Opposite: A detail of the Speaker's House in London's Palace of Westminster reveals the hand of A.W.N. Pugin who was made responsible for much of the interior design. The quality of workmanship is self-evident.

With Pugin the Victorian Gothic house had arrived too; his St Marie's Grange, built for his own use near Salisbury, was finished in about 1835. For such an archetypal Victorian building this is an astonishing date; it could well have been built, without arousing comment, at any time over the next 50 years. In it are combined all the major characteristics of the "new" Gothic style: asymmetry, picturesque silhouette, texture and variety of material. It was according to its architect, "the only modern building complete in every part in the ancient style," that is, of the 15th century. To modern eyes St Marie's Grange looks like a gentleman's country residence and not an ancient manor, however scrupulous its ancient detailing. No matter, it is a fascinating building in spite of the perversity of its plan and idiosyncrasy of its concept, features which conspired to make it hard to sell in later years.

Ruskin, who never openly acknowledged his obvious debt to Pugin, continued the same medievalist line. In 1849, the year after his marriage, he went on a second honeymoon to Venice. He fell in love with the city and from this visit resulted, in 1851, *The Stones of Venice.* It is curious to reflect how a chance foreign trip could change the face of English architecture, but that is what happened.

Ruskin was acute enough to realize that the outward features of Gothic were not, by themselves, important. "The shape of the arch," he wrote, "is irrelevant." What mattered was that the craftsman should be free to express himself unfettered by outworn classical orders and ornaments. The craftsman working on his own, or as a participant in a small studio, is generally considered to be happier, more fulfilled, than his counterpart at a factory bench. The mistake the Ruskinians made was to believe that the whole accelerating process of industrialism, well under way by mid-century, could be reversed by dogma; that a half-understood picture of medieval society could actually turn back, let alone withstand, the pressures of mass-production. The truth was that artist–craftsmen were a dying breed and were to survive only as a gifted few, patronized by an elite and for the most part ignored by others except at second and third hand. This indeed is the unhappy situation that has continued unchanged to our own day.

By the last quarter of the century, the period Americans most closely associate with the term "Victorian," design trends on either side of the Atlantic were again diverging. During the 1870's the influential British "Arts and Crafts" Movement, an elaboration and extension of Ruskin's romantic ideals, became the new fashion rage. Partly a reaction against the standardized manufacture of the Industrial Age, and partly a protest against the decorative excesses of High Victorian design, this movement stressed hand-crafted decorative objects and a return to less complex historical precedents. Its principal champion was William Morris

(1834–1896) – designer, artist, poet and socialist – a true visionary whose ideas were to dominate British fashion for several decades.

Morris worked tirelessly to improve the standard of everyday design which, as a young man, he had despised at the flamboyant "Crystal Palace" Exhibition, in London, of 1851. "Have nothing in your home which you do not know to be useful or believe to be beautiful," he wrote. To this end Morris established craft workshops to put his principles into practice. He and his collaborators searched for pre-industrial forms of furniture and tapestries which they developed with their own distinctive idiom.

Morris was primarily concerned with the decorative arts and interior design but he also inspired a group of young architects who translated his ideas into the design of buildings. The most influential of these British Arts and Crafts architects was Richard Norman Shaw (1831–1912).

Shaw, who was to become one of the most popular and prolific designers of fashionable late Victorian houses, played a seminal role in the two sub-movements that came to dominate British domestic architecture of the period. Shaw's superb and widely reproduced architectural drawings have been credited with popularizing what became known as the "Old English" phase of the Arts and Crafts Movement. This drew inspiration from the picturesque steep-gabled and half-timbered town halls and manor houses of late medieval England. These were variously reinterpreted in an attempt to emphasize their pre-industrial and "hand-made" qualities. Shaw is still more closely associated with the second or "Queen Anne" theme of Arts and Crafts design. Loosely drawing on precedents from the early 18th century, Queen Anne architecture stressed a free and creative interplay of both medieval and Renaissance design elements. Typically, steep-roofed medieval forms with tall chimneys and projecting towers were used with regular rows of large sash windows of Georgian inspiration. Red brick accentuated by sharply contrasting white window surrounds and decorative bands was the favored wall treatment. The stylistic freedom of Queen Anne design led to still more revolutionary developments in Britain during the 1890's. Rather than mixing historical shapes and decorative detailing, creative architects began to experiment with stylized exaggeration of medieval shapes, and with a sharp reduction or even elimination of all decorative details. Clean stucco walls with a minimum of decorative detail were favored as a means of emphasizing these striking new designs, which provided England with the first glimpse of the new modernism that was to flourish in the next century. This last phase of the British Arts and Crafts Movement has been aptly named the "Free Style" and among its most distinguished practitioners were C.F.A. Voysey (1857–1941), Charles Rennie Mackintosh (1868–1928) and Edwin L. Lutyens (1869–1944).

(continued on page 34)

Left: Rows of late Victorian houses like this may be found in British and older American cities. Though despised by architects and many Victorian critics, these streets fulfilled a social and economic need, making affordable housing available for the ever-expanding middle classes.

Far left: A plate from Ruskin's *The Stones of Venice* illustrates an arch he describes in detail over three pages. Not only a persuasive writer of prose, Ruskin was also a fine draftsman; many of the plates from *The Stones of Venice* are by his own hand.

Left: An example of mass-produced decoration in a London street owes its origin to *The Stones of Venice.* Ruskin spent much of his middle life in the suburbs of South London surrounded by middle-class row housing finished with this kind of ornamentation, copied from illustrations to his books.

EARLY VICTORIAN SEMI-DETACHED

English cottages of *c*.1840's. The classical tradition still dominant. Rectangular box-like form follows the standard Regency villa, now divided into two semi-detached dwellings. Simple play of solid and void in keeping with Georgian architectural ideas. Applied decoration in artificial stone around windows and doors.

FLAT-FRONTED ROW HOUSE

Standard laborers' housing. In America found primarily in the cities of the Northeast and industrial Midwest. Built inexpensively to meet the housing needs of the workforce; front door alone allows for any individual treatment.

ITALIANATE VILLA

Italianate styles popular from 1845 to 1870; A. J. Downing's influence made the Italianate villa the favored suburban style. The stuccoed first floor highlights the equivalent of a *piano nobile* of the Italian villa or palazzo. Roof-line brackets given a picturesque emphasis.

BRICK GOTHIC REVIVAL

Standard house with Tudor dressings and Gothic asymmetrical plan. Roof given steep pitch and spiky details to suggest the vertical lift of medieval domestic architecture. Character comes from the use of historical detailings selectively deployed, such as Tudor-arched entry.

THE NEW YORK BROWNSTONE

Standard form of mid-century speculative housing on Eastern seaboard of the United States. Italianate palazzo design in a row house form. Round-arched windows and double front doors are typical.

APARTMENT HOUSE
Apartment buildings, traditional in Scotland and on the Continent. This English version, known by the nickname Pont Street Dutch, is built of red brick with white-painted Queen Anne windows; buildings of this type began to appear in England after the 1870's.

CARPENTER'S GOTHIC
Original American style of building dependent on the plenteous timber and space of the United States. Decorative Gothic forms, often taken from pattern books, re-interpreted in wood. Timber-based house construction kept alive by a very high standard of carpentry in North America.

MIDDLE-CLASS ROW HOUSES

Built in England from 1880's onwards, following success of the Utopian London suburb of Bedford Park. Queen Anne style dominant: red brick, white woodwork, smaller panes for upper part of the windows, Dutch or Flemish door surround. Flemish strap-work on gable end.

THE ARTS AND CRAFTS COTTAGE

As developed in further suburban zones and garden cities. Stuccoed walls with stone dressing. Strong horizontal lines create an artificially low, cottage look. Given artful informal character by its asymmetry. In America this led to the popular early 20th century Tudor style.

AMERICAN QUEEN ANNE HOUSE

The American vernacular from 1885 to 1905. Asymmetrical with high-pitched roof, front porch and ornamental shingles. Turned spindlework porch supports shown here were supplanted by classical columns in examples built after 1895. Bold paint colors were widely used during the era.

C F.A. Voysey embarked on his architectural career during an economic recession. Because of the scarcity of jobs, his older friends advised him to try his hand at decoration and interior design, which he did with great flair. When architectural commissions came in later, he took as his inspiration the English small manor house and cottage, and in a sense he reduced all his designs, however big, to this simple model. The house, he maintained, should always be subordinate to nature. In his respect for the site, he draws comparison with his American counterpart Frank Lloyd Wright, who was ten years his junior. Both architects liked low-ceilinged rooms fitted and furnished with unpainted woods, set off against Art Nouveau decorations and hangings. Of course, Wright's talents were unquestionably greater and led to higher flights of spatial imagination, but Voysey with quiet integrity anticipated much of the better modernism now associated with the 1920's and 1930's. His love of simple stucco as an external finish is acceptable, sometimes even inevitable, given his sensitive handling. Voysey was a revolutionary with a distaste for revolution itself. As a young man he had deplored the less healthy manifestations of Art Nouveau, a movement in which he himself had played a role. Living on to 1941 he also came to detest the Modern Movement for its bigotry and lack of soul.

Mackintosh, a more passionate genius, was influential in the birth of modernism both in America and on the Continent, but was unappreciated in British design circles outside of his native Scotland. With his wife Margaret Macdonald, he developed a distinctive version of Art Nouveau decoration that achieved wide acclaim. His architectural works, mostly in Glasgow, are an eclectic mixture of Voysey and traditional Scottish architecture, distilled through the vision of a powerful if idiosyncratic mind. Ignored in England, he was fêted abroad where a joint exhibition with his wife in Vienna in 1900 caused a sensation. His influence has leapfrogged several generations, providing inspiration, much of it sadly

Opposite: Morris & Co.'s Strawberry Thief, although unmistakably 19th-century, has a bold and simple treatment that comes near to Gothic wall and tapestry designs.

Top: Stepped brickwork supports the curious bay window in the Red House, designed for William Morris by Philip Webb. The windows themselves are plain: some have pointed heads or Gothic relieving arches set flush in the brick. This is an English manor house look, somewhere between medieval and Queen Anne.

Above: One of the beautiful wallpapers designed by Morris is still hand-printed by Sanderson from the original blocks.

Left: At the Great Exhibition of 1851, held in the Crystal Palace in Hyde Park, London, many designs of High Victorian taste at its most ostentatious were on view. To the young Morris, as to many others, the display was full of bad design and a cause for grave concern.

Left: "When Adam delved and Eve span" is a Morris design with a Pre-Raphaelite flavour. The naturalism is in contrast with the bird design shown above.

Far left: This cxccllcnt design was produced by Watts & Co. of Westminster, a firm still in existence.

35

Top: A contemporary lithograph of Queen Anne Gardens, Bedford Park, London, was produced from a painting by H.M. Paget. Pictures like this were used to advertise the benefits of life in the new garden suburbs.

Above: Built for the first Lord Armstrong by Norman Shaw, Cragside in Northumberland was an extraordinary venture, set on a barren hillside outside Newcastle. The building is an extravaganza of eclectic styles, adapted to late Victorian comfort.

imitative, to the young British designers of our own times. What his influence on British architecture would have been if he had continued his practice into middle life can only be conjectured. As it was he declined into professional inactivity and we have only the exquisite watercolors of his later years as compensation for an abandoned talent.

Lutyens was a very different figure, the urbane Englishman opposed to the awkward Scot. Like Shaw, his sympathetic and witty character endeared him to his clients. He started off with small houses and alterations around his native Surrey. His collaboration with Gertrude Jekyll, the garden designer, expanded his clientele and the practice grew. He was never addicted to movements nor apparently was he much interested in current trends. Clearly influenced by the Morris–Shaw designs of his youth, he nevertheless went his own way, adopting Old English or Queen Anne as the fancy took him or the latest commission suggested.

Marriage into the aristocracy served him well and his country house commissions became larger, followed by public buildings. Somehow, in domestic architecture, his much simplified Old English vernacular always seems his happier inspiration, more personal and idiosyncratic than his version of Queen Anne. His work in the latter manner was much imitated by other architects, but there it commonly graded into the more historically correct neo-Georgian.

To Lutyens was granted the unique honor, if that is the right word, to preside over the end of an era, exemplified in great and different commissions. His extraordinary and subtle Castle Drogo, built of local granite on a lonely moor in Devon, is the most remarkable example in the dying tradition of the large country house. Later came the great colonial commission of the Parliament buildings in Delhi which he undertook with Herbert Baker, completed just before colonialism itself was extinguished.

All of this architectural ferment of late Victorian Britain was more than matched by developments in America during the years from about 1875 to 1900. Both spread from the same spark, for Shaw's dramatic designs were much esteemed on both sides of the Atlantic when first published in the early 1870's. In America, however, windshifts led the flames in directions only remotely related to the Arts and Crafts phases of contemporary Britain.

The more conservative American movement grew from Shaw's Old English designs as reinterpreted by the most influential popularizer of the period, Henry Hudson Holly (1834–92). Holly is a much-neglected figure in 19th-century American design because the fashions he passionately advocated were those that fell farthest from favor with the rise of 20th-century modernism. Historians searching for the roots of this modernism have by now lionized those late Victorian architects, Louis Sullivan and H.H.

Opposite: This Voysey house, The Orchard, Chorleywood, Hertfordshire, was sensibly adjusted to the needs of contemporary families. The high stylization of interiors such as this had a profound influence on the architects of the Modern Movement in Germany – a fact that Voysey resented.

Baillie Scott was the architect of this house at Knutsford, in Cheshire, built in 1895, a typical "Artistic" house in an informal garden suburb. Garden cities were popular at the turn of the century for their Utopian socialist charms as well as for their new, fashionable architecture. The American equivalents were Tudor revival houses in suburbs reached by newly popular streetcars.

Standen, at East Grinstead, West Sussex, was built by Philip Webb in 1891. Designed as a weekend house for a successful London lawyer, Standen shows Webb in his typically unpretentious manner. The careful assemblage of vernacular details intentionally avoids any grand or classically coherent architectural statement. Standen and its fine Morris & Co. interiors has been miraculously spared by the 20th century; it is now open to the public.

Richardson for example, whose work they perceive, sometimes with difficulty, as having led to the new orthodoxy. Holly on the other hand, a man who set the theme of popular domestic design for over two decades with his 1878 book, *Modern Dwellings*, is yet to receive more than a derogatory footnote or two in the literature of architectural history.

Critics notwithstanding, Holly's steep-roofed, rambling designs, all with generous porches wrapping around front and side, became the mainstays of local architects and builders throughout the country in the 1880's and 1890's. In the first decade these were mostly decorated with fanciful mock-medieval friezes and balustrades made of turned spindles that are today nicknamed "gingerbread" ornamentation. In the 1890's this changed to "Free Classic" ornamentation – Greek-inspired columns, pediments, and garlands. Rather confusingly these Holly-inspired and loosely medieval designs, mostly built in wood, have also come to be called "Queen Anne" even though most have little resemblance to their masonry British cousins which bear the same name. For this reason it is important, when speaking of "Queen Anne" houses, to make clear whether the reference is to the American or British version.

The second American design trend of this period has no direct British counterpart and was largely the creation of a single towering figure, Henry Hobson Richardson (1838–86). Richardson was an early admirer of Shaw as shown by some of his first commissions, particularly the Watts Sherman house, designed in 1874 to be built in Newport, Rhode Island. He soon, however, evolved his own very personal style based on a free interpretation of much earlier medievalism – the massive walls and round-arched openings of Romanesque architecture.

Richardson was a larger-than-life figure in every sense of the word. A three-hundred-pound giant of a man, he was born on a prosperous plantation near New Orleans, the son of Catherine Priestley, granddaughter of the great British chemist who discovered oxygen. Richardson attended Harvard where he maintained an active social, if not academic, schedule and apparently first developed his interest in architecture, a subject then taught in America only by apprenticeship rather than as a formal academic discipline. Determined to pursue architecture as a career, and fluent in French from his Louisiana childhood, he became only the second American to enrol in Paris' prestigious Ecole des Beaux Arts, then the great mecca for aspiring architects everywhere.

After six years of study and apprenticeship in France, Richardson opened an architectural practice in New York City in 1867. His Staten Island neighbor was a young landscape designer and follower of Downing, Frederick Law Olmstead (1822–1903), whose long and distinguished career become intertwined with that of Richardson. Equally gifted as designers, the two men became

A black and white house by Charles Rennie Mackintosh owes more to English models than to his native Clydeside.

Above: One of the studio houses that Voysey built in the 1890's, on the edge of the garden suburb of Bedford Park, London, has horizontal windows, wide eaves and pebbledash that mark it as "Modern."

Below: A well-to-do middle-class interior of about 1900 recalls an earlier taste in its general clutter; more modern fashions are reflected in the display of china and the elaborate classical revival mantelpiece.

Above: Hill House, Helensburgh, was built by C.R. Mackintosh for clients on a hill outside Glasgow overlooking the Clyde. Everything in the house was designed by the architect, or his wife, down to the humblest fittings and fabrics. The term "Art Nouveau" may be applied, but cannot begin to convey the intensely personal genius of this striking house and its extraordinary interiors.

Top: Lutyens's house at Munstead Wood, Surrey, built for Gertrude Jekyll in 1896, takes Tudor a step further towards simplicity. Any fussiness has been subordinated to pure form and textural contrasts.

Above: Little Thakeham, in Sussex, is an impeccable exercise in symmetry, demonstrating Lutyens's versatility in harnessing romantic styles to classical discipline.

Left: A typical country bedroom of the end of the period at Lindisfarne Castle, Northumberland, has a wide-board floor with rugs, unpainted furniture and functional fittings.

life-long confidants in spite of, or perhaps because of, their very different personalities. Olmstead was the introspective philosopher – a man whose humanitarian and environmental interests led him to champion many causes beyond his profession. Richardson, in contrast, was an impatient and flamboyant aesthete who burned the candle at both ends. Fond of lavish dining and lively intellectual soirées, he lived in the continuous company of admiring apprentices and stimulating friends, interrupted only by recurring bouts of illness. Cursed with a chronic kidney disease, he apparently knew that he faced early death and determined frantically to make the most of his remaining years.

In 1872 Richardson's neo-Romanesque entry won an important competition for Boston's new Trinity church and his success was assured. Soon he had so many New England commissions that in 1874 he moved his practice to the then pastoral Boston suburb of Brookline, where Olmstead also later moved. There, in a studio wing added to his house, he and a dozen or so assistants spent the next twelve years, until his death in 1886, feverishly designing dozens of churches, train stations, public buildings and dwellings – works that were to become the widely copied models for much of the nation's monumental architecture of the late 1880's and 1890's. So original was Richardson's influence that this movement is known as "Richardsonian Romanesque."

Many large and costly dwellings were designed and built in Richardsonian Romanesque but these required elaborate and expensive stone masonry so that the style never extended to the great mass of wood-based American housing. Richardson's free shapes and rounded arches were, however, translated by the master and his pupils into an equally influential wooden innovation, the "Shingle style," which became a favorite of fashionable American architects designing sea-side summer "cottages" for the affluent. The simplified lines and open interior planning of these new designs, which were to remain relatively rare and avant-garde, led to a still more revolutionary change – the first wave of modernism in housing design which quickly swept the country during the period from 1900 to 1915. Following the lead of Frank Lloyd Wright in the Midwest and the brothers Charles and Henry Greene in California, unprecedented "Prairie" and "Craftsman" designs dominated American housing during the first two decades of the new century. No comparable trend appeared in Britain where this "Edwardian" period was marked by the last phase of the earlier Free Style and by a return to historically correct Renaissance designs in the "neo-Georgian" movement. Thus the fashion trends that bear Victoria's name were ending in America at the time of her death in 1901 but, as if in mourning, lingered on in Britain until interrupted by the outbreak of war in 1914.

Above: Castle Drogo, Devon, on the edge of Dartmoor marks the end of the era. The Victorian castle tradition might have seemed to end with the neo-Gothic Arundel, Sussex, in the 1890's, but less than a decade later Lutyens began sketches for Drogo. Embellishment is confined to the entrance, with only mullioned casement windows to modify the austere granite walls.

Winslow House, River Forest, Illinois, was built by Frank Lloyd Wright in 1893. Wright was influenced by the British Arts and Crafts Movement and by the great Chicago architect, Louis Sullivan, in whose office he had worked. Also, Wright was interested in the idea of a Midwest vernacular architecture which was subservient to the surrounding landscape. He quickly assimilated these and other influences to produce a style uniquely his own, of which this house is a striking early example.

Chapter Two
EXTERIOR FEATURES

Architecture is always a compromise between style and technology. Whatever the period, whatever the school of thought, the fierce aesthetic arguments of the protagonists are tempered by the available materials and their intrinsic properties, however unwelcome this limitation may be. In ancient Greece and Rome, and in northern Europe during the Middle Ages, great architecture could be said to have grown out of the material technology of wood and stone, "honest" materials later seized upon and celebrated by such Victorians as Ruskin and Pugin. By the Renaissance, building materials such as stucco were known to have allowed a certain degree of fakery, that element of deception which so offended the Gothic revivalists. Modern archaeology has since shown that, even in the ancient world, thin marble veneers and painted plaster were in widespread use. But the structural purity of strong natural materials – wood, stone and, later, fired clay – remained unsurpassed.

Sometimes, as we have seen only too clearly in our own age, doctrinaire aesthetics run ahead of technology. The Modern Movement made demands which could not be met by the existing construction methods. By the time technology had caught up, an irony of taste decreed a return to the old traditions, and pitched roofs, pediments, ornament and color have all made a strong comeback.

Although great strides were made in civil engineering and industrialized building in the 19th century, domestic architecture remained, in structural terms, relatively unchanged. Houses continued to be constructed of load-bearing walls of brick, stone or wood. Across this basic frame wooden joisted floors provided essential lateral bracing. Roofs were made of wood trusses which were generally clad with tiles, slates, thatch or shingles. Foundations did gradually improve, mostly as a result of new building codes, although footings were still only taken down to plain earth or, at best, compacted rubble mixed with lime. F.P. Cockerell first used concrete for footings in 1850, and the first British building to be constructed from poured concrete, Down Hall in Essex, dates from 1871, but the material did not come into ordinary domestic use in America until the turn of the century. At this stage it was often used in the shape of concrete blocks and often shaped to imitate rusticated stone. Improving concrete and steel construction

The crisp, well proportioned architecture of this shingle house makes a focal point of the main entrance. The color scheme gives due prominence and dignity to the front porch, bringing it forward from the body of the house.

Left: Illuminated from behind by stained-glass windows, this Australian verandah, with its florid cast-iron brackets and balusters, becomes a welcoming exterior living space for long summer evenings.

techniques made possible larger and stronger spans needed for the popular high-rise apartment houses which began to appear in New York and other cities across the United States late in the century.

More obvious changes resulted from improvements in transport. Whether these can be judged beneficial is open to argument; what is unarguable is that the face of Britain was changed for ever by the expansion of the railroad and canal systems and the subsequent accessibility of building materials hitherto considered too cumbersome to move. In the United States the general availability of wood produced a coherent translation of current European fashions into frame and clapboard, leading, for a few decades at least, to the delightful domestic architecture that gives such grace to the towns of the East Coast and southern states. In Britain it meant only that much of the intrinsic character of local building became blurred. Slates, produced by the million in North Wales and Cumbria, were transported by rail to all corners of Britain. Being much less heavy than tiles, they made possible shallower pitches and lighter roof construction. In the same way, brick buildings turned up in what had hitherto been stone country or among the wood and plaster towns of East Anglia. Identical terracotta ornaments could now be incorporated in houses throughout the United States and Britain. New brick fields turned out the strong red facings so favored by High Victorian architects, who positively delighted in their raw appeal and decorative possibilities when mixed with blue engineerings or ochre terracotta.

Improvements in glass manufacture brought radical changes to window designs. Panes grew larger, and if this did not always enhance the proportions of the façade, it was not yet as destructive as the large sheets of cheap plate glass in the 20th century.

In perspective, Victorian architecture can be seen as the bridge between the hand-crafted building that went before and the bleak but eclectic houses of the post-war West. Today's buildings may be superior in terms of stability, insulation and convenience, but the constituent parts are often applied without love or understanding. It would be frivolous to pretend that the Victorians were substantially different in their attitude, but they caught the tail-end of a centuries-old tradition of craftsmanship that ensured a certain solidity of construction and a generosity of finish.

With their sublime lack of self-consciousness about class, British Victorians openly distinguished between the social status of different house types, categorizing them as Class I, II, III or IV

Exterior details make a statement about a building: the ornamental keystone at Burleigh Mansions in St Martin's Lane, London *(left)*, confidently exudes neo-classical grandeur, while the simple but elegant lancet window of a Sussex farmhouse *(above)* unpretentiously signals a solidity of craftsmanship within.

Above: Foot scrapers were an important fixture at the entrance, marking the transition from the muddy outdoors to the cosy Victorian interior. They were usually of cast iron, and were often embellished with charming ornamental details.

Right: The overhanging roofs, elaborate corbels, cast-iron balcony rails and exuberant dormer of this house in Washington, DC, present a distinctly Spanish aspect to the world.

according to their prospective owners or tenants. A Class I house is what would now be called a small estate in the United States, with a substantial villa standing on its own in 50 or so acres of land. Smaller Class II houses stood in a modest acre or half acre, served by a short drive from the road, forming part of a development of similar houses. The present inner suburbs of most towns in Britain and the United States (formerly the outskirts, of course) have examples of such houses set in leafy avenues, groves and crescents – for example Castle Park in Nottingham, England, and Brookline in Boston.

Next down the scale came the semi-detached villa or two-family dwelling. Although such duplexes were built in the Georgian era, their popularity dates from Victorian times, as do their bay windows, an essential ingredient of their design.

Class IV was the row house, called a terraced house in Britain because the ground was terraced flat before building. The great glory of the 18th-century British terrace declined over the early decades of the 19th century. As the cost of road frontages increased and building regulations discouraged basements, single- and double-story rear additions became common, housing the new bathrooms and closets as well as the servants' quarters. The removal of rooms to rear additions reduced the height of the house and concentrated the architectural treatment on the façade; anyone

traveling through the suburbs by train cannot fail to notice how plain and even brutal the treatment of the backs of these houses is in comparison with the fronts.

In the United States, cheaper land deferred such economic measures except in the largest cities. In the suburbs the concept of a single-family detached house sitting in its own plot of land was possible to realize for much longer; indeed the American suburbs today still continue this tradition, though the architecture grows simpler and the yards smaller.

It is always difficult to assess the extent to which social changes have influenced the architecture of a previous age. What may seem to later generations to have been eras of modesty and taste may not have appeared so to contemporaries. Seen through early 21st-century eyes, the snobberies, enthusiasms, revivalisms and aesthetic battles of the Victorians have dulled with the passage of time. We can only judge their buildings on our own terms, and our judgements are tinged with our own peculiar nostalgia, that mixed emotion which our Victorian forebears would surely have understood and, above all, condoned.

Above: This richly ornamented door handle, with more than a suggestion of Art Nouveau about it, gives the visitor an impression of artistic flair.

Left: Many Victorian town residences had a door plate such as this. A sliding brass panel – now missing – would have indicated whether the occupants were in or out.

THE MASONRY HOUSE

Underlying the almost infinite variety of Victorian houses were a few basic structural forms, repeated millions of times over by builders following well established principles.

Of the three types illustrated on the next six pages, the first is the detached masonry house, built of load-bearing brick or stone with a single masonry cross-wall, the remaining interior walls being non-load- bearing wooden stud partitions. From the early part of the century the foundations were a series of brickwork steps laid directly on to the excavated trench, diminishing as they rose to the width of the wall.

The first part of the wall above the ground is the plinth, generally a few courses of different-colored brick or perhaps a different finish of stone. Above the plinth, there rises the rest of the wall, in this instance stone facing bonded, for economy, into a brick backing which provides structural stability. Then comes the cornice, consisting here of a stone coping, to throw water away from the wall, and finally, to complete the composition, the roof.

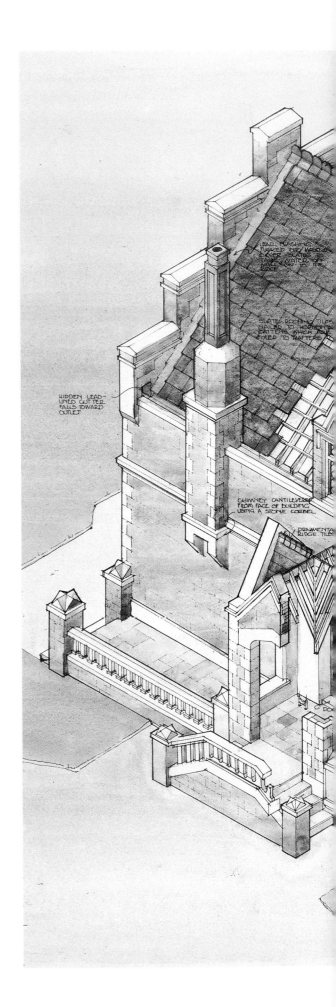

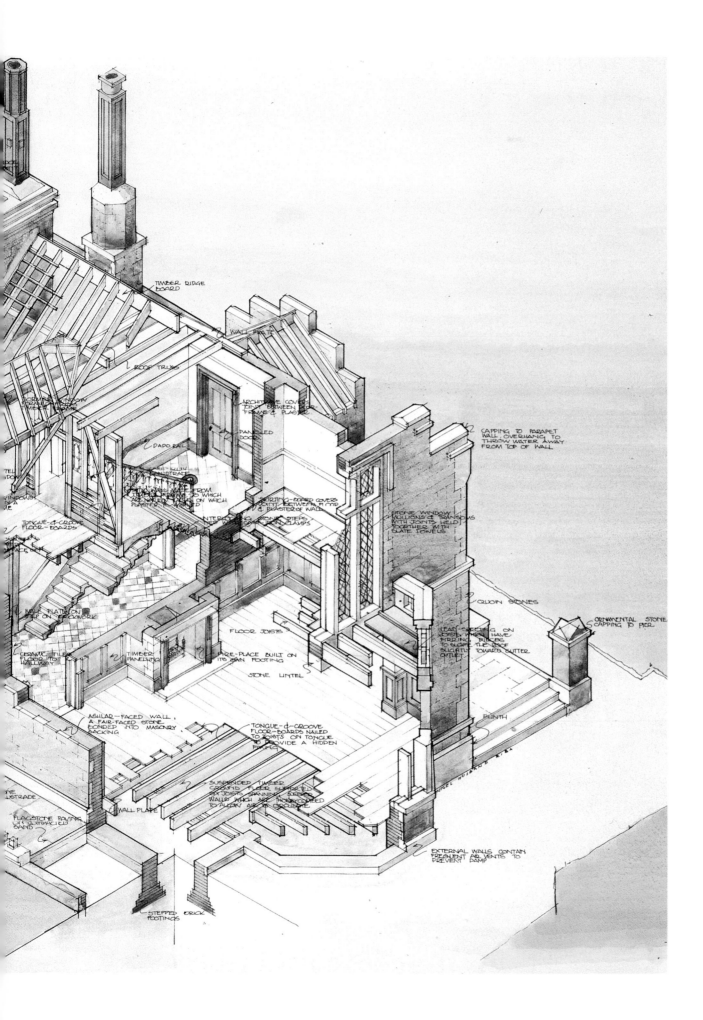

TIMBER RIDGE BOARD

WALL PLATE

ROOF TRUSS

ARCHITRAVE COVERS JOINT BETWEEN FRAME & PLASTER

PANELLED DOOR

DADO RAIL

CAPPING TO PARAPET WALL OVERHANG TO THROW WATER AWAY FROM TOP OF WALL

BALUSTRADE

WALL MADE FROM TIMBER FRAME TO WHICH ARE NAILED LATHS ON WHICH PLASTER IS WORKED

SKIRTING-BOARD COVERS JOINT BETWEEN FLOOR & PLASTER OF WALL

TONGUE-&-GROOVE FLOOR-BOARDS

INTERLOCKING STONE STEPS HELD WITH CAST-IRON CLAMPS

STONE WINDOW MULLIONS & TRANSOMS WITH JOINTS HELD TOGETHER WITH SLATE DOWELS

WINDOWS IN A FRAME

WALL PLATES ON DPC ON BRICKWORK

QUOIN STONES

ORNAMENTAL STONE CAPPING TO PIER

CERAMIC TILES FLOOR INTO HALLWAY

TIMBER PANELLING

FLOOR JOISTS

FIRE-PLACE BUILT ON ITS OWN FOOTING

STONE LINTEL

LEAD SHEETING ON JOISTS WHICH HAVE FIRRING PIECES TO SLOPE THE ROOF SLIGHTLY TOWARDS GUTTER OUTLET

ASHLAR-FACED WALL, A FAIR-FACED STONE BONDED INTO MASONRY BACKING

TONGUE-&-GROOVE FLOOR-BOARDS NAILED TO JOISTS ON TONGUE TO PROVIDE A HIDDEN FIXING

PLINTH

STONE BALUSTRADE

FLAGSTONE PAVING ON COMPACTED SAND

WALL PLATE

SUSPENDED TIMBER GROUND FLOOR SUPPORTED ON JOISTS SPANNING SLEEPER WALLS WHICH ARE HONEYCOMBED TO ALLOW AIR TO CIRCULATE

EXTERNAL WALLS CONTAIN FREQUENT AIR VENTS TO PREVENT DAMP

STEPPED BRICK FOOTINGS

49

THE
ROW HOUSE

T he row house (called "terraced house" in Britain) was rarely designed for an individual occupier. Most of these were built, often streets at a time, by speculative builders using the cheapest convenient wall materials and details purchased from a catalog.

Row houses were only rarely over three stories tall, and inherited their basic characteristics from their Georgian predecessors, including stylistic patterns that continued to be built right up to the 1850's. Row houses were constructed with load-bearing masonry external walls and an internal masonry cross-wall. Remaining internal walls were non-load-bearing partitions made of wooden studs covered by wooden lath and plaster. Basements and semi-basements provided a service area at the bottom of the house, giving way as the century progressed to back extensions. This house has both.

Save in the very late Victorian period – and then often only for the most modest examples – row houses in the north and west of England were built of stone. In the Midlands and the south-east, the long tradition of brick building dominated, while most American examples also had walls of brick.

Row house blocks were frequently designed to be read as a whole from a distance, with prominent buildings at either end and often in the centre. External details – such as whether a bay carried up to the first floor or was, more economically, restricted to the ground floor – gave a precise indication of status. Stone lintels, brick voussoirs, pillars, capitals and terracotta details all played their part in announcing the social standing of the occupants. Many of the rows that still make up much of the inner-city housing stock in Britain and in the larger cities of the northwestern U.S. were originally built for those of very modest means.

RAFTERS SITTING ON A
TIMBER WALL PLATE.

NEY POTS
ED IN
NT MORTAR

LINTRAY LEAD
LINED BOX GUTTER;
STEPPED TO PROVIDE
WATERTIGHT JOINT
BETWEEN SHEETS

LEAD LINED BOX
GUTTER BEHIND
PARAPET WALL
AND TUCKED INTO
MASONRY

RE-TILED
SQUENCE
DROP OR

LEAD SHEETS
JOINTED OVER
TIMBER RAFTER

HARDWOOD
HANDRAILADE

STONE
TIED TO WALL WITH
METAL CRAMPS

ARCHITRAVE
COVERS JOINT
BETWEEN DOOR
FRAME & PLASTER

FLAT ROOF GIVEN
FALLS (SLOPE) BY LAYING
A CUT STRIP OF TIMBER
A FIRRING PIECE

EXPOSED ARCH;
BRICKS CUT TO
SHAPE

STONE WINDOW
SILL TO THROW WATER
AWAY FROM BUILDING
FACE

FIBROUS
CORNICE COVERS
JOINT BETWEEN
WALL &

FLOOR BOARDS
WITH TONGUE &
GROOVED EDGES
NAILED TO JOISTS

SKIRTING TO COVER
JOINT BETWEEN
FLOOR & PLASTER
OF WALL

TIMBER
LINTEL

EXTERNAL WALL REDUCES
THICKNESS AS BUILDING
HEIGHTENS

SASH WINDOW
TWO VERTICAL
WHICH SLIDE
CHANNELS

CAST-IRON LINTEL
SPANS CORRIDOR

TONGUE & GROOVE
VERTICAL BOARDING
WAS USED FOR SOME
PARTITIONS

QUARRY TILE FLOORING
LAID ON A COMPACTED
SAND

SUPPORTING ZONE
ARCHED TIMBER
FACING TILE

TIMBER STAIRCASE
CONSTRUCTED WITH
STRINGS WHICH
PROVIDE THE SECTIONAL
FORM FOR TREADS (HORIZONTAL)
& RISERS (VERTICAL) PARTS
OF EACH STEP

SOLID BASEMENT
FLOOR

STEPPED BRICK
FOOTING (OR
FOUNDATION)

THE BALLOON FRAME HOUSE

The balloon frame is a method of building unique to the United States and perfectly suited to the expanding Midwestern states where it originated. Drawing on the nation's all but unlimited supplies of timber, it was a cheap, easy-to-erect system using a wooden wall frame of simplified design.

Unlike earlier wooden framed houses, in which a few heavy timbers were the load-bearing units, the balloon frame – perhaps so called because the houses went up like balloons – consists entirely of a great many small-dimension wooden "sticks" nailed together with machine-made wire nails. No one part of the structure supports any greater load than any other. There are no corner posts or heavy load-bearing timbers to cut by hand. Instead principal members are made of two or more standard timbers, usually two inches thick by only four or six inches wide, nailed together. The walls are then clad in timber or a decorative masonry veneer and the house is finished off with a roof usually of varying design.

This streamlined system greatly lowered the cost of house construction by using less expensive wall materials assembled by a foolproof methodology which did not require highly skilled labor. First used in Chicago in the 1830's, it became the dominant building method in the Middle West by the time of the Civil War, and by early in this century was used for all but the grandest masonry dwellings. With slight modifications, it is still the most common method of house construction in America today.

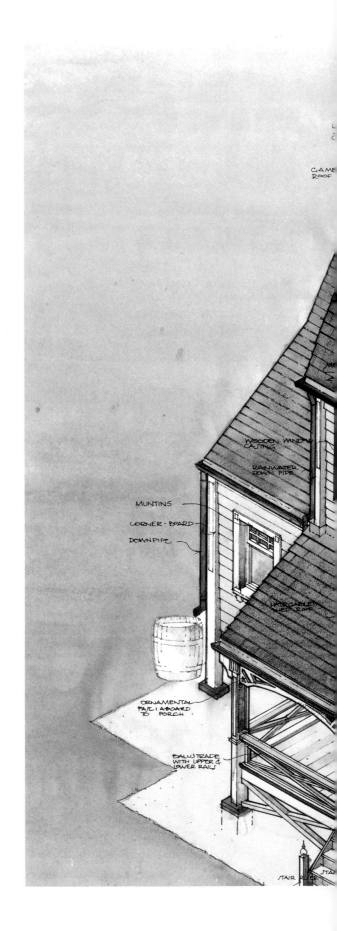

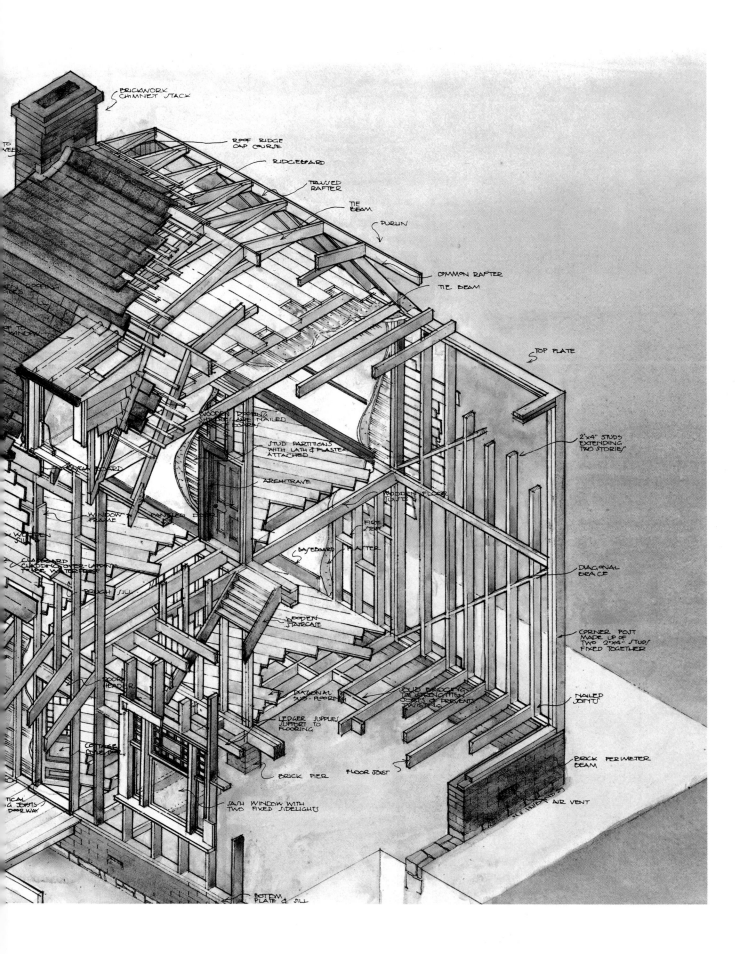

BRICKWORK
CHIMNEY STACK

ROOF RIDGE
CAP COURSE

RIDGEBOARD

TRUSSED
RAFTER

TIE
BEAM

PURLIN

COMMON RAFTER

TIE BEAM

TOP PLATE

2"x4" STUDS
EXTENDING
TWO STORIES

WOODEN ROOFING
SHINGLES LAID & NAILED
IN COURSES

STUD PARTITIONS
WITH LATH & PLASTER
ATTACHED

ARCHITRAVE

WOODEN FLOOR
JOISTS

WINDOW
FRAME

PANELED DOOR

FIRE
STOP

BASEBOARD

PLASTER

DIAGONAL
BRACE

WOODEN
STAIRCASE

CORNER POST
MADE UP OF
TWO 2"x4" STUDS
FIXED TOGETHER

DIAGONAL
SUB-FLOORING

STUD BRIDGING
TO STRENGTHEN
JOISTS & PREVENT
WARPING

NAILED
JOINTS

LEDGER SUPPLIES
SUPPORT TO
FLOORING

DOOR
HEADER

BRICK PERIMETER
BEAM

BRICK PIER

FLOOR JOIST

AIR VENT

SASH WINDOW WITH
TWO FIXED SIDELIGHTS

BOTTOM
PLATE & SILL

53

THE FRONT ENTRANCE

Before the Victorians, only a rich minority were able to pay for an imposing doorway or porch – now the growing middle classes could afford them too. As long as the materials had been just wood, brick or stone, a certain homogeneity had been assured. Now the introduction of stucco, decorative tiles, cast iron and cheap colored glass led to a confusion of design and ornament. Early entrances continued the classical themes of the Regency, somewhat coarsened in detail. Later, the medieval revival played a part, though classical grammar was generally found to combine the requirements of public presentation more satisfactorily than Gothic. In smaller urban row houses, such niceties of style were usually ignored or misunderstood, resulting in a cheerfully eclectic marriage of the two leading schools.

Left: A lace-like double staircase and entrance, from Queensland, Australia, shows how British colonial architecture often went one further than the home product, employing cast-iron products exported as ballast in the holds of ships. The nearest to such exuberance in Britain was usually confined to the seaside or health resorts.

Opposite: Nothing could better exemplify British upper-middle-class town houses of the 1850's than this grand parade with its Tuscan columns. The relatively modest doorcases of the previous century have been replaced by heavy stucco entrance porticoes. Above, the walls are so ornamented with architraves, cornices and balustrades that the brick is dominated by the applied decoration.

RAILINGS AND GATES

In early town houses, the front door opened directly on to the street; railings became popular during the 18th century to define the property and protect the strip of land in front, as well as to add another touch of elegance. In the 19th century the wish to enclose the property became stronger, reflecting the growth of private ownership and the simultaneous transformation from a rural to an urban society. The new owners of suburban villas wanted to mark out their territory, just as the landowners of the 18th century had done.

Gates and railings afforded another opportunity for decoration and display. Whether the enclosure is of iron or wood, the gate should generally be of the same material, though some delightful hybrids of wood and wire panels were concocted. In cases where dwarf walls and piers are made of brick or stone, iron railings usually look best. They should be 18 inches to 2 feet (45 to 60 cm) high.

In general, cast iron was popular in the early years of the century while wood and wrought iron, beloved of the Arts and Crafts Movement, came into their own later, to persist into early 20th-century designs.

Right: A classical revival entrance, wrought-iron railings and grandiloquent overthrow with hanging lantern all derive from English baroque models, but interpreted by later eyes.

Left: The wood and wirework fence, with ornamental gate, casts its pattern upon the pattern of the tile path which leads up to a delightful porch of turned spindlework.

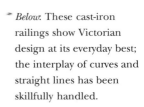

Below. These cast-iron railings show Victorian design at its everyday best; the interplay of curves and straight lines has been skillfully handled.

Left: Porch and railings combine in an artless but charming ensemble of decorative ironwork. Classical features and nearly Gothic ones have been gloriously mixed up.

Left: Though at first glance elaborate, this front gate is made up of simple rails decorated with standard finials and rosettes from an ironwork catalog; the white paint is effective against the dark background.

P A T H S ,   T I L E S   A N D
O R N A M E N T S

The strip from front gate to entrance door provided another chance to proclaim the status of a house. Traditionally the materials had been, in descending order of quality, flagstone, brick, gravel and beaten earth. Horse traffic alone provided sufficient reason for keeping dirt out of the entry hall, necessitating pathways that were hard and easy to clean. The new Victorian tessellated tiles, recently reintroduced through the rebirth of interest in medieval flooring, met this need and became particularly popular in Britain. Made of dense clays baked hard, they either drew their color from the clay itself, giving dull reds, browns, ochres and near blacks, or were artificially colored by more elaborate techniques. Glazing produced tiles which, too delicate for flooring, gave ample opportunity for pictures or patterns on adjacent walls. Many of these showed pastoral scenes of hunting, shooting and fishing.

Above: An Australian tiled path is a good match for the bright sunlight and a luxuriant border.

Left: A typical British tiled entrance of the second half of the century looks like a hall floor which has been rolled down to the gate.

Right: This sphinx is an example of the new range of cast sculptures made possible by advances in cements and mass-production techniques.

Above: The quality of Victorian clays and glazes is shown by these tiles with their sunshine motifs.

Left: The plant forms in the small roundels betray the familiar influence of William Morris.

Far left: In England, a popular place for tile pictures was in the return of an entrance wall, no doubt to impress and divert the waiting visitor.

Far left: This dog shows some of the lighter touches a little imagination can lend to an entrance.

Left: Door scrapers came in a variety of cast-iron patterns of which the harp was a favorite and one which remained in production for decades.

PORCHES

The porch has always had a dual function: to call attention to the entrance door and at the same time to provide temporary shelter for the visitor.

In Britain the word porch is used only for the small entry area, which might be either recessed in or exterior to the house itself. In the United States and other former British colonies such as Australia and the West Indies, porches assumed a different guise – they became outdoor living areas, made attractive or even necessary by the warmer climates. In these places the expanded porches provided a perfect setting for elaborate decorative detailing in supporting columns, balustrades and friezes. During the early Victorian years, the classic columns of the Greek revival were most typical as were squared vernacular imitations of the same. During the middle years, Italianate houses tended to have square columns with beveled corners. The late Victorian years brought the Queen Anne house with its marvelous turned spindlework porch supports and balustrades. Finally, at the turn of the century, the influence of the World's Columbian Exposition in Chicago in 1893 made classic columns once again popular.

The Victorians understood the importance of bravura around the entrance, from the garden gate into the hall itself. One has to remember the added effect that servants had on the Victorian entrance. Brass was polished regularly, often daily, and similar treatment was accorded to the steps and pathway. Everything sparkled and shone – those who for reasons of poverty or laziness did not comply would have been regarded by their neighbors with contempt. Nor was this attitude merely a middle-class fetish; such pride was also found in working-class neighborhoods.

Entrances to Victorian houses have sometimes been spoiled by modern signs, bells, lights, and alterations to the doors themselves. However, reinstatement and sympathetic painting can restore much of the original effect.

Top: This deep porch in East Hampton, Long Island, possibly a Victorian era addition to an earlier design, complements a traditional New England clapboard house.

Above: This late Queen Anne house in Austin, Texas, has the classic columns which became so popular on this style at the turn of the century.

Opposite: These doors were probably made by a local craftsman, but their simple carpentry is very effective.

Above: The Victorian porch was not entirely for show, but had a protective function too, to shelter visitors alighting from carriages. The invention of large sheets of glass made glazed entrances such as this possible.

Above right: The squared porch supports with beveled corners seen here were most typical on American Italianate houses. The balustrade, cut from softwood, is probably a modern addition, as is the window scrollwork.

Right: American Queen Anne houses built between 1880 and 1895 almost always featured the turned spindlework columns seen in this Rhode Island example.

Far right: This British entry porch is greatly enhanced by the use of trellis in the side panels, betraying its rural origins. A standard iron cresting gives it a fretted roofline.

Above: Porches-cum-bays like this were popular at the seaside. The Regency tradition of slim panes of border glazing has lingered on, filled with colored glass to provide a decorative frame round the windows. The square corner panes were usually picked out in a strongly contrasting color or, as seen here, with decorative rosettes.

Left: In England a projecting porch was a social signal, implying that a house was occupied by a wealthier family than one would expect if the porch were recessed. Some regarded an elaborate Gothic house as an advertisement for their success.

Above: This type of enclosed exterior entry porch, on a house in Cornwall, England, is rarely found in the United States.

FRONT DOORS

There can be no denying the importance the Victorians placed on first impressions – the visitor had to be left in no doubt as to the owner's position in society.

However charming the gate or imposing the porch, it is the entrance door which captures the eye of the visitor as he waits to be admitted. Up until the Greek revival, front doors had all been solid, made up of panels of wood held together by framing called styles (vertical) and rails (horizontal). The only way of introducing light into the hallway was by means of graceful semi-circular fanlights. Fanlights of this kind continued into the 19th century, particularly where the accent was classical. With the introduction of cheaper and stronger glass, it

Left: The door becomes a work of art at Old Swan House, on the Chelsea Embankment in London, designed by Norman Shaw. Traditional panels are limited to tiny inserts at the bottom of each door. It is not too difficult to see how Art Deco grew out of such precedents; indeed the sculptured panels already seem to be ahead of their time.

Above: Color is an integral part of this Australian entrance. The miniature broken triangular pediment above the door, the use of turned spindles beside the door and the decorative glazing are all quite inventive.

became possible to incorporate quite large panes into entrance doors.

With this new plate glass came glass engraving, stained glass and, for the first time, obscured glazing of all kinds.

Gothicists brought back pointed doors to some houses, but the practical difficulties of their geometry meant that the new medievalism was usually confined within the old and convenient rectangle. As a tribute to the past, however, many of these doors were given leaded lights, the only method by which early Elizabethan windows could be put together from the small glass sizes then available.

Decorative fun could be had by baroque treatment of the door panels themselves and the adjacent columns and supports, elaborations made easier by new machinery.

A British Queen Anne door surround is embellished with brick and terracotta details.

Ruskinian capitals decorate plain columns supporting a top-heavy surround.

Paint has given a sugar-icing effect to this variation on the same theme.

Cheap but effective moldings decorate these handsome doors in San Antonio, Texas.

A Queen Anne revival doorway makes rich use of mixed window panes.

This typical American Italianate door has elaborate door panels and railings.

NUMBERS

As Victorian architecture grew more ornamental, so did typography and graphic design. In the 18th century classicism had provided the basic grammar for lettering and numerals, but the interest in medievalism brought new influences to typefaces. Elaborate variations were played on the old Roman fonts, expanding and condensing the letters and enlarging the serifs to create some fanciful and often bizarre styles. Most people will be familiar with the typical Victorian poster or billboard, each line set in a different type and weight, producing an effect which is at the same time both chaotic and vigorous. New techniques of engraving and painting on glass enlarged the scope for signing and lettering buildings, as can be seen here. American Victorian houses rarely embraced the use of large numbers to the extent of their British counterparts.

These examples show the variety of design and material used on English Victorian doors and their surrounds. No. 71 shows a standard number and knocker which would have been familiar to Dickens. No. 42 is straightforward signwriting on glass, while 5 and 23 are in tailor-made metalwork. The blue and white enamel 72 is an appropriate modern alternative.

DOOR FURNITURE

The fitting out of hundreds of thousands of front doors provided great opportunities for the foundries and engravers of the day, and one is struck by the sheer fertility of ideas and excellent craftsmanship of these quite humble artifacts. Some were undoubtedly commissioned by an individual client, but the majority were made to fill those extensive catalogs which are one of the pleasures of Victorian manufacturing. In general, American versions were less elaborate than their British counterparts.

Early knockers repeated the classical themes of the previous century, such as shields, lion heads and medusas; later there are clear influences of Morris & Co., later still the sensuous forms of Art Nouveau.

Mail slots only became really useful after the introduction of uniform prepaid rates in 1845. The addition of "Letters" or "Newspapers" was perhaps more a symbol of literacy and self-importance than any instruction for deliverymen. Materials for this hardware were brass, gun metal and bronze. Cheaper models were made of cast iron.

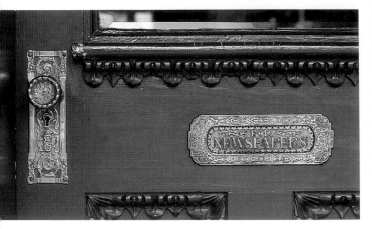

The invention and quality of Victorian hardware is exemplary. These designs range from Georgian classical through Arts and Crafts to Art Nouveau. One of the most beautiful (*opposite, bottom right*) is a purely functional bell pull which would have won the admiration of the Modern Movement. Doors with patterns of glass obscured by various methods (*top*) were almost never found in the United States and invariably look wrong on an American restoration.

TYPES OF ENTRANCES & BOUNDARIES

RECESSED OPENING   FRAMED DOOR   SIMPLE CANOPY   BRACKETED CANOPY

CORBELLED DECORATIVE CANOPY   WOODEN CANOPY   WOODEN PORCH   GLAZED PORCH

COLUMNED PORCH   TRELLIS PORCH   CLASSICAL PORCH   'GOTHIC' WOODEN PORCH

BAY WINDOW & PORCH   METALWORK VERANDAH PORCH   WOODEN PORCH   ARTS & CRAFTS PORCH

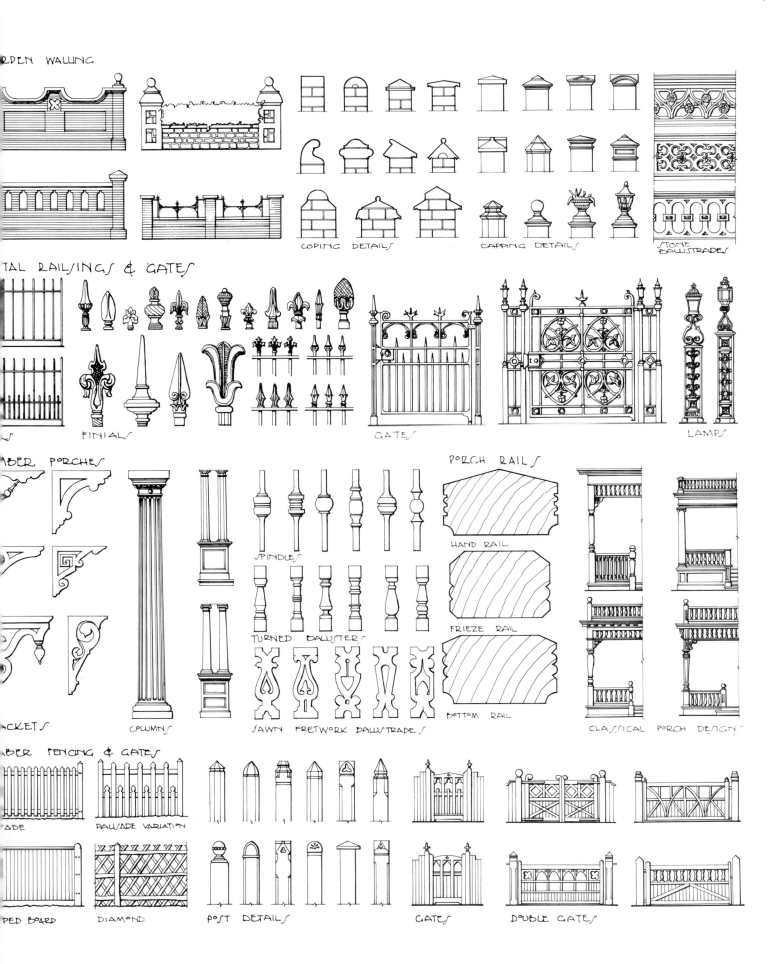

RDEN WALLING

COPING DETAILS   CAPPING DETAILS   STONE BALUSTRADES

TAL RAILINGS & GATES

FINIALS   GATES   LAMPS

BER PORCHES   PORCH RAILS

HAND RAIL

FRIEZE RAIL

BOTTOM RAIL

SPINDLES

TURNED BALUSTERS

CKETS   COLUMNS   SAWN FRETWORK BALUSTRADES   CLASSICAL PORCH DESIGNS

BER FENCING & GATES

ADE   PALISADE VARIATION

PED BOARD   DIAMOND   POST DETAILS   GATES   DOUBLE GATES

EXTERNAL WALLS

A beautifully textured or ornamented wall surface is one of the delights of most High Victorian houses. In Britain this was most often obtained with decorative patterns of brickwork. Brick was also a common wall material in Victorian America, but was vastly overshadowed by wooden-framed walls clad with wooden clapboards and shingles – all products of America's enormous forests.

During the early Victorian era American houses continued to use the plain clapboard siding that had dominated the preceding Georgian and Federal eras. An attractive variation appeared on wooden Gothic revival houses of the 1840's and 50's. In this the siding was applied vertically, rather than in the more usual overlapped horizontal orientation. Joints between the flush-mounted vertical boards were then covered by smaller vertical strips known as "battens," from which the ensemble came to be called "board-and-batten" siding.

By the 1870's mass-production woodworking machines were turning out enormous quantities of inexpensive decorative architectural detailing, among which were patterned wooden shingles. Produced in diamond-shaped, fish-scale, hexagonal and other decorative patterns, these quickly became the most popular means for achieving an ornamented wall surface. By the 1880's houses of almost every style and size had some part of their walls covered with patterned shingles.

Bricks could be cut or molded to a variety of shapes, for construction and ornament and perfectly answered the 19th-century passion for pattern. All of these bricks were at first distinctly local and are still found in greatest quantity close to their place of manufacture. But matters were complicated by the introduction of a national railroad system in both Britain and the United States. This meant that bricks, like other building materials, could be transported cheaply throughout the country. The bringing together of bricks of many hues from different points of origin had a delightful side effect, for it allowed Victorian builders to indulge in an ever more flamboyant brick polychromy, creating wall patterns obtained by mixing bricks of contrasting color or tone.

In brick construction the "facings" or outer

Opposite: Molded brick tiles were made out of dense clays burnt hard, and were very durable, as can be seen from their precise profiles after a century of use. These dark reds provide a sharp contrast to the soft yellow stocks of the main wall, which has been unsympathetically repointed during the 20th century.

Below left: These decorative lintels are ultimately derived from Venetian and oriental sources. The unusual pointed keystones tie in with the central mullion.

Below: A simple diamond pattern was a favorite device to liven up large areas of brickwork. Color variations were achieved by using headers, the smaller end faces of the brick, which often came out darker than the stretchers, or long sides.

skin of brickwork are placed together in "bonds": particular, recognizable arrangements which guarantee strength and cohesion. Not only is the choice of bond structurally important, it can also have a radical effect on the appearance of a building. All Victorian brick houses were built with deep enough walls for a brick to be laid crosswise on the wall, showing only its end face or "header," as it is called. This allowed for variation between header and "stretcher", a brick laid lengthwise along the wall. The characteristic variations of bond were thus composed of varying mixtures of header and stretcher, their syncopation giving a wall both character and strength.

Stone continued to be used for economy where it was locally available, and elsewhere for effect, sometimes in combination with brick. Ornamentation is naturally more expensive in carved stone than in mass-produced brick. Even so, remarkably elaborate work can be found where quarries produced stone soft enough to be easily workable by the carver.

Heavy rusticated stone was a favorite wall material in one American Victorian style, the Richardsonian Romanesque, and was also used as a first-story material in many examples of the related Shingle style. This stone might be applied as a veneer on a brick wall or used as the actual wall building material.

Apart from brick, there were a number of other man-made building materials or finishes to external walls. The period opened with extensive use of stucco, a type of plasterwork with an exceptionally smooth finish. Greek revival architects and builders continued to use it for several decades, often in combination with brick or stone. It could provide columns and cornices at a fraction of the cost of stone. It was also invaluable for false stone walling which could be marked out like regularly hewn stone, then either painted or left to revert slowly to the natural color of its basic constituent, sand.

Terracotta was held by Victorian architects

Above: Ogees over the windows and a mock-Jacobean pediment give this early 19th-century English house its playful "Gothick" charm.

Center: A Queen Anne house in Newport, Rhode Island, incorporates numerous elaborate patterns in decorative shingles and carved panels.

to be a more natural material than stucco and it played a major decorative role in both Britain and the United States. Like brick, terracotta is made of fireclay. It could be molded to virtually any form, then finally fired to give it a finish which could be vitreous if desired. It was thus both water-resistant and suitable for all forms of decoration, no matter how elaborate. Terracotta could be used as a simple facing block like brick, as well as for molded features such as cornices, swags and sculptured panels. Only a few large houses used this material comprehensively – it was still more expensive than brick – but for more modest houses it provided a cheap decorative accent for exterior brickwork.

Left: This American house, if executed in brick and stucco, would not look out of place in a British suburb, but its wood construction has allowed a lightness and exuberance impossible in other materials.

Above: Careful examination of these rusticated quoins shows them to be mass-produced. The squiggly incisions, or vermiculation, give strength and character to the corner stones.

Left: Some cheaper examples of Victorian decoration, like this pierced balustrade, were made up from ready-made components.

ROOFS AND GABLES

With the exception of a few great houses, the Georgians never took roofs seriously. In the English row house, in particular, Georgian designers often sought to suppress roofs as far as they could, reducing their pitch and hiding them behind parapets. The same was true in American Georgian, Federal, and Greek revival houses. Then, with the Gothic revival, there came a full-scale return to dominant roof forms, a celebration of the steep and picturesque rooflines of medieval England.

Dramatic roof forms reached their apex in the popular housing styles of the late Victorian United States. American Queen Anne designs were dominated by tall and steeply pitched hipped roofs that were further elaborated by lower, intersecting gables on two or more sides. This complex "hipped with cross gables" form was used for Queen Anne houses of all sizes and costs, from the grandest mansions to the most modest cottages. The same roof shape persisted in two later styles – Shingle and Richardsonian

Opposite: The inspiration for this lodge cottage is Elizabethan, but the carved bargeboards, bay windows and decorative roof tiles are typically Victorian.

Above left: The influence of Second Empire France is apparent in this American house. The almost vertical mansard is clad in thin metal tiles.

Left: A wedding-cake house in Connecticut blends a classical façade with Carpenter Gothic details.

Above: The crow-stepped gable of this neo-Elizabethan building has stone dressings and dark headers forming diaper patterns in the brickwork. This rather aggressive effect is common in Victorian buildings, improving durability at the expense of homogeneity.

Romanesque – that developed from the American Queen Anne Movement in the last decades of the century.

Gables, too, became a major feature, with the walls rising to the level of the top of the roof not just at either end of the building but on other elevations or faces as well. This led to complicated roof plans with a resulting delightful confusion of hips and valleys.

Nothing about the roof was left undecorated. Ridges were fretted and crested. The apex of the gable often had square wooden posts like balusters, heavily decorated, both rising upwards and extending downwards. The bargeboards suspended underneath the gables met centrally at the downward-pointing post. The bargeboards themselves were elaborately carved and provided further opportunities for elaborate posts, balls and finials.

The building's silhouette became all-important. Frequently the age of a house can be told by a glance at its outline, a Victorian country house positively identified by a fragment of roof or chimney rising above the trees. Chimneys were particularly emphasized in Victorian buildings. The Greek temples so admired by Georgian and Greek revival designers had no chimneys and even the precedents of Renaissance Italy were unhelpful. But in the twisting, soaring chimneys of late medieval England, the Victorians found an answer to their craving for the picturesque.

Chimneys on their own were not enough for the Victorians. Their taste also ran to a picturesque crown of chimney pots, and they did much to refine the quality and design of the rather crude versions coming in towards the end of the 18th century. Whether chimney pots are needed at all is a matter of debate. Some maintain that brick chimneys properly built are

Right: These astonishing bargeboards, conveniently dated to 1892, have suspended decorations which hang like icicles from the gables.

Far right: The tall roofs of 19th-century houses provided ample opportunities for decoration, as in this polychrome example from New England.

Right: A high standard of workmanship was needed to make a success of this ornamental detail, applied like a frieze under the eaves.

Far right: Pointed slates, called fish scales, had to be trimmed by hand, but help to break up the monotony of a tall roof.

adequate on their own. But pots do provide an easily weather-proofed wind protector at the end of the flue and increase flue height without the cost of extra brickwork. More important still, from the Victorian point of view, they made another distinctively medieval addition to the roofline. The Victorians sought out models with enthusiasm and some of these, castellated like chess pieces or twisted in Elizabethan chevrons, are now collectors' items.

The main British roofing materials were clay tile, stone, thatch, and, increasingly, Welsh slate. In the United States, wooden shingles were the dominant roofing material, although slate or seamed metal roofs were common on larger and more pretentious dwellings. Towards the end of the era, shaped metal shingles and asphalt shingles were introduced. Not content with plain slates, or plain shingles for that matter, the Victorians invented patterns, introducing

courses of rounded shingles to break the rhythm of an otherwise unbroken and regimented roof pitch. Surprisingly, they seldom competed with the extraordinarily decorative roofs of France and Belgium, where elaborate patterns were created with vari-colored slates and parts of the roof were sometimes gilded. In the United States, vari-colored slate patterns are found on the mansard roofs of some Second Empire style houses, which mimic their colorful French counterparts.

Skylights were normally confined to internal roof slopes invisible from below and were simple in construction – a pane or two of glass set in a hinged wooden frame or, more basic still, metal-framed and fixed, the whole let into the roofing material and flashed with lead. They would probably have been more widely used if there had been a foolproof way of making them watertight. Where central roof lighting was

Above and top: Rainwater heads often carry the date of the building, while the pipes could be elaborately decorated.

Far left: Comparatively restrained bargeboards complement the Gothic gable of this row of East Anglian almshouses.

Left: Harder bricks and stronger cement allowed the Victorians to produce bigger and better chimneys.

Far left: Lively chimneys brighten an otherwise undistinguished roofline.

Left: Elaborate chess-piece chimney pots harmonize with the finials, hood molds and castellations of the rest of the building.

needed, for example above an internal staircase, a flat roof with a solidly constructed lantern light or dome would have been usual, like a miniature greenhouse or conservatory. High roofs, of course, provide immediate opportunities for loft conversion (see page 297). In many Victorian designs the traditional Georgian dormer survived, but with modifications. Each had a little pitched roof of its own, happier in appearance than a flat one and affording further scope for ingenious decoration.

Drainage of the roof was achieved by a wide variety of external cast-iron gutters and downpipes, with hidden gutters behind the parapets of houses. Where an external gutter met a downpipe, it often debouched into an ornamental collecting sleeve or basin called a hopperhead, wider than the downpipe itself. The new and higher roofs, however, brought problems of drainage. Their steep pitches increased the area of the roof and added to the catchment rate of the rain-water, in turn increasing its discharge rate into the gutters and hopperheads. Downpipes were often far too narrow, 3 in (60 mm) or less. They looked elegant, but were quickly blocked with leaves in the fall. Regular inspection and maintenance was vital. In large houses, gutters were checked regularly by the gardeners. In smaller homes the householder no doubt took responsibility, while in cottages, clearing of gutters and downpipes was a continuous necessity, since the only water supply was often provided by means of water butts filled from the roof.

As is common today, except in towns with mains drainage, rain-water was taken to soakaways. Sometimes, in an excess of medievalism, gargoyles were used to throw the rain-water clear of the building.

As in earlier centuries, hopperheads were used decoratively, often carrying the date of the building and initials of the owner. They were usually made of cast lead, although cast iron became more common in the 19th century.

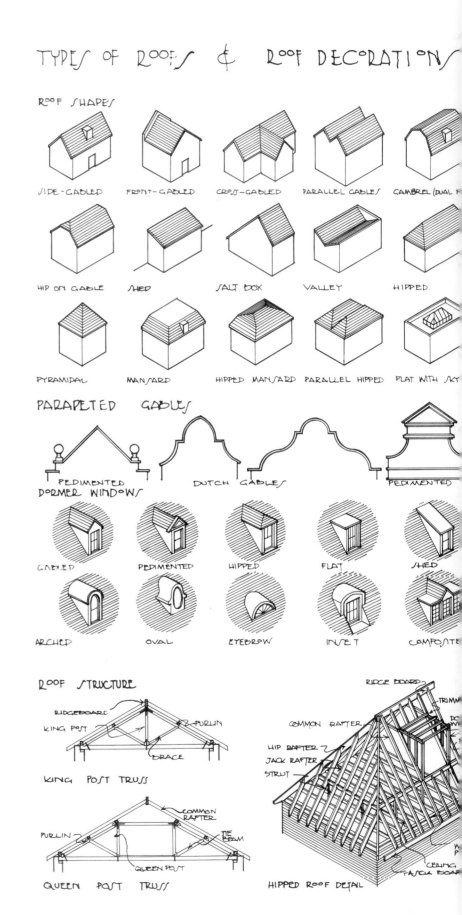

TYPES OF ROOFS & ROOF DECORATIONS

ROOF SHAPES

SIDE-GABLED · FRONT-GABLED · CROSS-GABLED · PARALLEL GABLES · GAMBREL (DUAL P...

HIP ON GABLE · SHED · SALT BOX · VALLEY · HIPPED

PYRAMIDAL · MANSARD · HIPPED MANSARD · PARALLEL HIPPED · FLAT WITH SKY...

PARAPETED GABLES

PEDIMENTED · DUTCH GABLES · PEDIMENTED

DORMER WINDOWS

GABLED · PEDIMENTED · HIPPED · FLAT · SHED

ARCHED · OVAL · EYEBROW · INSET · COMPOSITE

ROOF STRUCTURE

RIDGEBOARD · KING POST · PURLIN · BRACE

KING POST TRUSS

PURLIN · COMMON RAFTER · TIE BEAM · QUEEN POST

QUEEN POST TRUSS

RIDGE BOARD · TRIMM... · COMMON RAFTER · HIP RAFTER · JACK RAFTER · STRUT · CEILING · FASCIA BOARD

HIPPED ROOF DETAIL

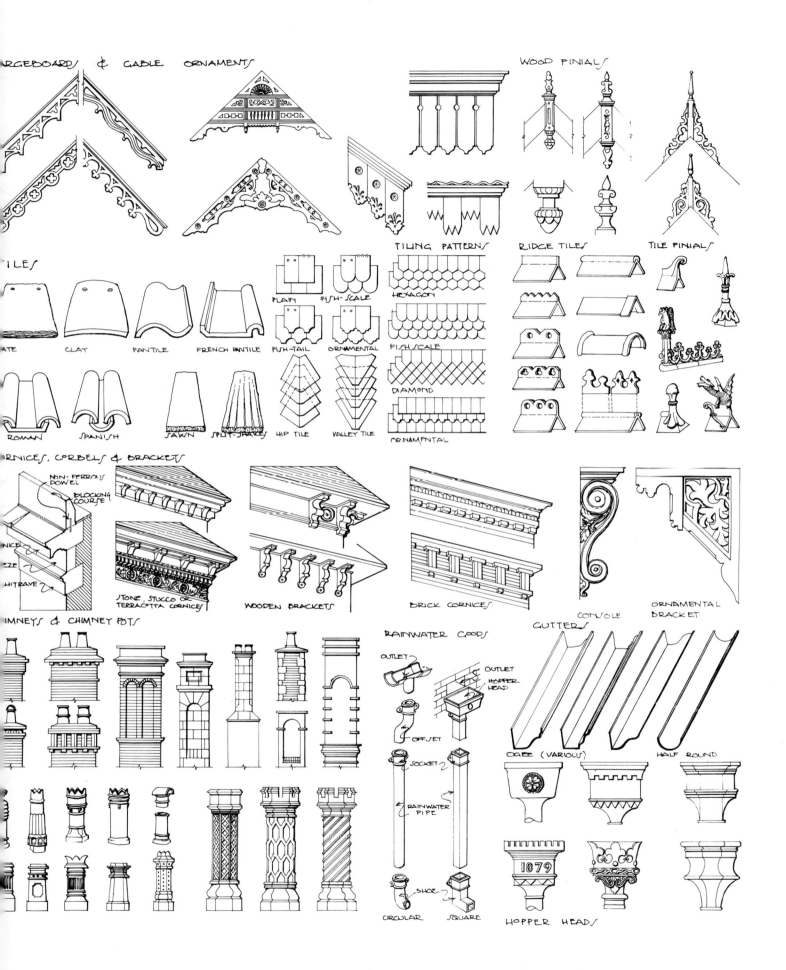

BARGEBOARDS & GABLE ORNAMENTS

WOOD FINIALS

TILES

TILING PATTERNS

RIDGE TILES

TILE FINIALS

PLAIN FISH-SCALE

FISH-TAIL ORNAMENTAL

HEXAGON

FISH SCALE

DIAMOND

ORNAMENTAL

SLATE CLAY PANTILE FRENCH PANTILE

ROMAN SPANISH SAWN SPLIT-SHAKES

HIP TILE VALLEY TILE

CORNICES, CORBELS & BRACKETS

NON-FERROUS DOWEL

BLOCKING COURSE

CORNICE

FRIEZE

ARCHITRAVE

STONE, STUCCO OR TERRACOTTA CORNICES

WOODEN BRACKETS

BRICK CORNICES

CONSOLE

ORNAMENTAL BRACKET

CHIMNEYS & CHIMNEY POTS

RAINWATER GOODS

GUTTERS

OUTLET

OUTLET

HOPPER HEAD

OFFSET

SOCKET

RAINWATER PIPE

OGEE (VARIOUS)

HALF ROUND

1879

SHOE

CIRCULAR SQUARE

HOPPER HEADS

81

EXTERIOR COLOR SCHEMES

We know that Victorian builders loved color, texture and pattern in their buildings, yet it is hard to be dogmatic about the actual paint colors they applied to their external walls and details. This becomes especially important in America, where painted wood-clad houses dominated throughout the period. Photographic records, of course, are all in black and white, and scrapes (the method by which layers of paint are methodically exposed down to the bare wood) are not always reliable because pigments can change color with age, and undercoats may be mistaken for surface finishes. Contemporary oil paintings are a useful source of information, as are books and magazines of the time. Most valuable are the color charts and sample paint schemes, issued as advertisements by paint manufacturers from the 1860's.

These lines of evidence indicate that the range of external paint colors was somewhat more restricted than it is today. According to Webster and Parkes' *Encyclopaedia of Domestic Economy* (1844), the tints most frequently employed were grey, pea, sea and olive green, and fawn. Originally, these tints would have been mixed on the spot from a narrow range of basic pigments, such as Prussian blue, yellow ochre and burnt umber. As the century progressed, manufacturers started to produce ready-mixed paints, and the range of colors widened. These were still limited, however, by a shortage of color-fast pigments: bright reds, purples, yellows, blues and blue–greens faded too quickly (even today's blues and purples are notoriously fugitive); the

Right: The olive green and cream of this San Francisco house has an authentic air and conforms to the color schemes suggested by contemporary trade catalogs. Sometimes a third color, usually dark, would be applied to the window sashes in order to recede and so emphasize the large expanse of glass.

normal Victorian range included black, white and cream, dark reds, browns and ochres of all shades and a wide variety of greens.

The ideas of Michel Eugène Chevreul, who was Director of Dyes at the Gobelins tapestry works, were widely influential. His *Principles of Harmony and Contrast of Colours,* translated into English in 1854, pointed out that some colors change their values when put alongside other colors. Charts of compatible colors soon appeared in manufacturers' catalogs.

The colors favored in America during Victoria's long reign were different during the four sub-eras, each of which had its own color palette and preferred patterns of application. Before about 1840, Greek revival houses dominated American building, and houses, new and old, were primarily painted white with dark green accents. Color use was simple – a white house body, white trim and green shutters.

Between about 1840 and 1870 Gothic revival and Italianate designs became popular, largely because of the writings of Andrew Jackson Downing who had strong feelings about appropriate colors for his designs. He decried the ubiquitous "white house with green shutters" and advocated a change to softer and more "natural" earth tones. Downing published a color card in 1842 which showed three shades of warm grey and three shades of fawn or drab, tones he felt were "pleasing and harmonious in any situation." These neutral colors gradually increased in popularity through the 1860's. It was considered fashionable to use a paler tone for the body of the house and a slightly deeper tone for trim, though an opposite scheme was also used. Window frames and sashes were both customarily painted in the same trim color. Thus a light grey house might have a darker grey trim. Shutters were painted a still darker neutral tone or reverted to the familiar dark green.

From about 1870 to 1900, colors became deeper and more varied, with the addition of full browns, rich reds and dull greens. Simpler

homes still tended to use two closely related colors, one for the body and one for trim, although these were likely to be somewhat stronger and more contrasting than in the preceding era. The trim color was applied to corner boards, window frames, cornices, brackets, porch supports and railings – indeed for all of the "structural" looking members. Porch balusters and bits of detail such as inset panels or bracket details (but not the bracket itself) might be "picked out" in the body color. A third, deep color was sometimes added for the window sashes in order to recede and give the feeling of a large expanse of glass.

In a scheme published in Philadelphia in 1887, the body of the house is painted in drab and the trim in brownstone, with a third color for the sashes and the door and shutter moldings. The colors could be reversed, to give a light trim on a dark body. Both effects were considered superior to the earlier tradition of white for the house body, white trim and green for the shutters.

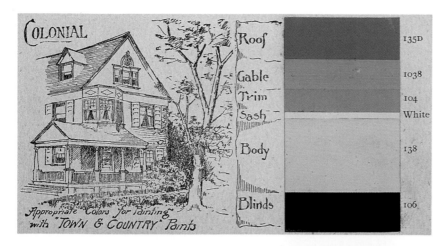

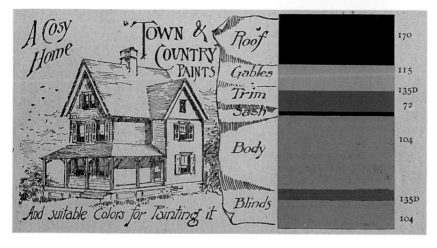

A manufacturer's advertisement of about 1890 helps customers resolve the choice of colors by suggesting how to paint the different parts of the house and achieve a harmonious result using related tones.

Larger and more elaborate Queen Anne houses were commonly painted in complex, multi-hued schemes, becoming a veritable symphony of rich color. The body of the first story might be one tone, the second another, and exposed gable ends painted in yet a third. A fourth and related trim color would be added to corner boards, window frames and "structural" members. Finally, the window sashes would be painted in one of the deep, almost black tones.

Around the turn of the century, softer pastel colors were added to the palette, primarily for houses in the newly popular Colonial revival style. The pastel tone, usually a pale grey, yellow or blue, was used for the body of the house and all trim was painted white. This included both window frames and sashes, for now designers wished to accentuate the multiple small window panes, rather than obscure them. Shutters were again being used, painted either traditional dark green or a deep tone of the body color.

Graining, the painting of ordinary wooden surfaces to imitate fine hardwood, was a favorite Victorian decorative technique. In Britain, particularly, it was commonly used on entrance doors and was also applied to window joinery and other external woodwork. Although graining fell out of favor during the late Victorian years, when more "honest" real woods were preferred, it did not die out completely until the 1930's, and is now enjoying a modest revival.

Some examples of original Victorian paint can still be found, even outside, and this longevity is almost certainly due to its high lead content, in proportions not permitted today but which certainly extended the life of the material considerably. Country paneling which has survived with its original paintwork is almost always in brown or green and is likely to be a good guide to the color of an exterior. Right up to the 1930's most suburban houses in Britain were painted green or brown, some of the browns approaching red. There was a kind of "bull's blood" which was very popular, as was Indian red.

Owners of Victorian houses today are turning to the original color schemes, and some excellent guidebooks are available to aid in this process. Among the best for American dwellings is Moss and Winkler's *Victorian Exterior Decoration* (Henry Holt and Company, 1987). Several major paint manufacturers also now offer a complete range of ready-mixed and harmonizing exterior colors for Victorian houses.

The "earth" colors favored by the Victorians are not only among the cheapest and most readily available pigments but are also fast, retaining their color for decades without noticeable fading (a factor which has remained influential in paint manufacture right up to the present day). Beautiful greens and browns can be obtained by taking the time to add small quantities of black or umber to everyday trade colors, and the extra time spent in experiment can be well worth while when the result is something which is to last for five or ten years.

Top: The pure white trim of this West Coast Italianate house contrasts sharply with the dark body color. This cocoa red was a Victorian favorite, and traces can still be found on many houses.

Above: A typical Italianate house has been demurely painted in lavender and white.Using such pastel tones is sometimes called the "boutique" approach to painting Victorian houses.

Left: Victorian color schemes, such as the Neapolitan paint effects of these houses in San Francisco, can come as something of a surprise, so strong is the impact of black and white and sepia photographs on our image of the period. The deep red scheme on the left is in authentic colors, whereas the pale green, one of the pastels so commonly used in San Francisco, is a less authentic choice.

Below: A traditional, early 19th-century color scheme adds dignity to this Italianate house in the United States. Many such houses were painted in this classic earlier palette despite Downing's efforts to promote drab colors.

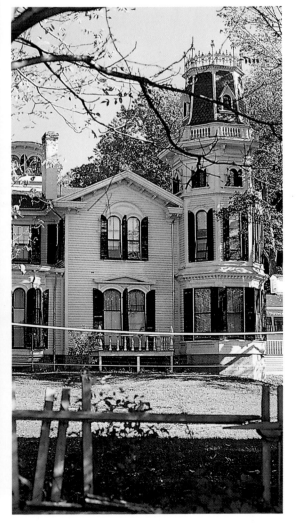

Right: A simple combination of sandpaper brown and white is perfect for the unpretentious classicism of this façade.

Far right: The purplish-brown woodwork of the Mark Twain House in Hartford, Connecticut, relieved by thin red bands, echoes the tone of the brick.

Right: The colors for this window surround, lilac and pink restrained by bands of darker grey, represent a carefully selected but less authentic "boutique" scheme.

Far right: The red and white scheme brings life and accent to a plain façade, enhancing the architecture without undue effort.

Above left: The paintwork brings this ordinary bay window to life.

Left: The blue and cream color scheme gives maximum support and dignity to another fairly commonplace bay window.

Top: The decision to use light orange against a powder blue background shows the delicate wrought iron of the balcony to fine advantage.

Above: The quiet color scheme of this Victorian bay is probably close to the original, although the terracotta decorations would have been unpainted.

DECORATIVE IRONWORK

The art of wrought-iron working reached its peak in the 18th century, but some of the refinement already achieved carried over with continuing momentum into cast-iron technology developed in the 19th century. Wrought iron, as its name suggests, is iron hammered into shape while hot, the traditional art of the blacksmith, who was called upon to make the hinges, latches, and gates for the builders of early Victorian houses and cottages. Some of these craftsmen became distinguished artists, called upon by leading patrons and architects to provide the railings and ornamental gates for grander homes.

The introduction of casting, pouring molten iron into molds, meant that gates and railings could be replicated by the thousand. Wrought iron continued to be cheaper than cast for custom jobs, just as it is today. But the new labor-saving method was naturally adopted for the large-scale production necessary to meet the swelling demand in the early Victorian period for balconies, railings, grills and so forth. Coalbrookdale became the English center for this new industry of cast ironwork. In America the iron industry was more dispersed, with major manufacturers like Wood and Perrot in Philadelphia and Hutchinson and Wickersham in New York joined by numerous local pattern- and mold-makers in cities where cast iron was particularly popular, such as New Orleans.

Aesthetically, it is is difficult to make hard and fast judgements between the two types of ironwork. The greatest English work is undoubtedly wrought, yet the standard achieved generally in, say, Regency balconies in cast iron, was probably higher than could be achieved by local blacksmiths using traditional methods. The hardness of wrought iron is excellent, while cast is relatively brittle and will break if dropped. On the other hand, cast iron is slow to rust and develops a patina which cuts down the rate of oxidation. It also has a grainy quality, caused by the coarse sand used in the casting molds which gives it a pleasingly robust character.

The British Victorians saw in the new technology almost infinite possibilities for decoration while in America Victorian detailing was more commonly executed in factory-turned wood, rather than cast iron. Both materials were inevitably repetitive, a characteristic which caused little concern until the appearance of the Arts and Crafts Movement which called for a return to the hand-made. Some cast ironwork had undoubtedly grown coarser and heavier. But cast iron in the hands of a sensitive designer could be refined and attractive. The marvelous ironwork of New Orleans and Savannah, exceptions to the dominance of wooden detailing in America, has many admirers, as has that of colonial Australia, much of it shipped as ballast from the works at Coalbrookdale.

Modern interest in old buildings has created a demand for iron replacement components and new firms are being formed to answer this need. Long-established manufacturers like Ballantine in Scotland publish specialist literature devoted to traditional patterns and many new foundries will turn out replicas from original samples at modest rates.

A final point on the maintenance of cast iron: its characteristic grain becomes invisible after the application of a few layers of paint. Removing the paint with liquid strippers is a long and arduous process. Sand blasting produces none of the deleterious effects associated with its use on stone or wood and is generally the best method. Ideally this process should be carried out, under workshop conditions and care should be taken to employ the appropriate size of grit.

Opposite: The repeated panels of these Australian balustrades show how mass-produced cast-iron components could be used with grace and delicacy.

DECORATIVE METALWORK

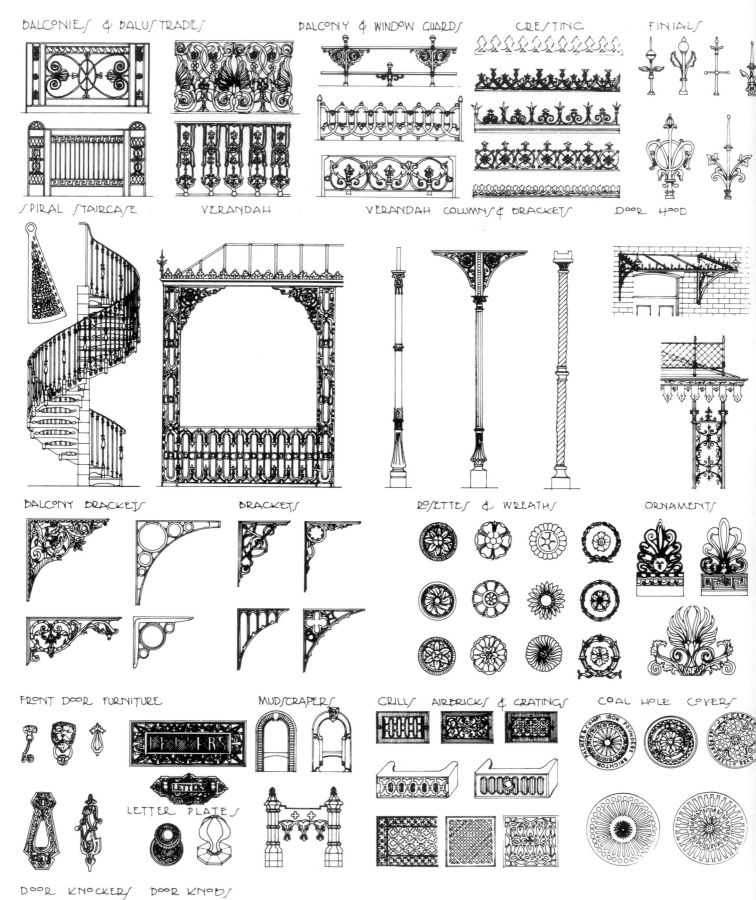

BALCONIES & BALUSTRADES

BALCONY & WINDOW GUARDS

CRESTING

FINIALS

SPIRAL STAIRCASE

VERANDAH

VERANDAH COLUMNS & BRACKETS

DOOR HOOD

BALCONY BRACKETS

BRACKETS

ROSETTES & WREATHS

ORNAMENTS

FRONT DOOR FURNITURE

MUDSCRAPERS

GRILLS AIRBRICKS & GRATINGS

COAL HOLE COVERS

LETTER PLATES

DOOR KNOCKERS DOOR KNOBS

Far left: Delicate railings in Charleston, South Carolina, harmonize perfectly with the foliage that trails around them.

Left: Dark paintwork sets off the exquisite tracery of this cast-iron balcony in Savannah, Georgia, against the white walls and matching shutters.

Above: Commercial pride and advertising are combined in this decorated coal-hole cover.

Overleaf: The juxtaposition of plain uprights and louvers set against highly ornate brackets and railings has produced a sophisticated abstract composition, enhanced by the chic dark green and white color scheme.

Above: Robust cast-iron window box guards were popular in the mid-Victorian era.

Left: Cast-iron vent grills are more attractive than those in brick or terracotta, and worth emphasizing.

WINDOWS

The range and variety of windows increased dramatically during the 19th century, though essentially all derived from two main types – sash and casement. In medieval times and down almost to the end of the 17th century, the casement was the universal model, a window hinged vertically to the window frame and opening inward or outward like a door. The sash window is believed to have originated in Holland. It arrived in Britain in the 1670's and reached the American colonies shortly after 1700. It consists of two framed sections, one above the other, which overlap at the dividing transom bar, and slide up and down in grooves instead of opening in or out. In early examples the upper sash is fixed and the lower held in position by pegs or pins. Later the movements of both sashes came to be controlled by weighted pulleys hidden behind the sides of the window frames.

Sash windows rapidly replaced casements on the main façade of more formal houses during the 18th century, but casements also continued in use in dormer windows, in basements, and in modest houses of few pretensions. Casements are cheaper to produce than sashes, particularly by less skilled carpenters.

With the Gothic revival, a return to appropriate casements is seen in many high-style houses. Most examples, however, retained more convenient, if less authentic, sash windows. Casement windows made a comeback in prestige late in the century and were common in at least some focal windows in Tudor revival houses which spread widely throughout the United States and harked back to English medieval precedents. Frank Lloyd Wright also used casements glazed in modern decorative patterns in his revolutionary "Prairie" houses.

Though Victorian designers were reluctant to abandon the sash, new ways of incorporating it were devised early on. The most obvious of these was the bay window, by no means a

Right: More expensive suburban houses had double decker bay windows, often with sculptural panels between the stories.

Far right: When the roses round this cottage gable fade, the terracotta quoins and polychrome string course will ensure that the house still looks pretty. The casement windows are simple but appropriate.

Opposite: Thatch and wood combine in this example of country Gothic: short branches (from which the bark has long since dropped) set diagonally and studded with oval sections nailed round the edge.

Victorian invention but one which was revived with great enthusiasm. Pre-Victorian bay windows were unusual in America, but were often found in England where they enabled the occupant to look out on a particular view. The enjoyment of views, it should be remembered, was a recent phenomenon, starting in about the 1760's in England, but not reaching America until about 1840, when the growth of romantic sensibility lent a new importance to all that was rugged or picturesque or which stirred the emotions. The arrival of the mass of Victorian bay windows may have included an element of ostentation, but also fitted well with the romantic enjoyment of view and landscape.

Another Victorian favorite, borrowed from an earlier England, was the oriel window, a little bay on its own on an upper story, supported by corbels of some kind or else internally cantilevered so that it appears to be hanging in

Right: This window in "Victoria Cottage," more Georgian than Victorian, was built when the Queen was only two years on the throne. The shaped Gothic tracery has been comfortably placed within a round-headed sash, and the rubbed brickwork joints are particularly fine.

Far right: Grey brick headers were a common device to create pattern interest in brickwork, and provide an attractive foil to a simple classical window.

Right: Narrow side panes, which came in with the Regency, are also found in Victorian windows.

Far right: The medievalists hated large panes of glass and sought to decorate their windows like everything else.

the air. Among many other architects, Norman Shaw was fond of oriel windows and they appear on some of his Queen Anne façades.

Much was made of decorative window surrounds. The abstract counterpoint of solid and void seen in Georgian and Adam designs was too bleak for later tastes. The Gothic revivalists, in the full flood of their initial enthusiasm, were all for making the window panes in the pointed form of the Gothic arch. This was frequently accomplished in one or two main windows, but expense and practicality of opening for ventilation made these not feasible for the whole of the house. More typical were square or rectangular windows set in square or rectangular openings but decorated above with Tudor hoods or pointed moldings. The windows themselves could then be either casement or sash. Gothic arches in flush brickwork were also quite easy to form and after Ruskin's *The Stones of Venice* many

Above left: The use of steel and concrete allowed window openings to become larger. To fill the wide span created here, four simple sashes have been grouped side by side with decorative lights above.

Left: This bay shows how the development of larger panes of glass made large, unobstructed windows possible; the starkness of the window voids is offset by the strength of the surrounding architecture.

Above: This remarkable terrace with vaguely Venetian arched windows crowned with semicircular dormers, each with a spiky finial, reflects the influence of Ruskin. The dormers are new, and much superior to most efforts produced by modern builders.

FIXTURES AND FITTINGS

Much of the character of a Victorian house lies not in the furnishings, nor even in the furniture, but rather in the fixtures and fittings with which the Victorians embellished the interior. Fixtures and fittings are, as anyone who has dealt with house sales and rental property knows, quite distinct both in law and in practical terms. There is no hard and fast rule for distinguishing between the two categories, but in general fixtures are the immovable features such as decorative plaster and tiling, fireplace surrounds, moldings, doors, bath and kitchen installations, the staircase, built-in cabinets and shelving. Fittings are the door handles, door scrapers, curtain fittings, stair rods and other easily removable items.

Most of the architectural details of a house are functional in origin. To take an example, the often glorious moldings surrounding doors, called architraves, have their origins in the humble need to conceal the junction between wood and plaster. It is interesting to find that, whatever the style, similar devices have been designed all over the world and at many different times to answer the same functional needs. Similarly, baseboards have the practical purpose of protecting wall plaster from damage by furniture and feet; they also hide the awkward gap between the wall and the floorboards. In the same way a cornice hides the cracks that inevitably appear at the joint between ceiling and wall. Dado-, or chair-rails, were intended to protect walls against being knocked by furniture (in the 18th century it was customary to place chairs and tables round the perimeter of a room, leaving the center more or less free). The picture rail's function is self-evident.

In addition to fulfilling a distinct function, ornamentation was used to alter the proportions of a room or accentuate its features. Ceiling roses, wall brackets and plaster wall frames introduced additional elements within which different decoration could take place. Dado-rails came to serve a double purpose as it was found that they could adjust the scale of a room, allowing contrasting colors and patterns to be applied above and below. The same is true of the picture rail which, together with the dado, created a tripartite division of the wall which was much favored by designers towards the end of the 19th century.

The fixtures and fittings even in a modest room can add up to

Opposite: Flintham in Nottinghamshire, built by T. C. Hine between 1851 and 1854, is a fine example of the High Victorian grandeur to which many lesser homes aspired. The Corinthian columns that frame the library would be out of place in all but the most generously proportioned rooms, but many of the fixtures such as the corbels, brackets and plaster moldings were echoed in countless humbler dwellings.

Right: With its magnificently paneled walls and spirited plaster molding on the ceiling, the drawing room at Wightwick Manor near Wolverhampton draws its inspiration from the Elizabethan and Jacobean periods.

Below: This charming early Victorian hob, with its unpretentious overmantel, shows how simple fixtures can be put to elegant use today. Later in the century, more elaborate register grates came into widespread use.

a surprising number. Imagine a small Victorian living room or parlor. The floor may be of simple pine boards, probably wider than most modern examples, or it may be wood strip or parquet. The hearth to the fireplace may be stone or tile, and the fireplace itself will have a surround and a basket grate of some kind, most probably of some mass-produced pattern in cast iron. Close to the fireplace may be the remains of an old bell system with a cranked handle. Then there is the door to the room, its architrave, the baseboards, a dado-rail perhaps, and the window and shutters, if any. There will almost certainly be a cornice in any principal room and possibly decorative ceiling plaster as well.

Despite the stylistic changes that occurred over the century, the basic pattern of the Victorian house remained remarkably consistent. Whatever the size or status of the house, the focus of the building remained the entry hall, stairway and upper landings off which the many, often small, rooms led. In great houses and estates, the hallway was a grand affair boasting a magnificent fireplace, and possibly an elaborate beamed ceiling. This "living hall," as it was called, was intended to replace the earlier pattern of the hallway as simply a passage with a warm, welcoming room which immediately made one feel at home and could even be lived in. At the other end of the scale, row houses had a narrow entrance hall, with a door opening immediately to right or left into a drawing room or parlor. This arrangement was intended to give the visitor an immediate view of the most impressive room in the house, finished with the finest cornices, fireplace and baseboards. The staircase led up straight ahead and past it ran a passage leading to the dining room and kitchen at the rear. In many row houses a large double door linked the two principal ground-floor rooms.

Staircase, doors and fireplace were supplied by the builder. Indeed, most of the fixtures of the house including cornices and ceiling roses formed part of the builder's finish. The majority of homeowners were happy with this ornamentation, which was updated in line with the latest technological advances and supplied an air of fashionable elegance. At the lower end of the scale, ornamentation served to hide the skimped construction of the cheaper houses. As today, ornamentation or "design" was cheaper than good, solid construction, and since it was to the financial advantage of each member of a production line to follow a tried and tested formula, the finish of many houses was monotonously repetitive. Some features were straight shams. The ubiquitous arch in the hallway and the corbels supporting it were both made of plaster and served no structural purpose. Influential writers and artists decried this trend, but to little avail.

Like 19th-century society, the fixtures and fittings followed hierarchical, not to say patriarchal, principles. Decoration was concentrated in the hall, living room, dining room and the first

Below: As the density of urban housing increased, stained glass was used to ensure privacy and to disguise the proximity of other buildings.

Above: This illustration from the Edinburgh decorators Purdie & Lithgow's 1856 catalog shows how elaborately the divisions of a wall, from baseboard to cornice, could be treated.

flight of stairs. These were the public parts of the house where guests were received and impressions made. The remaining family rooms, such as the bedrooms, were not seen by people that mattered and were furnished and decorated at little expense. In many cases the height of the bedroom story was sacrificed to achieve a spaciousness in the drawing room below, and the upstairs architectural detailing was reduced. Main bedrooms might have a much simpler cornice than the public rooms, and children's and servants' rooms generally had none. The fireplaces shrank in size and were less ornate on the upper stories, reducing to simpler versions in the main bedrooms and sometimes to none in the attic rooms.

The dining room – which often faced west to catch the evening sun – was traditionally "masculine." The somber tone might be set by wood paneling and a deep toned fireplace; dark family portraits were traditionally displayed on the walls and dark wood predominated in the furniture. The living room might have a white or white-veined marble fireplace, and was decorated in a so-called feminine idiom. "Feminine" was a license for ornate cornices and even more ornate furniture and an array of soft furnishings which were felt to exemplify elegant comfort and coziness. Soft pastel colors were often introduced.

In Victorian times the utilities of the house were of the simplest nature. Electricity was not available to most houses until well into the next century. Some houses may retain the original piping for gas lights intact, usually concealed in the plasterwork and covered by layers of wallpaper. Plumbing is likely to have been equally skeletal. Water, in lead pipework, was introduced from the street into the basement or ground floor, to serve the kitchen sink and closet. Piped water was rarely taken above this level until more

Left: These delicate Gothic alcoves make an attractive feature out of an awkward corner and provide a good example of how original architectural detailing can be used to enhance a modern decorative scheme.

reliable water pressure was available in this century. Most existing utilities found in Victorian houses are therefore early 20th-century or later in origin.

Central heating was found only in the larger and more expensive houses, and reflected the Victorian enthusiasm for invention. Books and magazines of the time reveal a strong market for patented inventions for radiator systems, back boilers, warm-air under-floor heating and new types of forced air heating. None, however, completely supplanted the traditional open fireplace, for that had functions far more significant than the simple process of heating, and the Victorians recognized the strong emotional significance of the hearth as the center of the home.

PLANNING AHEAD

Victorian house always has character. It is a quality that comes first and foremost from age, and from the pleasure of rediscovering the past. Anyone walking along a street in any city or town will see examples of buildings awaiting the restorer's hand. Often they have lost the status they once enjoyed, especially if they are no longer lived in as family houses. Many delightful villas set back off the road in wide avenues, now enjoying planting in full maturity, advertise the plight of multiple-occupancy with six bells by the front door, uncherished drives choked with weeds and parked cars and gates rotting or removed. Inside they may have lost many of their original fixtures and fittings, and acquired unwanted partitions and jerry-built baths. But their original status as a gentleman's residence remains indestructible.

A great deal of forethought is required to decorate a Victorian house and make it a comfortable place to live, much more than when moving into a modern house. Structural alterations may be needed to adapt the interior layout to modern requirements (see Chapter 8 for the technical aspects). Decisions will be required on which fixtures and fittings to restore or reinstate. Heating, electrical, and plumbing facilities may have to be relaid. Even the color scheme, and whether to paint or paper a wall in one color, two or three, will be influenced by the architectural detailing of the house.

It is extremely difficult to visualize how a house will be used when all the work has been finished. Surprisingly few decorators and designers use any methodical system for working out the requirements of everyday living. My own method is to prepare a full interior design plan (see page 109) before calling in the builders. It can be used both to plan a scheme for fixtures and fittings – the subject of this chapter – and to think ahead to the decoration of the house, discussed from Chapter 4 on.

Many people delay getting builders' estimates because they do not know how they are going to decorate. This is an unnecessary worry. It is best to think of work on a house as a two-stage operation – building first and decoration second. The first phase takes the house to what may be termed builder's finish, with the interior ready to receive the chosen coat of paint or wallpaper. Decoration can be thought about – and costed – separately. The only important decision to make in advance is whether a room is to be papered or painted, because the sub-preparation will be different in each case.

Before getting down to detail, a question of priorities must be decided. How much importance should be placed on the structure of the building and the internal fixtures, and how much on decoration? My own answer is a simple one. Everybody, whether carrying out their own plan for a house or using a designer to help them, inevitably has to set themselves a budget. Somewhat to my detriment, I always argue that the major part of the cost should be spent on the architectural fabric, and that includes internal architectural detailing. Decoration is secondary. Get the architecture right, and the rest will follow.

The guiding principle in all decoration is, do not do anything that destroys the proportion and form of the original architecture. In a Victorian house the interior architectural features reflect the character and period of the building and are nearly always worth preserving however humble or simple they may be. They are as much an integral part of the architecture as the structure itself. Anyone first viewing a house will find it is prudent to ask the real estate agent which fixtures go with the house, and which are fittings to be taken away by the owner. Needless to say, doors should come complete with the knobs and hardware, but with the rise in value of antique ironwork the temptation to remove

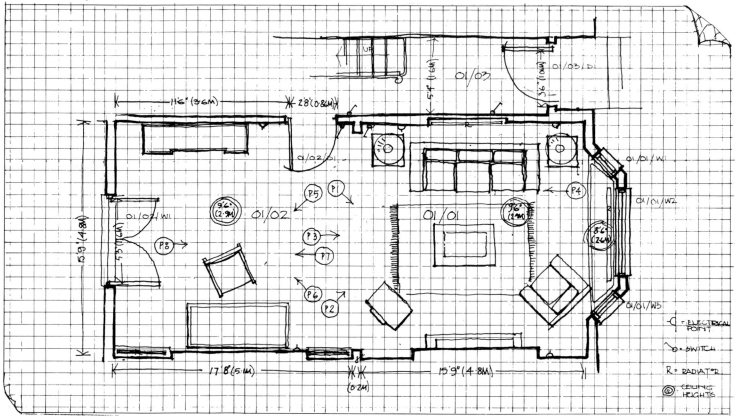

The key to good interior design is a complete floor plan and furniture layout. By working out what furniture you want and where you plan to put it, you will be able to form a fairly exact idea of how you intend to use the house. Once there is a furniture layout, it can be used to work backwards, to plan the infrastructure which will be needed, the wiring, heating, plumbing and all the rest of the "mechanicals." At the same time the layout will enable you to look ahead to the final goal, the fully decorated house.

My own approach to any house is first to draw up a proper floor plan, with measurements marked on it. The simplest method is to use graph paper, first setting a scale. In the center of each room, I put a circle with the ceiling height on it. If

the ceiling height alters, say under a bay window, I note the fact in the appropriate spot. Next I mark any existing electrical outlets and radiators or heating registers. I also like to note which way the doors are hinged, and whether they open inwards or outwards.

Once I have completed the floor plan, I photograph every room, numbering each shot and marking its direction on the plan with a small arrow. I make sure I have a photograph of each window to give to the curtain-maker.

Then I number each room, door and window on the floor plan, so that I have a quick method of reference. A number of systems will do equally well. My own is to number floor level first, then give each room its number, rather like the system in many

hotels – basement 00, ground floor 01 and so on upwards. This might yield the number 02/01 for the master bedroom and I would add the number of each window and door to the same series: 02/01/W1/ W2/D1 and so on. Alternatively, start with the basement B, the ground floor 1 and number on upwards from there.

Once the house is mapped out on paper, with doors and windows numbered, and room sizes, ceiling heights, electrical outlets and heating apparatus noted, I make three lists of furniture. The first contains items that will definitely be used – furniture to be moved from the owner's old house and pieces that have been bought specially for the new home. The second list is more tentative – items that may be used if they fit and seem appropriate. The third

list covers items of furniture that must be bought.

Now I mark on the floor plan the kind of furniture layout that might be expected, using a different color for items from each of the three lists. Then I can see at a glance what is available for a particular room and what is still needed. This layout phase requires the most detailed thought.

A complete floor plan and furniture layout make it easier to see how the utilities should be arranged, that is to say, where radiators or heating outlets will be convenient and where they will not, where electric plugs are needed and, consequently, wiring.

Now, on a separate set of plans, I mark the intended position of electrical services and wiring, and on another I make the heating plan. These drawings are not

intended as great works of art but purely as an *aide-mémoire* for the homeowner which may later be passed on to builder or architect. But they do have the great merit of focusing one's view of the house.

A carefully prepared plan should also help with decisions about changing the structure of the house or altering the fixtures and fittings. Does a door need to be moved to accommodate a built-in closet? Should the swing of a door be reversed? Is a door needed at all? What will the circulation patterns be? Would it be a good idea to provide an additional exit into the garden? The answers to all these questions become much more evident when you are able to look coolly at a piece of paper.

Now, and only now, begin to think about decoration.

it and replace it with cheap new fittings may be irresistible to the greedy. The same is true for faucets, shower fittings, cabinet furniture, curtain hardware, even fireplace surrounds and decorative tiling. Some sellers are quite unscrupulous and have been known to remove handles, knockers, door scrapers and so on just before they leave.

Of course, today it is increasingly rare to find a house with very many original interior details still in place. Either they were swept away by "modernization" during the 1950's and 1960's or they have been badly mauled during past conversions into apartments or boarding houses.

Before carrying out any extensive repair or restoration work it is a good idea to use the interior design plan to catalog, room by room, what remains that is worth preserving and what missing features might reasonably be replaced. Think of the relative ease or difficulty of replacement – replacing broken stained glass in a door or window, for instance, may be done at leisure, whereas the repair of broken cornices, worn flooring or wood paneling will only cause disruption if delayed until the house is occupied.

Deciding which features to restore is not simply a question of cost or practicality. Some kind of cornice, however simple, is important to get the best out of a room; likewise a fireplace, which gives a focus and personality to a room. The re-installation of a handsome mantelpiece is a good starting point and, with the cornice, will establish a character from which all other decoration will ultimately derive. The typical Victorian four- or five-paneled door is also an essential feature of a well-finished house. Such doors are frequently found in attics, or can be bought from salvage yards. Sometimes they were made of handsome woods, which when stripped have wonderful graining patterns.

The other fittings that formed an integral part of a Victorian interior, such as door furniture, handles, locks and escutcheons, can be reinstated at a later date. The perfectionist will even want to go into such details as door hinges, window handles and remnants of old curtain hardware. Attractive finger plates, for instance, may be found quite by chance in an antique shop. Whether the list leans to the practical or decorative side will vary with the individual – many houses are bought for impulsive reasons, and what may seem frivolous to one buyer may be crucial to another. There are no rules in restoration, only a few guidelines which may be of help to the inexperienced. It is important above all that the design should be personal.

ALTERATIONS

The Victorians were more formal in their social habits than we are today. They preferred many small rooms with different purposes whereas we are often more at ease in an open, multi-functional living space. Nevertheless, in spite of the arrival of the automobile, the television and modern kitchen gadgetry, our lives have not altered all that much, and a Victorian house will meet most of our needs extremely well with only minor alteration. We still need a living room, bedrooms, kitchen, bathroom and garden. We no longer need a scullery (it vanished with the scullery maid), but we can convert it into a utility room; nor do we need a parlor, but we can combine that with the living room. Instead of wardrobes, we fill in corners and alcoves with built-in closets. We need another bathroom, so we convert one of the bedrooms.

The chief problem in adapting Victorian houses to modern living occurs in small row houses and some larger ones where, in an effort to create an air of spaciousness and light, the wall between the front and back rooms on the ground floor is removed to create one through room with large windows at either end. The result is generally a long, thin space with two doors, which is not infrequently difficult to heat and awkward to decorate. Attempts to give two dissimilar rooms some contemporary homogeneity are frequently unsuccessful. In the section below on the styling of these "through" rooms I have suggested solutions to some of these problems. Often the wall that has to be removed is the principal structural cross-wall of the house, and considerable engineering work is necessary to provide a replacement (see Chapter 8).

Less drastic is a change I often advocate in reception rooms, where the swing of the door may be reversed. Victorian doors always opened inwards into rooms, and swung not back towards the nearest wall, but out "against" the room,

blocking the view so that servants could withdraw if unwanted, before they could see what the occupants were doing. In bedrooms this practice is retained today, but in other rooms many now prefer to open the door against a wall and so provide a more spacious feel to the house.

Sometimes the position of a door may need to be changed, especially if it is close to an end wall where a built-in closet could be installed. By moving the door along 2 ft (60 cm) space can be obtained for the closet, but the baseboard and dado-rail, if there is one, will have to be cut and moved too, as will any light switch. This is just the sort of decision that must be made early, when building work is in the planning stage.

THE STYLING OF THROUGH ROOMS

Combining the two main ground-floor rooms in a row house is the most drastic departure we are likely to make from the original architecture of our Victorian forebears (see the technical discussion in Chapter 8). By using the architectural detailing of the period, however, it is possible to make the opening look an integral part of the house.

Victorians generally had double doors between the two reception rooms. These tend to be most inconvenient. When folded back there always seems to be a piece of furniture standing in the way. If major work is to be done to the house, and double doors seem suitable between two rooms, then a solution may be to build a false wall with a new cornice around it in one of the rooms, so the doors can slide into the space created between the old and new walls.

If doors are not wanted, the opening may still be constructed like an enlarged door frame, with architrave to match the other door openings.

Sometimes the two rooms to be linked are so small that there is a strong desire to make the opening as large as possible. It is very difficult to take an arch right up to the ceiling. Because space has to be left for a supporting beam, the arch generally stops about 1 ft or 18 in (30 or 45 cm.) below cornice level, so the cornices in each room stay separate. This is preferable since normally they do not match; the room at the front will generally have the grander fixtures and fittings.

An arched opening may be embellished with plaster corbels. Although serving no structural purpose, they are no more

(continued on page 112)

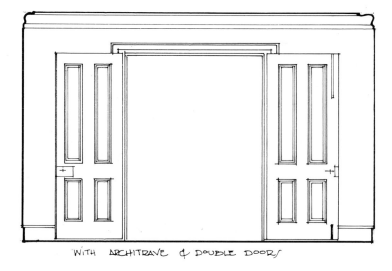

WITH ARCHITRAVE & DOUBLE DOORS

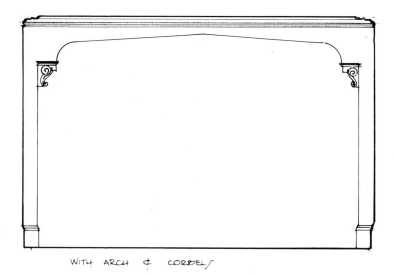

WITH ARCH & CORBELS

UTILITIES

The provision of plumbing, central heating and wiring in a Victorian house requires just as much forethought as the fixtures and fittings. Not having been included in the house originally, these utilities are likely to have been installed in a piecemeal fashion, at the whim of various contractors and owners over the years, and they may well not suit the patterns of contemporary use.

There is no reason to attempt to preserve the old plumbing and wiring found in an unmodernized house. Most of it will be post-Victorian, and either in poor condition or unsafe. Where cast-iron radiators have survived, flushing and cleaning can extend their life, but the old steel large-bore pipework should be discarded and replaced with copper. Original gas piping, if intact, may be restored and used, though such a relish for authenticity is likely to attract only the most fervent period enthusiast. Gas provides a very agreeable light source, soft and white, and is accompanied by a faint hissing; but in terms of convenience it is no rival for electricity. There is no reason, however, why a single room or perhaps two should not be provided with this form of illumination, run as an occasional pleasure.

(continued from page 111) false than the corbels found "supporting" the arch in the hall. For the sake of symmetry, care should be taken to ensure that any brick pillars supporting the cross beam project equal distances from the side walls. In large houses it may be possible to give extra style to an opening by introducing pilasters or even slim cast-iron columns with decorative capitals.

When two rooms have been combined into one, many people choose to seal up the door between hallway and front room and instead use the door to what was originally the back room. Usually, the hinges will be on the side of the door nearer the back of the house. As the door opens, it offers a wide view through the opening towards the front of the house and the main fireplace.

An alternative is to seal up the door to the original back room and then, if there is a single door from the hall into the front room, open up a big double doorway. The new door space can be left open so that on entering the house the visitor sees the whole of the hall and living room.

Each room originally had its own fireplace, but it scarcely seems worth keeping two in what has become a single through room. If the mantelpiece in the back room has gone, one solution is to cover the whole wall with shelving, including the chimney breast. If shelves are made deeper than the recesses, and they cross the chimney breast; with the baseboard mold taken through at the bottom and a cornice at the top, there will be a sense of continuity.

An alternative is simply to shelve the recesses and leave the chimney breast bare. A large piece of furniture serves the same purpose as a fireplace in providing a focal point.

Generally through rooms are best treated as a single unit when decorating, with floor and wall surfaces the same. Apart from that, symmetry may be ignored. Hang a chandelier in each room – they do not have to match – or in one and not the other. Mantelpieces, area rugs and seating styles can also differ.

WITH DECORATIVE GRILL

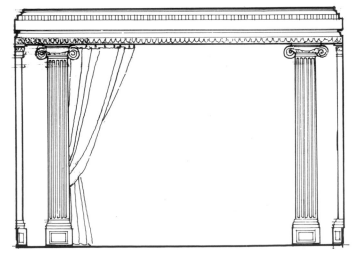

WITH PILASTERS & COLUMNS

WIRING

The wiring plan for a house should be worked out from the interior design plan and furniture layout. The positions of beds, sofa, easy chair and kitchen table will determine where reading and working lights ought to be.

Many people believe their problems will be solved if they put in enough 220 V plugs, but this may not be the answer. Apart from a few major appliances like refrigerators, few items need to be run off 220 V plugs. Of greater help is converting one plug of the usual two plug outlet to a switched lighting point. These can be placed on one continuous circuit controlled from the door of a room. If the circuit is to be dimmed, it is worth adding up the number of lamps that might be used on one of these circuits and telling the electrician what the load is likely to be, as dimmers do vary in size.

The best place for the lighting circuit is behind the baseboard. This low-level arrangement allows table and standing lamps to be connected at the most convenient points. Later, if a wall or picture light is needed, the wiring can be run straight up the wall and chased into the plaster with a minimum of damage. For replica Victorian light fittings, brass ducting fixed to the surface of the wall can look effective.

Even with a properly prepared furniture layout, it is difficult to foresee all necessary wiring. To decide where to put switches, and which lights have to turn on where, try walking around the house at night, flashlight in hand, and see where you have to turn the light on. That is where you need a switch. If you are uncertain where the television will go, add cable outlets and plugs for every likely position. The cost of wiring at the outset is not prohibitive, but the cost of alterations later can be. The same is true of the sound system. For the sake of flexibility and neatness, it is worth running concealed speaker cables to several spots.

The doorbell is one of the easiest items to overlook. It should probably ring at the front door, in the kitchen so that it is not drowned by the noise of kitchen machinery, and even, perhaps, upstairs.

It is also worth paying attention to the placing of controls. An electrician, acting without instructions, is likely to position the central heating thermostat at eye level in the middle of the drawing room wall and to put the doorbell in the most visible place in the hall. Many burglar alarm control panels are in impossible places because they have been positioned as an afterthought. Door entry-phones, and even more so the new TV door entry-phones, should be tactfully placed. The fuse box should be a system of modern circuit breakers placed at eye level in a closet with its own separate lighting supply that comes on when the door is opened.

The following workmen and perhaps some others besides may all need to put in wiring – an electrician, telephone engineer, heating engineer, sound system engineer, security firm, cable television and intercom expert. To avoid the constant lifting of floorboards or the confusion of a multitude of different tradesmen on site simultaneously, it is possible – if wiring runs are planned early – to install plastic ducts down which wires may be threaded by each expert in turn.

By avoiding unsightly cables and electric outlets, the effort that goes into good architectural detailing in a Victorian house will not be wasted and the result will be modern facilities with period charm.

HEATING

By using an interior design plan, it is possible to work out the best positions for the radiators or heat registers in advance. The pipes or ductwork can then be laid when other major works are carried out.

Ductwork should be placed where it does not lower main ceiling heights and registers where they will not be covered by furniture.

Traditional cast-iron radiators were handsomely designed and well suited to Victorian interiors. Modern replicas are available in both pressed steel and cast iron. These radiators closely resemble the originals, but they run on modern small-bore heating systems.

Radiators should not generally be boxed in unless there is a functional reason for doing so, such as their position under a window seat. Where radiators are placed under bookcases in a recess, they would look strange if not boxed in.

Victorian houses with central heating had the hot water heater at the bottom of the house close to the point of coal delivery. This remains the usual site for them, but with gas-fired water heating other positions are possible.

There is no good reason to run the whole of a house on the same central heating system. In some homes the heating runs all day in cold weather and is turned off at night. But many people prefer to keep their bedrooms warm at night. The answer is to have the upper floors of the house on one circuit and the lower floors on another, with two separate air systems or pumps (or alternatively a single pump with two sets of motorized valves), two thermostats, and two time clocks.

VICTORIAN CAST-IRON RADIATORS

RADIATOR SCREEN WITH MARBLE TOP

HALLS, STAIRS AND LANDINGS

Opposite: A grand newel post at the foot of an otherwise modest staircase provides a strong and unmistakably Victorian accent in an American hall. North America, with its strong woodworking tradition, produced halls that were brighter and much more elegant than their British counterparts.

Below: In this generously proportioned hall the staircase turns three times between first and second floors, and the Gothic-style door closes into a standard square-arched frame to which a shaped header has been added. Parquet flooring was a common alternative to encaustic tiles in larger hallways.

Today, with our less visible air pollution, we forget that entry halls once had to act as *cordons sanitaires* between a comfortable indoors and a horse-driven, dusty or muddy world outside. A hall also had to impress the visitor and set the tone for entry into the public rooms. Despite the fact that many hallways in row houses were poorly lit, often only by a fanlight above the door, dark colors were widely used. They lent an air of authority to what were often thin party walls and, along with the encaustic tiles and marbleized papers, gave an impression of security to resident and visitor alike.

For the entry hall walls of the urban row house, Victorians favored hard-wearing materials. The most common mid-19th-century covering for the hall dado was marbleized paper designed to look like a wall of individual marble building blocks. Cutouts of individual blocks could be replaced singly if any damage occurred. Not all Victorians favored this effect, however; Charles

Eastlake's *Hints on Household Taste* (first published in the United States in 1872), was a compilation of articles that had first appeared in the women's journal the *Queen*. It disagreed and attacked this aping of palatial marble panels as an ugly and unnecessary delusion of grandeur in the hallway of an ordinary house. Eastlake favored encaustic tiles (solid-color tiles laid in varying geometric patterns) as a washable and hard-wearing finish, both for the floor and also as a wall covering to a height of about three or four feet. The most common dado coverings in the second half of the century were leather-paper; anaglypta, an embossed and strengthened paper; and Lincrusta, an embossed linoleum-like product.

The fact that a hall is not a room where you spend much time gives you a little liberty to decorate with extravagant color schemes, using a profusion of colors and patterns that is exciting when passing through but would become infuriating in a room in which you wanted to work or relax. Another difference is that the wall divisions in a hall are related to people standing.

Given the narrowness of some halls, it is questionable whether any furniture is needed beyond hat-and-coat-rack and umbrella-stand. The hall table of the Victorians with a tray for visiting cards and a drawer for a clothes brush, flanked by two chairs, or a bench with a wooden seat for waiting workmen, may not quite tally with a modern lifestyle. Nowadays a chest or table with a looking-glass above may serve for all purposes.

Relatively narrow halls were given fireplaces, and their minimal size needed all the support it could get from draft excluders to keep the staircase warm. A cold staircase inhibits movement and makes for a house divided against itself, creating a sense of claustrophobia. The area immediately inside the front door is

Opposite: Dark and hard-wearing surfaces such as encaustic tiles and anaglypta paper were an advantage in halls, which saw heavy traffic. Here the radiator has been painted the same color as the anaglypta, which is the right thing to do.

Below: Vestibule doors and arches were used to break up the space in a hall, which can so easily look like one long, somber passageway.

sometimes divided off from hall and stairs by glass-paneled double doors. Like so much else in the Victorian house, this arrangement worked on three levels: the social, the aesthetic and the functional. A lobby or vestibule was a regular feature in grand houses, and thus lent status and dignity to a humbler dwelling. The vestibule doors are often an attractive feature in their own right, with fine carving and elegant beveled, frosted or stained glass, and the division improves the proportions of a long, narrow hallway which might otherwise seem like an endless corridor. This second set of doors also served to prevent drafts, often with the help of a heavy curtain, and the vestibule provided a useful space for coat-hooks and umbrella-stands.

The living hall revived by the Arts and Crafts Movement was a rather different kind of entrance. In essence a modest great hall, harking back to medieval origins, it was strictly more of a living room than a hall and stressed simplicity as a theme. H.H. Richardson first introduced this

concept to the United States in two Newport, Rhode Island, houses in the early 1870's. The large hall became the central core of the house and focused on a welcoming, wide hearth, and handsome stairway. The decoration was plain, dominated by woodwork, beamed ceiling, and massive open fireplace. By the end of the century, the living hall was frequently invaded by the clutter from which it had originally provided an escape. The British architect Voysey complained that many a hall was full of "vulgar glitter and display," a "vast expanse of advertisement" that reminded him of a railway station.

A hybrid living hall and great hall became part of the basic vocabulary of both large and modest Victorian houses from the 1880's onwards, lined with dark woods, filled with museum-like displays of trophies and decorated in a vaguely "Jacobethan" manner, a revivalist mix of Elizabethan and Jacobean styles. The ceiling would be relatively low and might be elaborately stenciled or left as open oak beams.

Right: The stenciled decoration above the baseboard cleverly picks up the pattern of the border tiles.

A porch with a staircase leading off it fulfilled the strictly utilitarian functions of insulating the front door area, with all its comings and goings, from the rest of the house.

Interior stairs were generally of wood and were often elaborately decorated, even in quite ordinary houses, with a hardwood handrail, turned balusters and prominent newel posts. Of the many different baluster designs, "spindle" was the commonest, largely because it was easy to mass-produce on a lathe. Stone staircases were common on the exteriors of larger houses and row houses. They are most often found in the kind of large Victorian row house now converted into apartments. Metal staircases were less common, and normally reserved for external use.

The simplest way to deal with the stairs and landings of the row house is to run the same colors and carpet from top to bottom. This will supply a basic unity within which to arrange decorative features, built-in cabinets, pictures and furniture. Old-fashioned stair-runners with brass rods remain the most attractive way to treat

(continued on page 122)

Below: These attractive stone stairs at Cragside in Northumberland are enlivened by the thin band of tiles at the bottom of each riser.

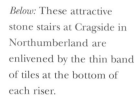

Left: The blue tiles on this staircase at Leighton House in Holland Park, London, date from 1866 and combine beauty with resistance to wear.

Above: Pugin's ornate staircase at the Speaker's House in the Palace of Westminster is a classic example of High Victorian Gothic.

Opposite: First-floor landings were relatively large, as it was here that the hostess would greet her guests as they came up to the drawing room.

Above: Stairwells can be more excitingly exploited for both storage and display than is achieved by the usual row of prints on the wall.

Right: Decorative schemes should give landings and staircases a warm and friendly aspect, so that they become extra living spaces for the family. In this country cottage with ledged and braced doors, fretwork motifs in the Victorian manner have been used successfully for both the balusters and boxed-in radiator.

(continued from page 118)

wooden or stone staircases. However, narrow and more cheaply made stairs may look better with fitted carpet – the narrowness will make the rods seem awkward, and the wood may not be strong enough to hold the fasteners for the rods. Except when graining or marbling is used, baseboards and the edges of the stairs are best painted the same color; this will add to the sense of height.

On the top landing, where the balusters meet the floor above the last flight of stairs, it is often difficult to finish the carpet neatly. The best method is to abut the carpet against a strip of flat molding cut to the width of the handrail and laid in front of the balusters.

If you need to build an additional flight of stairs, it is worth searching for balusters that match those in the original staircase. When you are building an entirely new staircase, the designs shown opposite may prove helpful in planning an attractive scheme.

Another feature that benefits from close attention to detail is the doormat inside the front door. The bigger the mat, the better it will look. The best treatment is to sink it into a mat-well. Suitable matting can be bought in rubber-backed rolls and cut to fit. In carpeted floors, carpet can be turned over the edge of the well to form a lining. Where a hall is divided by doors, the entire vestibule can be carpeted with matting.

Long, thin landings and halls pose special challenges. For many years, designers have been tackling the apparent endlessness of corridors in the larger hotels by incorporating arches, columns and alcoves. Some of these ideas can be applied in a domestic setting. Alternatively, if a long corridor leads to just one bedroom, it can be shortened and the space incorporated into the room, forming an inner entry hall.

STAIRCASES & THEIR DETAILS

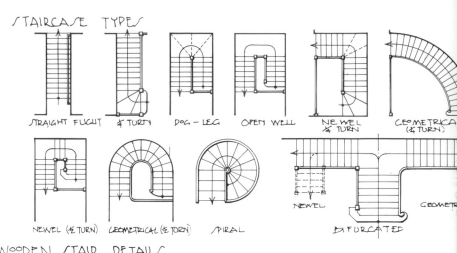

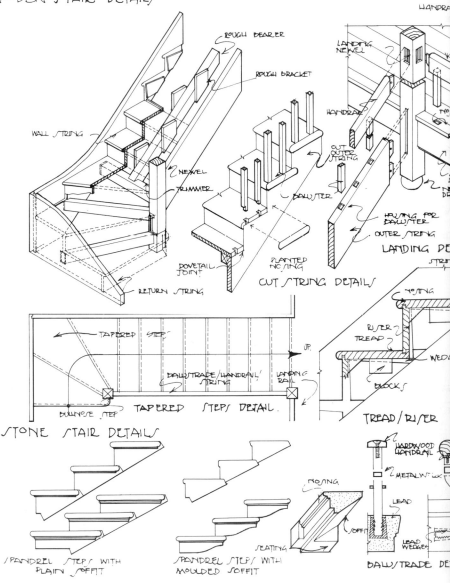

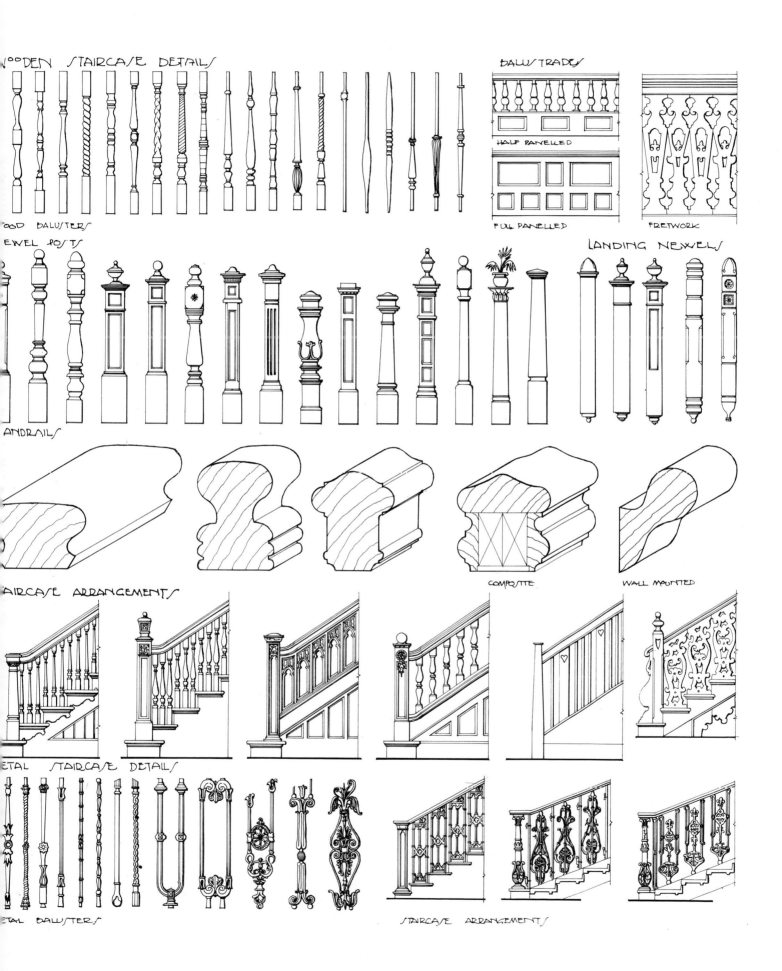

WOODEN STAIRCASE DETAILS

BALUSTRADES

HALF PANELLED

FULL PANELLED

FRETWORK

WOOD BALUSTERS

NEWEL POSTS

LANDING NEWELS

HANDRAILS

COMPOSITE

WALL MOUNTED

STAIRCASE ARRANGEMENTS

METAL STAIRCASE DETAILS

METAL BALUSTERS

STAIRCASE ARRANGEMENTS

INTERIOR WALLS, CEILINGS AND THEIR DRESSINGS

A Victorian wall is generally made up of three main parts: dado, field and frieze – each with additional divisions within. Beginning at the baseboard and moving upwards are the dado and dado rail; above this the field or main body of the wall; and above this the third part of the wall beginning with a picture rail (or simple horizontal band of paint or paper), the frieze and finally the cornice which can be very simple or elaborate depending on the pretensions of the room.

Baseboards were generally made of wood; their nickname, 'mop-board', commemorates their utilitarian origin as a surface which protected the wall when the floor was being washed or polished. They are butted together at the corners of the room and angles of the fireplace and attached to the wall.

In the humbler rooms of Victorian households, such as the kitchen or the servants'

Opposite: The elaborate cornice and niche in this dining room offer a spirited Gothic pastiche that exuberantly mixes the elements of different medieval styles. The way the leafy finial of the arch breaks into the cornice is a nice touch, bringing the niche forward and into the room.

Right: A ceiling rose need not necessarily be the suspension point for a light fixture, but can look effective simply as an ornamental centerpiece. Whereas some Victorians wished to be rid of the ubiquitous rose, most people today prefer to keep it as a valued period detail.

quarters, the baseboard might be a simple plank squared off without molding. Oak was for the top end of the market; painted, grained or marbled softwood was more usual. The baseboard in richer houses could be an extremely ornate, complex piece of joinery made up of several parts that create a layered profile narrowing towards the top and capped with a deep molding.

The dado rail, or chair rail, had largely lost its function as a buffer between the wall and furniture by the Victorian era. It was retained as a decorative feature since it created a section of the wall that could be decorated differently than the field, hence eliminating the monotony of an overall wallpaper. The leather-paper or anaglypta generally used for this section of the wall was designed to imitate the decorative wooden dadoes of the Georgian period. Of course, wooden dadoes still continued, and in the 1890's the Aesthetic Movement introduced a number of alternatives, including matting and even Japanese fans. Walter Crane's designs for dado papers rejected the bland solidity of anaglypta and leather-paper, introducing highly imaginative patterns, but the excesses of the Aesthetic Movement quickly made excitingly decorated dados passé, and tame Jacobethan designs on leather-paper never had a serious rival.

Cornices are best considered as part of the wall and not the ceiling. In 18th-century houses, a cornice was often made of wood; by the Victorian era, plaster-work cornicing was mass-produced and arrived on site in standard lengths to be sawed into sections and put in place with wet plaster. These mail order sections were made of wooden laths covered in scrim or hessian rag covered in wet plaster of Paris and then molded into shape. Simpler cornices for bedrooms were made of lime, sand and horse hair and "run" on site. The plasterer mixed the plaster wet, and then ran a zinc template with the chosen profile over it to form the finished molding.

By Victorian times, cornices had evolved from simple moldings to unrestrained confections that in the most extreme cases threw design conventions into one vast visual melting pot. They were sometimes painted in several colors picking out different bands of motifs and relating to the colors used on the wall; the most elaborate designs had gilding applied. In grand reception rooms, it is not uncommon to find classical egg-and-dart friezes in combination with dentil molding, fruiting vines, swags, husks and flowering garlands. The multi-colored cornice is the key to many Victorian rooms; surviving cornices, unfortunately, are almost always clogged with more recent paint, leaving few details visible. Cleaning off the paint is a labor-intensive operation; with a very good cornice this may be a rewarding effort, but with a run-of-the-mill Victorian molding, probably not. Painting with a single color may then be the best solution. Above all, if you have a cornice, keep it. The very simplest molding is valuable to soften the bleak right angle between wall and ceiling.

Even the most modest house came complete with ceiling medallion. The medallion gave a center to the room; from it hung a single gas light or gasolier. It also hid the ugly pipework associated

Opposite, right: A florid coffered ceiling with applied decoration evokes the Rococo era. The pictures hang from brass picture rods.

Opposite, far right: The rich reds and gold of this ceiling, with its Tudor rose and scrolls, combine to produce a particularly lively piece of Victorian historical fantasy.

Opposite, right: Sometimes a relatively plain cornice was edged by an elaborate ceiling frieze; like the cornices, they were made from pre-cast panels, and are here left unpainted after laborious cleaning with paint stripper.

Opposite, far right: An attractive sunflower motif lends a simple grace to this ceiling frieze.

Left: This typical Victorian hallway still has its original baseboards, dado and richly painted cornice, as well as a small fireplace and gas wall lights.

with gas. Early medallions might incorporate ventilation holes to trap gas fumes and funnel them under the ceiling to an air brick. In later Victorian houses light fixtures were either a combination of gas and electric or simply electric.

Victorian ceiling medallions, or roses, were different from the insubstantial pastiche Victoriana sold by mass market home improvement stores today. Like the icing on an over-the-top Christmas cake, they appeared to defy gravity. Acanthus leaves, flowers, honey-suckle anthemion style motifs competed in eye-catching display. Medallions could be gilded or painted in vivid colors matching the cornice or in hues complementary to the wallpaper. A ceiling might have a pattern stenciled with paint, or have ordinary wallpapers or special ceiling papers with a circular repeat applied right up to the edge of the medallion. In addition, a ceiling might be further decorated with additional plasterwork, such as raised strapwork that divided the ceiling into geometric shapes, or more inexpensively the ceiling might be covered with large sections of patterned tin.

For the ceiling of a modest Victorian drawing room, two colors are all that is necessary, as it rarely receives much scrutiny. Professional decorators of the late 19th century advised against a white ceiling: it tended to show off the inevitable cracks and had the distressing effect of making the rest of the room seem dirty. Victorian decorators either papered or painted it a lighter shade of the same color as the walls.

Plaster ornaments were the cheapest form of decoration available to the builder. Much of Victorian decorating was finding ways to make a virtue of necessity. Today, we can simply remove a ceiling medallion whereas a Victorian decorator had to spend effort making them inoffensive when a room was not to have a central suspended light, even going so far as putting up a second and lowered ceiling to hide the original one. These should be removed carefully to reveal any surviving original details.

THE ANATOMY OF WALLS & CEILINGS

PLASTER WALL & CEILING DRESSINGS

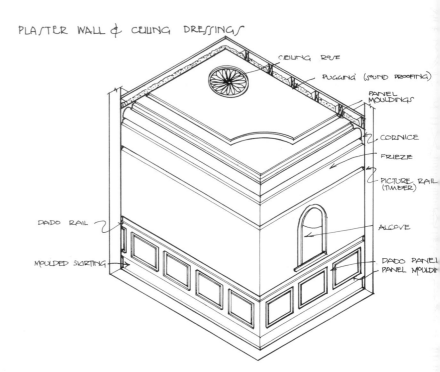

TYPICAL FIXING DETAILS

WALL / CEILING JUNCTION

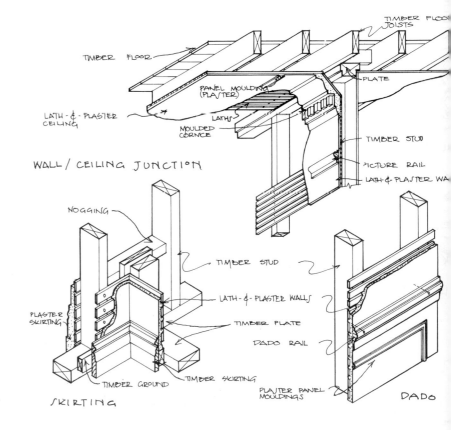

SKIRTING

DADO

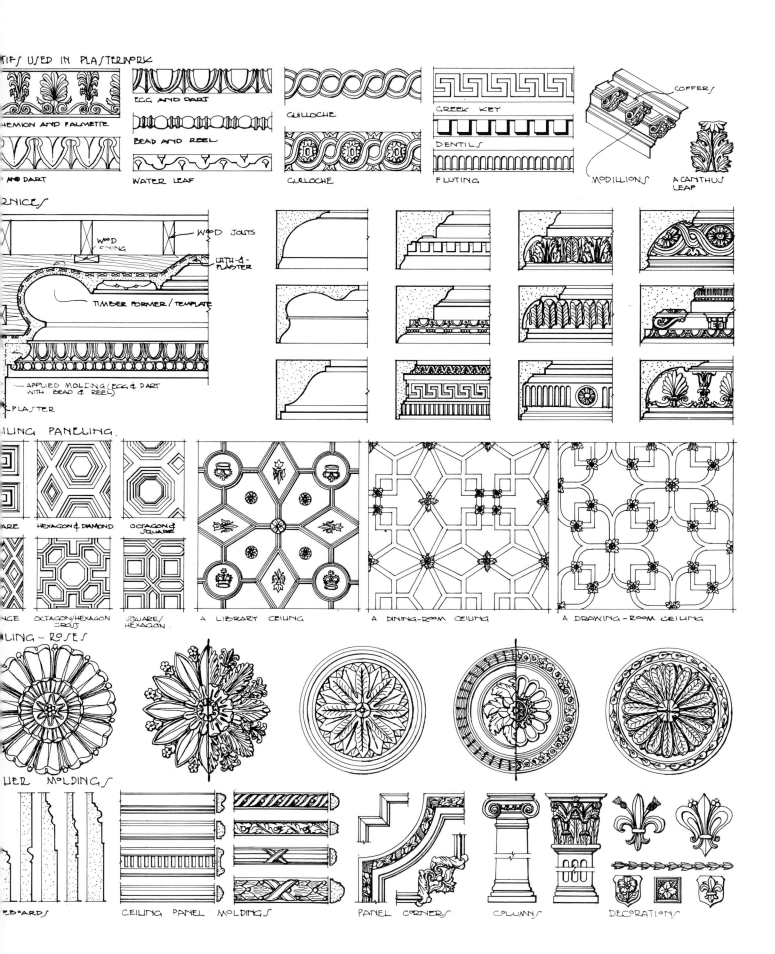

MOTIFS USED IN PLASTERWORK

ANTHEMION AND PALMETTE

EGG AND DART

BEAD AND REEL

WATER LEAF

GUILLOCHE

GUILLOCHE

GREEK KEY

DENTILS

FLUTING

COFFERS

MODILLIONS

ACANTHUS LEAF

CORNICES

WOOD JOISTS

WOOD FIXING

LATH-&-PLASTER

TIMBER FORMER / TEMPLATE

APPLIED MOLDING (EGG & DART WITH BEAD & REEL)

PLASTER

CEILING PANELLING

SQUARE

HEXAGON & DIAMOND

OCTAGON & SQUARE

LOZENGE

OCTAGON/HEXAGON CROSS

SQUARE/ HEXAGON

A LIBRARY CEILING

A DINING-ROOM CEILING

A DRAWING-ROOM CEILING

CEILING-ROSES

OTHER MOLDINGS

BEDBOARDS

CEILING PANEL MOLDINGS

PANEL CORNERS

COLUMNS

DECORATIONS

JOINERY

At the back of the Victorian mind there was a nostalgia for oak-paneled rooms with oak doors. The ever-popular *Mansions of England in the Olden Time* by Joseph Nash (1845) carried illustrations of 16th- and 17th-century oak-lined halls, studies and dining rooms. Until well into the 18th century, wooden paneling was simply the most economical way of covering the walls; plasterwork remained expensive. By the 19th century, however, the roles had been reversed. Plaster became the cheapest and most reliable finish, and wooden paneling an expensive status symbol.

With their flair for technical innovation, the Victorians developed various methods of simulating paneling at a lower cost. The anaglypta or Lincrusta wallpaper used below the dado rail, where the Georgians would have paneled, was often embossed with wood-grain patterns. By the 1880's thick veneers glued on to heavy cloth were available as a form of ready-made paneled wainscoting. One hang-over from earlier days was the continued use in many houses of shutters, close cousins of paneling, which were still properly constructed of wood and hinged to draw across the window or close into a recess at the side of the window frame.

Full-height paneling of the Gothic revival was rare for most of the 19th century, partly because of the cost but no doubt also because large areas of dark wood made a room heavy and gloomy. It made a brief reappearance in grand English homes such as Red House in Bexley designed for William Morris by the architect Phillip Webb and built in 1860. Homes such as this provided the impetus for America's Queen Anne style homes. These might have entry hall and dining room with natural wood paneling of oak, chestnut, butternut or other hardwoods from America's seemingly endless hardwood forests. Other rooms, such as the living room, might have painted panel work, usually finished in an off-white which complemented feminine pinks, bright chintzes or William Morris wallpapers. The smallish, square panels often extended three quarters of the way up the wall, and the top provided a shelf to display china ornaments. The light and airy aspect of this type of Queen Anne room owes a lot to the large expanses of white woodwork.

The Arts and Crafts Movement at the end of the century appealed to the new class of industrial barons who wished to create estates that would announce their status. The solidity of heavy wood paneling was a fine expression of the aspirations of these *nouveaux riches*. The introduction of electric lighting meant that timber-lined rooms did not have to be gloomy, and paneled hallways, studies and dining rooms enjoyed a revival. Bleached and lightly polished oak, with its connotations of tradition and patriotism, was regarded as the most desirable wood.

Although paneling had attractive historical precedents, its practical advantages should not be forgotten. It provided extra sound-proofing and insulation, and in passageways its easy-to-clean paintwork was an asset. The introduction of machine-cut tongue-and-groove boarding made painted panels a cheap solution to architectural problems. There were several types of tongue-and-groove boarding in use. The simplest consisted of plain matched boards with flush edges. The more decorative types had a V-shaped groove cut into the joint, or were beaded at the joint on one or both sides of the board. Bead board was a widely used wall and ceiling covering particularly favored in kitchens, back porches and

(continued on page 134)

This door, in what the Victorians called a tack room, has tongue-and-groove boarding to fill the large panels, a style of joinery that was normally restricted to the more functional parts of a house, and to institutional buildings where large doors were necessary. Sometimes the boarding was placed diagonally inside the panels, producing a highly decorative effect.

Left: A ledged door hides the staircase in this Victorian cottage. The long iron hinges and thumb-latch are typical of 19th-century British rustic building, as is the decorative carved bracket of the high mantelshelf.

Above: At the other end of the scale, the arched doorways of a grand entrance hall, opening on to a magnificently paneled interior, reveal Victorian joinery at its most accomplished, with paneling inside the door-frame and elaborate carving above.

(continued from page 130)
bathrooms where an inexpensive yet durable finish was needed.

Under the influence of the Arts and Crafts Movement, with its celebration of the skills of the carpenter and joiner, Edwardian woodwork was as exciting as its Victorian equivalent. The importation of cheaper hardwoods from the rainforests of the Amazon towards the end of the century encouraged more adventurous joinery, as did the rising number of homeowners, which made serious home improvements worthwhile.

Rich and poor alike enjoyed what is to us the luxury of paneled or tongue-and-groove doors. Before the days of plywood and building boards, these were the only practical ways of putting together a large enough piece of wood to cover a door opening. Even the humblest Victorian door was a complex piece of skilled joinery. The frame was mortised and tenoned together, and grooved on the inside to receive the panels. The vertical members on either side were called styles; the horizontals, rails; and the vertical pieces which ran up the middle between the rails were known as muntins. Most doors had four panels, although six was not unusual. The edges of the panels were often beaded.

The door frame, for all its solid appearance, was made up of overlapping sections of wood fixed together using heavy

Above left: In this charming example of Queen Anne revival paneling, the shelves and dressers have been left in natural wood to look like free-standing furniture. The boarding has been continued around each dresser to complete a most effective treatment.

Above: The entrance hall of Wightwick Manor near Wolverhampton illustrates the Victorian taste for Jacobethan paneling.

iron brads. The same was true of the door casing, where one was featured.

The construction and the decoration of a door reflected the importance of the room it served. In the ground-floor reception rooms and master bedrooms substantial doors were fitted with styles thick enough to accommodate a mortise lock. Door panels would be decorated on both sides with moldings in a single or double ogee. Brass door hardware – knob, keyhole escutcheon and finger plate – would commonly have included a sliding brass curtain rod attached to the top rail on which was hung a *portière* – a heavy, usually velvet, curtain to prevent drafts.

The ideal material for a Victorian door was

Left: A light and vigorous sunflower motif designed by Pugin is one of the pleasant surprises to be found in the paneling at the Palace of Westminster, London.

oak; solid, sound-proof, authoritative. The more common reality was painted softwood. Ordinary doors were therefore often grained in imitation of hardwoods, and stenciling might also be applied to imitate marquetry. The upstairs doors would probably not have been grained, though lighter stenciled forms sometimes decorated the panels. Doors in the kitchen or back-quarters were flimsier, without molding, or they might be the cheaper ledged doors, which were five tongue-and-groove boards held by two back bars and diagonal bracing and sometimes strengthened with a frame.

This type of door made in oak was considered a proper door for the Arts and Crafts cottage when coupled with a thumb latch and hinges that stretched along both front and back. These hinges, in the hands of a C.F.A. Voysey, for example, became elaborate decorative features.

During the later 20th century, many paneled doors were removed and replaced by the characterless flush door. Reinstating a handsome paneled door bought from an architectural salvage yard can quickly give some prestige back to a room. From the same salvage yard, you may well be able to buy the odds and ends of paneling from which to rebuild rooms that have been vandalized and rearranged to no good effect.

Paneling can be used to unify a difficult room. It can also be overpowering, though, and if not used carefully may overwhelm any authentic subtleties. The height and size of the panels is more an architectural question than one of furnishing, and relates to the proportions of the room rather than to anything in it. If plain, polished wood is to be used, then it should be old wood adapted to its new situation. If the paneling is less than first-rate it should be painted, as should new timber. If you are mixing old and new timber, it should be painted or stained to give it a consistent look.

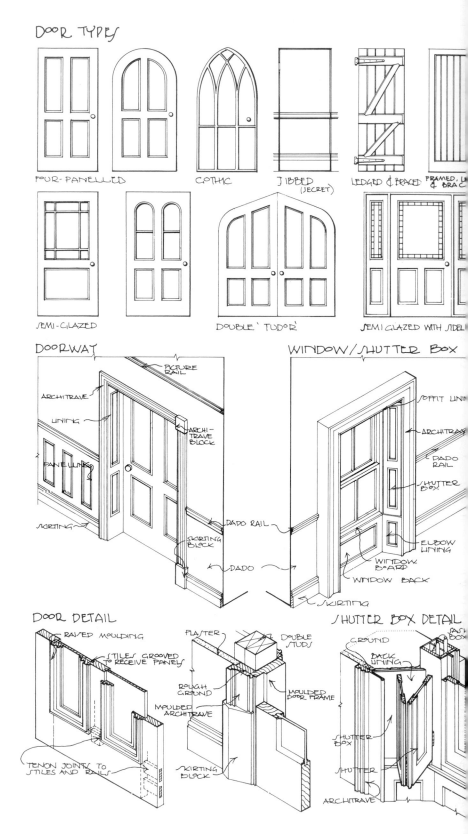

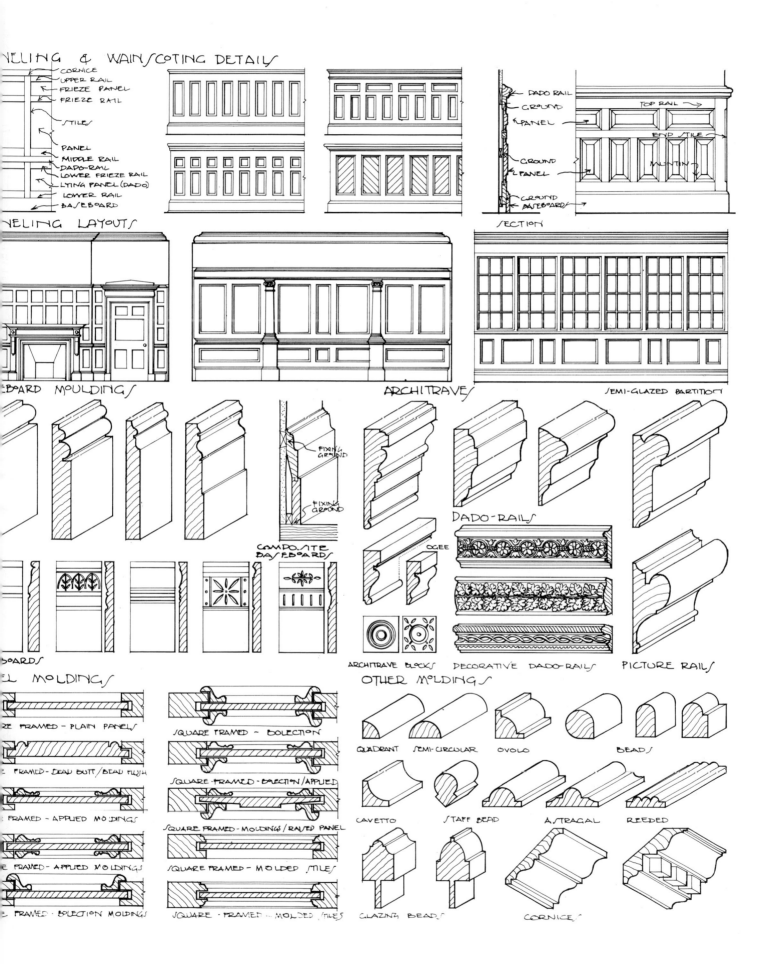

[PA]NELING & WAINSCOTING DETAILS

- CORNICE
- UPPER RAIL
- FRIEZE PANEL
- FRIEZE RAIL
- STILES
- PANEL
- MIDDLE RAIL
- DADO-RAIL
- LOWER FRIEZE RAIL
- LYING PANEL (DADO)
- LOWER RAIL
- BASEBOARD

- DADO RAIL
- GROUND
- PANEL
- GROUND
- PANEL
- GROUND
- BASEBOARD

TOP RAIL
END STILE
MUNTIN

[PA]NELING LAYOUTS

SECTION

[BAS]EBOARD MOULDINGS

ARCHITRAVES

SEMI-GLAZED PARTITION

FIXING GROUND

FIXING GROUND

COMPOSITE BASEBOARD

OGEE

DADO-RAILS

[BASE]BOARDS

ARCHITRAVE BLOCKS   DECORATIVE DADO-RAILS   PICTURE RAILS

[PANE]L MOLDINGS

- [SQUAR]E FRAMED - PLAIN PANELS
- [FRA]MED - DEAD BUTT/BEAD FLUSH
- [FR]AMED - APPLIED MOLDINGS
- [E] FRAMED - APPLIED MOLDINGS
- [E FRA]MED - BOLECTION MOLDINGS

- SQUARE FRAMED - BOLECTION
- SQUARE-FRAMED - BOLECTION/APPLIED
- SQUARE-FRAMED - MOLDINGS/RAISED PANEL
- SQUARE FRAMED - MOLDED STILES
- SQUARE - FRAMED - MOLDED STILES

OTHER MOLDINGS

QUADRANT   SEMI-CIRCULAR   OVOLO   BEADS

CAVETTO   STAFF BEAD   ASTRAGAL   REEDED

CLAZING BEADS

CORNICES

137

BOOKSHELVES AND CABINETS

Built-in cabinets did not enjoy the same prestige in Victorian times that they do today. The rich could afford elegant free-standing furniture; built-in fixtures were usually found in modest houses, or confined to the kitchen and servants' quarters. Made by a carpenter rather than a cabinet-maker, they were simply made with minimal ornament.

One item of built-in furniture that was frequently found in Victorian houses was the shelving for the library or study. This was very much a status symbol – books were still an expensive luxury – and would either have been designed by the architect or by the homeowner with the assistance of a pattern book and carpenter. Quite often an existing piece of furniture would be copied; a glass-fronted bookcase, for example, could be extended by constructing two matching wings.

Large closets were increasingly needed in the Victorian era as the ownership of clothes, particularly dresses, increased. Generous walk-in closets were provided occasionally in larger houses where they offered an efficient way of using space cut off in the search for a well-proportioned room, but the architecture of speculative row housing left no natural spaces for big closets. The larger row houses might have dressing rooms, and by the last decades of the century a built-in bedroom closet was an occasional feature in houses where space did not permit a separate room for storage. Arts and Crafts architects, who relished vernacular details, gave built-in furniture a new status and made it the basis for many of their rurally inspired interior decoration schemes.

In all houses, the traditional location for cabinets and bookshelves was in the recesses on either side of the chimney breast. The solidity of the chimney wall provided a firm support for the

Right: The recess beside the chimney breast is the natural place for built-in shelves. In this room the cabinet has been correctly designed so that it does not project in front of the chimney breast, and its height does not conflict with the line of the mantelshelf.

Far right: A plain, solid cabinet with traditional panel doors will stand the test of time and redecoration. In any built-in, the shelves should be slightly thicker than habit or instinct suggests, say 1 in. (2.5 cm.) rather than 3/4 in. (2 cm.).

Left: In a small house, display shelving can be hung from the level of a picture rail, where it will be out of the reach of children. The simple moldings along the leading edges of this attractive piece could easily be copied to give character to any set of newly built shelves.

Below: The fretwork surround of this niche in a child's room co-ordinates nicely with the bedstead.

woodwork. Equally widespread was a corner cabinet on landings which filled a space otherwise under-utilized.

Built-in furniture suits the demands of modern living, and can be installed in a Victorian house without violating its character; indeed, a built-in cabinet can actually enhance the architecture by disguising an ugly conversion. It should be plain and sturdy; decoration and paint can hide many things but not bad proportions and flimsiness. Plainness, however, is relative. A cabinet will be more satisfying to live with, and more authentic, if constructed from tongue-and-groove boarding rather than modern building board. If you can find simple paneling from architectural salvage yards, a good carpenter and a coat of paint can unite them into a passable whole. When boxing in electrical appliances, paneling or tongue-and-groove boarding will be less monotonous than plywood, and easier to paint. Arts and Crafts architects might take woodwork the whole way along a wall, embracing a bookcase with a bench underneath at one end, the fireplace in the center and a fitted

Above: Natural wood is an attractive medium for built-in kitchen fittings, especially when constructed with good detailing, such as the beading round these recessed shelves.

141

wardrobe in the second recess. To have one wall painted white may bring welcome lightness to a room. Benches or seats set into a bay window recess may be the most effective way to make use of that space.

When installing fixtures which do not exploit recesses or cover awkward corners, it is important to pay attention to the proportions of the wall and of the room generally. The lower section of a cabinet or bookcase ought to be more solid, brought a little forward or made of slightly thicker wood. The top can be given a pediment and architrave, or Gothic moldings. As a rule of thumb, such built-in furniture should reach to somewhere between the top of the door and the picture rail. Wardrobes in bedrooms, where the cornice is not so dominant, can stretch to the ceiling. Half-height cabinets which serve as sideboards should line up with the height of the dado. Beware of having the top of a bookcase or cabinet too close to the level of the mantelpiece shelf; the horizontal effect will upset the balance of the room, making it seem bottom heavy.

If you are not employing an architect, the choice of design for your bookshelves or other built-ins is most easily made by copying from furniture illustrated in this book or in other houses. A number of designs are included on page 144. It may be helpful to have some element

Basins in bedrooms, although useful, often detract from the appearance of a room. By fitting the basin inside a built-in cabinet, you can reduce its impact and use the area around and above the sink to good practical and decorative effect.

on which to focus your thoughts, be it an elegant door you wish to incorporate, a piece of china you plan to display or the dimensions of the books you want to shelve.

At a more practical level, the back wall of a bookcase or display niche ought to be painted before the carpenter begins work, and any damage can be touched up afterwards. Lighting for display cabinets or plugs for stereos needs to be planned in advance. Make sure not only that the wires have been run in to the bookcase before it is finished, but also that the wiring can be altered later on. Modern electronic equipment changes with confusing speed, so it is probably best to err on the side of elaboration

and run some form of ducting into the shelving; new wires can then be drawn through without having to dismantle the whole arrangement.

Although it may be tempting to accommodate as many books as possible, do consider how easy the shelves will be to use. If they are over seven feet high, you will need steps; if they start less than one foot from the floor, you will have to stoop to reach them, the books will get dusty and may be damaged by furniture being stood against them. When installing cupboards in difficult places such as under stairs, put lights in them; all too often, cabinets are built with no thought for the fact that a torch will be necessary to see what is in them.

Boxing in a radiator avoids the difficulties of papering or painting around and behind it, and can provide an attractive decorative feature, especially in this case where the Victorian art of the fretsaw has been so successfully recaptured.

SHELF & CUPBOARD DESIGNS

BOOKSHELVES

PLAIN

WITH ARCHITRAVE

WITH COLUMNS

DIVIDED

CUPBOARD DESIGNS FOR RECEPTION ROOMS AND HALLS

GOTHIC DRESSER

GOTHIC LIBRARY CUPBOARD

END OF THE ERA

CURTAINED CORNER CUPBOARD

WINDOW SEATS

TIMBER BENCH

SOFA

TIMBER/CUSHION

CURTAINED

RADIATOR

RADIATOR DETAILS

SHELF

TIMBER FRAME

METAL PERFORATED PANEL

SHELVES & CUPBOARDS FOR CHIMNEY RECESSES

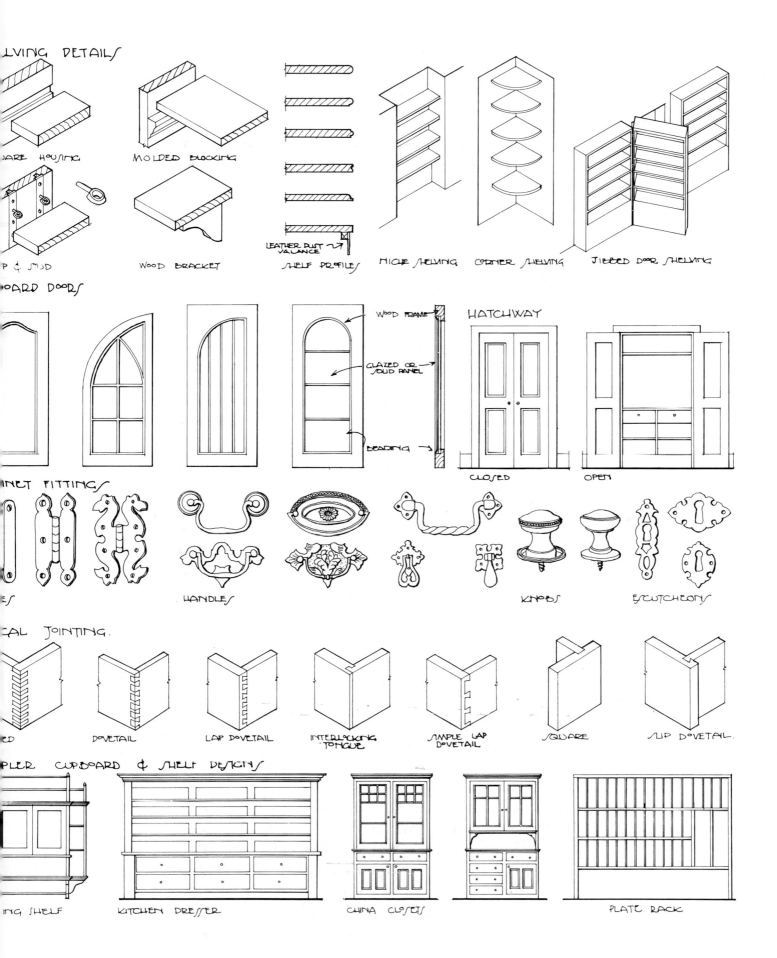

LVING DETAILS

ARE HOUSING MOLDED BLOCKING

P & STUD WOOD BRACKET SHELF PROFILES LEATHER DUST VALANCE NICHE SHELVING CORNER SHELVING JIBBED DOOR SHELVING

OARD DOORS

WOOD FRAME

GLAZED OR SOLID PANEL

BEADING

HATCHWAY

CLOSED OPEN

NET FITTINGS

ES HANDLES KNOBS ESCUTCHEONS

CAL JOINTING

D DOVETAIL LAP DOVETAIL INTERLOCKING TONGUE SIMPLE LAP DOVETAIL SQUARE SLIP DOVETAIL

PLER CUPBOARD & SHELF DESIGNS

ING SHELF KITCHEN DRESSER CHINA CLOSETS PLATE RACK

FIREPLACES

The importance of the fireplace was one point on which William Morris and the average Victorian homeowner in Britain would have been in perfect agreement. For Morris, a blazing hearth was the soul of a room; for the average homeowner it was the cornerstone of domestic comfort. From being a minor decorative feature in a Regency room, fireplaces became increasingly prominent in Victorian Britain. This was in part due to the Gothic revival, which brought back the big hearths and hooded fireplaces of the Middle Ages; it was also a result of the Arts and Crafts Movement which cherished the wide cottage-style fireplace. In the

more severe winters of the northern United States, open fireplaces were slowly replaced during the 19th century by more efficient free-standing stoves or central furnaces. By the early decades of the 20th century, American fireplaces were used more for their cheerful appearance than for essential warmth.

In Britain, most Victorian fireplaces were made up of two main parts – the fire-chamber or fire grate, which was manufactured as a total unit in cast iron, and the mantelpiece or surround, for which marble, slate, wood or, less frequently, cast iron were used. Advances in British fire-chamber design during the Victorian

Opposite: A circular-headed register grate with tiled jambs and elaborate cast-iron mantelpiece provides an eye-catching focus for a drawing room. The summer decoration used here is preferable to the traditional embroidered firescreen, which would hide the good features of the fireplace.

Above: A simple register grate with a minimal surround was typical in bedrooms. Painting the whole fireplace white is quite appropriate in a room with simple furnishings and light decoration.

Right: This Gothic revival fireplace retains the traditional hob grate; although the register grate was more heat-efficient, purists stuck to the historical form.

era created fires that threw a lot more heat out into the room. Early designs were mainly a framework of iron bars suspended above the ground (called a "hob" in England and a "grate" in the United States), designed to burn coal or wood efficiently. Later these were surrounded in Britain by masonry or iron panels and incorporated into one larger unit, called a "register grate," which combined the hob, chimney register (for controlling air flow), fire-back, and inner surround (see pages 152–53). Simple hobs continued to be used in modest houses and smaller rooms right up to the end of the century. Fireplaces in the United States rarely had the one-piece "register grate" and were more likely to use a simple grate. These were commonly supplemented by cast-iron self-contained stoves or central furnaces to improve fuel efficiency and heat production.

British Victorian register grates became very elaborate in design and proliferated in endless variety. At the same time architects devoted

Above: Mantelpiece mirrors were sold in standard sizes to match mass-produced fireplaces. The correct size mirror will be 6 in. (15 cm.) shorter than the mantelshelf at each end.

Right: In this magnificent French-style drawing room, the high-relief, fully arched mantelpiece has ironwork shuttering to close off the grate in summer.

Above: The generous marble surround of this drawing-room fireplace, still with its original marble fender, adds grandeur to a commonplace register grate.

Right: An Art Nouveau register grate has been attractively incorporated in an earlier dining-room fireplace which is somewhat large for the room it now occupies.

much attention to the design of the mantelpiece. At the beginning of Queen Victoria's reign, mantelpieces were mostly neo-classical in style, with simple brackets and plain pilasters. Good-quality materials were used. Marble was the most common, especially the white and veined varieties. Among the cheaper alternatives was the slate mantelpiece, which enjoyed great popularity in the 1880's. Many were cleverly painted to imitate inlaid marble panels on a black background with incised gold decoration. Wood lent itself to the older reeded designs with corner rosettes (see page 153) and other classical styles, which continued to be used according to the taste of the builder. Later mantelpieces began to sport carved brackets and became

heavier in appearance. Sometimes a cast-iron circular-headed register grate determined the shape of the mantelpiece, which itself became semicircular where it enclosed the grate.

At the Great London Exhibition of 1851 the firms of Carron and Coalbrookdale exhibited very ornate register grates incorporated into mantelpieces made entirely of cast iron, and by the late 1850's and early 1860's these cast-iron mantelpieces were being mass-produced, soon rivaling more traditional fireplace surrounds.

A subsidiary decorative feature in a fireplace was the area between the fire-chamber and the mantelpiece. Tiles were often used in this area and could be found by the early 19th century in some of the larger houses; by the 1860's and

Above: Valances and draperies on the mantelshelf were popular in the mid-Victorian era, adding to the coziness of the room.

Left: This cottage-style fireplace retains an open grate within a mantel of painted wood.

Far left: A German stove fits neatly into a traditional arched marble fireplace.

Left: The most basic form of register grate has been brightened up by a good set of patterned tiles.

151

1870's fireplace tiles were being mass-produced with an endless variety of plain and patterned tiles. Their popularity reached a peak in the early years of the 20th century.

A glance through a builder's or manufacturer's catalog of the late 19th century is a fascinating exercise. Many of the designs of the 1850's were still available, while Art Nouveau and other influences combined to produce styles that looked forward even to the 1920's and 1930's. A selection is given on the right. Many builders continued to use the traditional marble, slate, wood and cast-iron surrounds in the best rooms. Wood and cast iron were the norm in the bedrooms.

Today the owner of a Victorian house is likely to find that many of the original fireplaces have been covered over, partially destroyed or removed altogether. In public rooms, a fireplace without an appropriate mantelpiece will produce an incomplete and cheerless impression. When choosing a replacement, it is best to check on the size and design found in mantelpieces in neighboring houses of approximately the same date. However, exact sameness of design is less important than finding a fireplace that is the right size for the room. A full discussion of fireplace restoration is given on page 305.

Many Victorian fireplaces came complete with a matching fender or marble curb. An 18th-century fireplace had a spacious hearth jutting out into the room to catch sparks and falling coals, but in Victorian times the hearths were smaller and the fenders correspondingly more important. Apart from the purely precautionary function of stopping a crinoline dress catching fire as you adjusted your bonnet in the over-mantel mirror, and keeping small children out of harm, the fender was an integral part of the design. Finding the right one for your fireplace may be something of an odyssey, but a correctly restored mantelpiece and fire-chamber will greatly enhance the character of a room, and deserves the appropriate accessories.

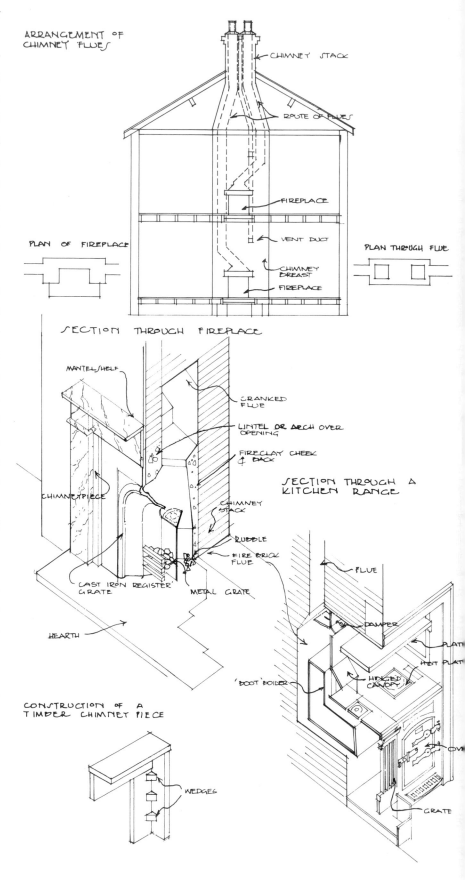

TYPES OF FIREPLACES & ACCESSORIES

ARRANGEMENT OF CHIMNEY FLUES

CHIMNEY STACK

ROUTE OF FLUES

FIREPLACE

PLAN OF FIREPLACE

VENT DUCT

PLAN THROUGH FLUE

CHIMNEY BREAST

FIREPLACE

SECTION THROUGH FIREPLACE

MANTELSHELF

CRANKED FLUE

LINTEL OR ARCH OVER OPENING

FIRECLAY CHEEK & BACK

SECTION THROUGH A KITCHEN RANGE

CHIMNEYPIECE

CHIMNEY STACK

RUBBLE

FIRE BRICK FLUE

CAST IRON REGISTER GRATE

METAL GRATE

HEARTH

FLUE

DAMPER

BOOT POLDER

HINGED CANOPY

CONSTRUCTION OF A TIMBER CHIMNEY PIECE

GRATE

WEDGES

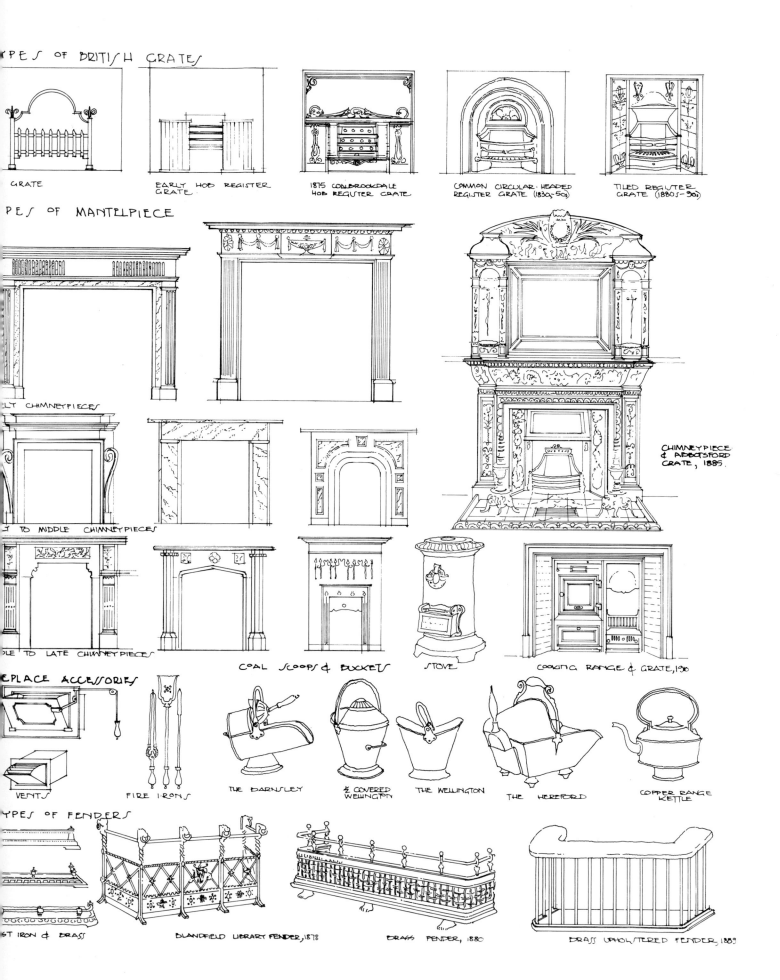

TYPES OF BRITISH GRATES

GRATE

EARLY HOB REGISTER GRATE

1815 COALBROOKDALE HOB REGISTER GRATE

COMMON CIRCULAR-HEADED REGISTER GRATE (1830-50)

TILED REGISTER GRATE (1880S-90S)

TYPES OF MANTELPIECE

CHIMNEYPIECE & ABBOTSFORD GRATE, 1885.

BUILT CHIMNEYPIECES

EARLY TO MIDDLE CHIMNEYPIECES

MIDDLE TO LATE CHIMNEYPIECES

COAL SCOOPS & BUCKETS

STOVE

COOKING RANGE & GRATE, 1910

FIREPLACE ACCESSORIES

VENTS

FIRE IRONS

THE BARNSLEY

½ COVERED WELLINGTON

THE WELLINGTON

THE HEREFORD

COPPER RANGE KETTLE

TYPES OF FENDERS

CAST IRON & BRASS

BLANDFIELD LIBRARY FENDER, 1878

BRASS FENDER, 1880

BRASS UPHOLSTERED FENDER, 1889

153

FLOORS AND FLOOR FINISHES

Most Victorians would have preferred oak floorboards scattered with oriental rugs, given the opportunity. Oak, however, was expensive, and was only to be found in grander houses. The average homeowner had to be content with softwoods. The parquet floor was popular in France, where great elaboration of design was practiced. In the United States it was less universal; parquetry floors are very expensive to install. Often a parquet border was laid around a room that had more modest flooring in the middle; expensive houses and apartments might have parquet in hallways. Stone flagstones were traditional but, like marble or mosaics, relatively costly; linoleum, a Victorian invention, was used mostly in the kitchen and back-quarters. Upstairs it might be laid in a children's nursery.

In the standard row house pine floorboards were the norm. These would have been stained and varnished and then covered to a greater or lesser degree with carpets or rugs. In the public rooms, the fewer the carpets, the easier it was to keep the rooms clean; in the bedrooms and the family rooms where the traffic was less, rugs might cover the whole floor.

Varnish was easy to maintain. Staining and then applying oil or wax polish was labor intensive; only when the wood was of sufficient quality did a floor merit the effort polishing involved. When a single carpet was laid in a room, stenciled patterns (in imitation of parquetry borders) might be painted on to the floorboards between the carpet's edge and the baseboard.

Today, vacuum cleaners mean that large carpets are no longer the same bother to keep clean. There remains, however, the same problem of what is to be done with the uninteresting wood floorboards. My preference is to cover them entirely unless the wood is of particularly good quality, or the floorboards are nicely tongued and grooved. The process of sanding and coating a floor with polyurethane varnish is unpleasant, and the result may not repay your labors. It is unfortunately in the nature of pine to turn yellow when sanded and treated and the result is all too often a jaundiced-looking floor. Sometimes, by applying bleach after sanding, you can stop the floorboards yellowing after the final finish. Staining, of course, is another answer. Before treating a whole floor you should test a small area to gauge the effects. The action of bleach and stain will roughen the grain of the wood and you will have to sand the floor again before sealing it with two coats of polyurethane. Beware, though, of bleaching parquet floors. Bleach attacks the black bitumen-like adhesive used to assemble the parquet, and may cause it to seep out and streak the surface of the floor irrevocably.

Above: In a suburban villa a patterned parquet floor has a simple border to delineate the edge of the room.

Right: Painting the floorboards is a good alternative to sanding and sealing with polyurethane; here it is used to provide a light background for country oak furniture.

TILES

The Victorians used tiles more widely and in a greater variety of designs than in any other period. The encaustic floor tiles laid in entrance halls, and the glazed wall tiles used to decorate fireplaces, bathrooms, friezes, and dados remain one of the most distinctive features of 19th-century interiors.

The British refer to tiles with inlaid patterns as encaustics and to small solid color tiles as geometrics. In the United States, however, patterned tiles were less often used and solid color tiles were often called encaustic tiles. This difference can cause great confusion. Inlaid tiles were a medieval invention rediscovered by the

Right and opposite: Most tiles took their colors from the natural tones of the clay – red, buff, black, white, grey and ocher, although brighter colors such as lilac were used occasionally.

Victorians and widely used in English Gothic revival churches. The basic tiles were made from red clay – sometimes with a coarser clay sandwiched in the middle – and fired in a mold with the pattern indented on the bottom. After firing, the pattern was inlaid with a lighter colored clay or "slip," and the tile was then fired a second time. Sometimes a lead glaze was added. Red- and buff-colored patterned tiles gave

way in the mid-1840's to greens with a blue inlay. Small, single-color tiles laid in geometric patterns – encaustics, in the United States – were the type of tile normally used in hallways.

The glazed wall tile was developed by William Morris, following 18th-century Dutch traditions. In the late 1850's, Morris had been hand-painting Delft blanks; by the 1890's, commercial processes of design transfer had

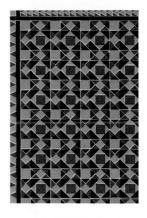

Above: These geometric pavements are designs for Minton tiles. The firm perfected the production of encaustic and patterned tiles in the 1840's.

become so efficient that a proposal was made to re-façade most of London with glazed tiles.

The hygienic advantages of pottery surfaces brought tiling into ubiquitous favor by the turn of the century. Glazed wall tiles became so common in restaurants and shops that resistance developed to their presence in the public parts of the house. For the kitchen or bathroom, however, they were perfect, providing a washable, hardwearing finish with a highly reflective surface that suggested an airy cleanliness.

Traditional patterned and encaustic tiles are still made and architectural salvage yards may also have second-hand ones ≈ both will be useful when you need to repair an original floor that has become loose and has lost some of its pieces. If the damage is extensive, the simplest solution may be to take up all the tiles and redesign the floor. Relay the original tiles in a smaller, central area and use new or second-hand tiles to make a larger border. When redesigning hall floors, the pattern should be kept simple; intricate designs will emphasize the narrowness of the space. A broad mass of a single color in the center with a simple border will be the most effective scheme and has the advantage of being easier to lay.

Good patterned Victorian tiles were never cheap, and today they are sold at prices which class them as works of art that you hang, rather than stick, on the walls. Tiles for hearths or fireplace surrounds provide a strong note of color, and it may be worth paying for old tiles which match damaged or missing ones in fireplace jambs. Anyone put off by the cost of installing or restoring Victorian glazed tiles, however, can take comfort from the fact that decorative tile panels would only have been used in the best rooms. For passages, kitchens or bathrooms, the plain, single-color encaustic tiles would have been used with decoration restricted to a border. Such middle-market tiles can be found in salvage yards and junk shops, and there are several firms making reproductions that are not prohibitively expensive.

Above: Glazed wall tiles displayed a wide variety of styles and motifs.

Above: Earthenware panels such as this were frequently used to decorate hallways.

Right: This panel reflects the then-popular interest in Persian styles.

Top: A Kate Greenaway centerpiece is set off by a *japonisme* surround.
Above center: Minton produced designs in most of the fashionable styles of the century.

Above: The flowing plant forms of Art Nouveau enjoyed widespread popularity in tiles of the late-19th century.

159

DECORATIVE GLASS

British architect Sir John Soane credits himself with the introduction of stained glass for domestic decoration. Previously, the ever-popular heraldic panels of painted glass used by architects had been treated almost like pictures set into windows, and added no color to a room. Soane's innovation was to use glass to impart picturesque tints to a room, adding variety as the sun moved round during the day.

The Gothic revival brought a renewed interest in the manufacture of all kinds of colored glass. Stained glass, which has its color fused into the surface during manufacture, had been a lost technology since the 16th century. Chemical analysis undertaken in the 1840's led to its rediscovery, and large British firms grew up between 1840 and 1860, initially making glass for churches. Stained glass enjoyed great vogue in British Arts and Crafts circles; William Morris's firm Morris, Marshall, Faulkner & Co., founded in 1861, was noted for church windows as well as wallpapers.

By 1870 stained glass was being made increasingly for the ordinary domestic market, and numerous firms were producing not only stained glass but also flashed glass, which is painted on one side, as well as frosted, pebbled, sand-blasted and etched glass. For reasons of health, Victorians were eager to see more light in their houses, and colored glass began to be utilized in surfaces that once would have been solid masonry or woodwork. Improvements in the manufacture of clear glass, which allowed larger panes to be made, also increased the ability to install obscured, or non-see-through glass in certain places. In the front entrance, colored glass acted as a translucent wall that let in light but perpetuated the sense of security. In internal doors, panes of frosted or pebbled glass could cast light from bathrooms or back-quarters into dim passages or landings. Frosted, painted and stained glass in hall and stair windows served to block out the unsightly backs of neighboring houses. Obscured glass made it easier for builders to crowd even expensive houses together while maintaining a degree of privacy.

The designs of colored glass available from the manufacturers' catalogs followed fashionable tastes with Ruskinian naturalistic motifs giving way to *japonisme* sunflowers in the 1880's and the sinuous forms of Art Nouveau by 1900. Under the influence of Art Nouveau the leaded joints of the glass came to play more of a role in the design than the colors, a trend that was particularly evident in the geometric style of Frank Lloyd Wright and his contemporaries, who produced designs of great virtuosity for ordinary domestic use.

Stained glass is expensive, whether you obtain it from specialist glass-makers or from antique shops and salvage yards. Victorian house decorating manuals contain detailed instructions for embossing glass with acid, using a stencil, or gilding using gold leaf and isinglass. This is sport for the adventurous. Certainly pebbled or frosted glass will be cheaper. Ordinarily, flashed glass will be the best way to restore a colorful *chiaroscuro* to a hall. Pollution and footballs do not encourage the use of antique or good Victorian glass as the window proper, but if affixed inside the window frame, so that it is protected by the outer glass, it will still catch the sunlight and blot out neighbors and passers-by. Large expanses of stained glass can grow wearisome to look at, but in a work room colored glass can be suitably placed to diminish the heat of summer light. W.H. Auden advised against working in a room with an interesting view; many offices seem to follow this advice. Colored panels can fulfil the same function; at Savonarola's cell in the convent of San Marco in Florence, you can still see a glass picture of the Devil set into the window to discourage the idle from gazing out.

Opposite: A front-door panel of obscured glass offers the waiting visitor a port-hole peep at a rustic scene, recalling the romantic idyll of the past so dear to the newly urbanized generations of the late 19th century.

Right: Obscured glass used as a translucent wall is given charm with the addition of a naturalistic bird.

Far right: A traditional diamond motif was adapted to glass patterns used in front doors from about 1870 onwards.

Below: Modern etched glass panels in a vestibule door show what can be done by present-day craft workers using traditional patterns and techniques.

Right: A roundel of decorative glass obscures a downstairs lavatory window.

Above: A cartoon for a Morris & Co. stained-glass window illustrates the high standard of design achieved by the leading studio workshops. Edward Burne-Jones, best known today for his Pre-Raphaelite paintings, was Morris's chief glass designer.

Above left: Stained and obscured glass with Art Nouveau designs became widespread at the end of the 19th century.

Overleaf left: Botanical subjects were very popular in painted glass decoration until more stylized Art Nouveau designs took over in the 1890's.

Overleaf right: An Aesthetic Movement glass design has been fitted into a standard door of the 1880's, still in everyday use as the front door of a school of English.

Above: Painted and stained glass with a wild strawberry motif is an example of more naturalistic design.

Right: A traditional Greek motif has been adapted to a design for a hall or stair window.

163

LIGHTING

Throughout the Victorian period, homeowners made do with lighting levels that would be unacceptably low today. Many still relied exclusively on candles and oil lamps, which had innumerable disadvantages. Tallow candles smoked and smelled, and wax candles were expensive. Until the 1850's oil lamps burned whale oil, and were manufactured to 18th-century designs. Their light output was low, and it was only after the 1846 introduction of kerosene, made from distilled coal, that significant improvements were made. With the discovery of the first oil well in 1859, kerosene's future was assured for it could also be distilled from oil. Between March 1 and December of 1862, 623 patents for petroleum lamps and

Above: A common type of gas bracket inspired the shape of this early electric light fitting; the continuity of style made the new fittings seem reassuringly familiar to their purchasers.

Right: Functional lighting works best when it is contemporary. This very Victorian assemblage of artifacts is given character by two downlighters directed across the corner.

burners were granted. New styles came in – pendant lamps, table and floor lamps, student lamps with burners that could be moved up or down on a central column, all provided with globes and shades that were painted, stained, frosted or etched, finished with crimped or tinted edges and hung with silk and lace fringes.

Gas lighting was slow to compete with oil, though it had first been demonstrated in Philadelphia in 1796. In 1817, Baltimore put the first gas street lighting system in the U.S. into effect. Boston and New York soon followed, and finally Philadelphia installed a system in 1836. Gaslight soon became common in large factories and commercial buildings but it met resistance for ordinary domestic interiors. The fishtail or batswing burners flickered and smoked, giving off sulphurous fumes which killed indoor plants, tarnished metal and discolored paintwork and furnishings. Ceiling roses helped to hide the

discoloration, and some had concealed grills and pipes to carry away the fumes. The standard of illumination was poor, and most people preferred wall brackets which were frequently designed to swivel from side to side, so that the light could be brought close to the task in hand. Gas brackets, like the earlier candle sconces of the Georgians, were often placed near wall mirrors to maximize the amount of light produced. Supply was uneven and at the discretion of the gas companies, who decreed the appropriate hour to turn it on and off.

The breakthrough in gas lighting came in 1886 when Carl Auer von Welsbach invented the incandescent gas mantle, or Welsbach mantle, a round or cylindrical net which, when placed over the jet, produced a light of exceptional brilliance. The flame itself was now hotter, thanks to improvements based on the newly invented Bunsen burner. Soon afterwards came the

Below: A Gothic revival bracket gas lamp has been adapted for electricity.

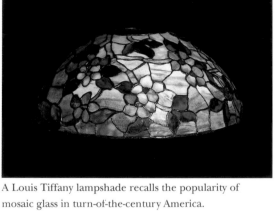

A Louis Tiffany lampshade recalls the popularity of mosaic glass in turn-of-the-century America.

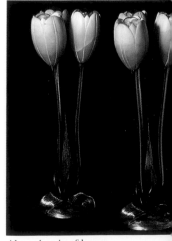

This fitting was designed by Philip Webb.

Right: A "Winfield" gas jet was one of many fittings designed for table-tops, complete with flexible gas pipes.

Above: A pair of lamps shows distinction in metal and alabaster.

inverted mantle, which directed the light downwards. By then gas was available in most towns and portable gas systems were bringing it into more remote locations. The new gas lights were instantly popular, and revolutionized the night-time character of the family parlor, making the whole room lighter and brighter.

Just when suppliers of gas lights were enjoying a huge demand, they found themselves facing a powerful rival. In 1878 Thomas Edison organized the Edison Electric Light Company and by 1879 had invented a commercially successful electric light bulb with a carbon filament. By 1882 the first electric system began operation in New York City; within twenty years more than 3,500 power plants around the United States were producing commercial electricity.

Early electric light bulbs produced much less light than modern versions and were made in clear glass only. At first many were left dangling naked on their cords, without shades. Later they might be provided with simple conical shades, maybe with reflective white or silver interiors to increase the light output, and green exteriors, to be restful to the eye. Holophane shades came in around 1907; made of ribbed clear glass, they were a scientifically designed means of increasing light by prisms and grooves. Electroliers could often be lowered or raised on pendant cords, so that the light source could be brought close for reading, sewing or other tasks.

The big advantages of electricity were its lack of flame and the ability to switch it on or off at will. Initially the high cost of installation was a disincentive, but the invention of the tungsten filament in 1906 doubled the light output of the electric bulb and signaled the death knell of gaslight. Glare became a problem for the first time, and numerous designs of shade were produced to create indirect lighting, particularly

The craft of mosaic glass, more popular now than at the end of the Victorian age, survives in this modern "Pyramid."

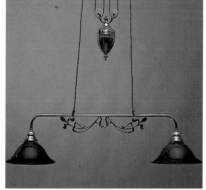

A rise and fall lamp with blue madeleine shades is a type used over billiard tables.

A "Beethoven" wall bracket has a shade typical of the oil and gas lamp era.

Above: A reproduction ceiling pendant with electric candle lights uses a hunting horn motif.

Above: A modern "Beethoven".
Left: An Art Nouveau light fitting.

the ceiling bowl, that archetypal central light so hated by later generations. When the frosted bulb first became commercially practical in 1925, accompanied by the first fuses, something approaching a modern lighting system was established.

The advent of electricity added to the already bizarre confusion of old and new fittings at a time when both oil and gas lighting were still undergoing improvement. A late Victorian parlor might have as many as 20 different fittings running off oil and gas, including alcove lights, table and floor lamps and a central chandelier – often one of the popular combination gas-electric fixtures, allowing the homeowner to "hedge his bets." Ceiling gasoliers made of copper or brass often had several burners shaded by etched glass or crystal globes designed after the oil lamp style. In the hall a gas lamp or later an electric globe on the newel post might be held aloft by a bronze figurine. Many private houses still have their original brass gas fittings, concealed under the grime of decades. Being non-magnetic, brass reveals its presence negatively by refusing to respond to magnets.

It is possible to echo Victorian styles in lighting in ways that are practical and decorative. A number of quite satisfactory reproduction wall lights are available, along with matching ceiling pendants (see page 309 for suppliers). Some are manufactured in the original lamp factories using original dies and molds, and may be obtained either wired for electricity or fitted with oil lamp burners.

PERIOD LIGHT FITTINGS

CANDLESTICKS AND CANDELABRA

C. 1820-40 C. 1800 SILVER CANDLESTAND, 1855 C. 1820 C. 1800

BRONZE GIRANDOLE, C. 1851 BRASS CANDLE LAMP, C. 1850s STORK CANDELABRUM, C. 1851

OIL LAMPS AND SHADES

MODERATOR LAMP PEAR SHADE CRIMPED SHADE DOME SHADE TULIP SHADE

STUDENT LAMPS

OIL RESERVOIR

SINGLE LAMP WITH INTEGRAL OIL RESERVOIR SINGLE LAMP WITH SEPARATE OIL RESERVOIR DOUBLE LAMP

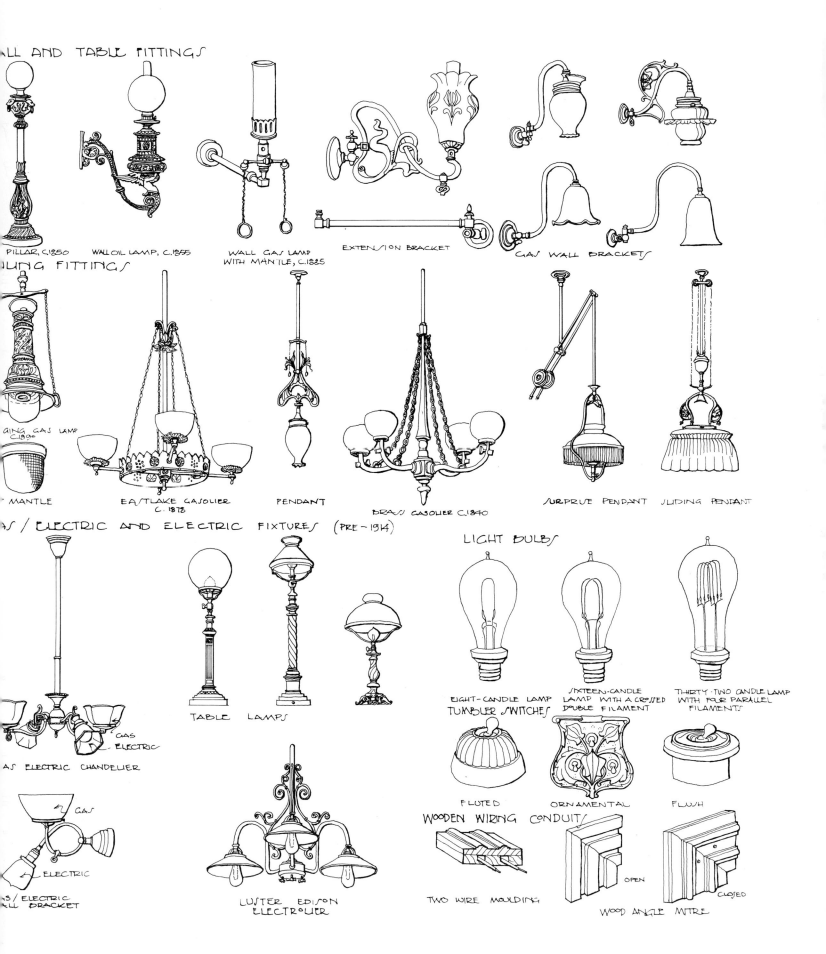

LL AND TABLE FITTINGS

PILLAR, C.1850   WALL OIL LAMP, C.1855   WALL GAS LAMP WITH MANTLE, C.1885   EXTENSION BRACKET   GAS WALL BRACKETS

ING FITTINGS

GING GAS LAMP C.1890

MANTLE   EASTLAKE GASOLIER C. 1878   PENDANT   BRASS GASOLIER C.1840   SURPRISE PENDANT   SLIDING PENDANT

AS / ELECTRIC AND ELECTRIC FIXTURES (PRE-1914)   LIGHT BULBS

TABLE LAMPS

EIGHT-CANDLE LAMP   SIXTEEN-CANDLE LAMP WITH A CROSSED DOUBLE FILAMENT   THIRTY-TWO CANDLE LAMP WITH FOUR PARALLEL FILAMENTS

GAS

ELECTRIC

AS ELECTRIC CHANDELIER

TUMBLER SWITCHES

GAS

ELECTRIC

S/ELECTRIC LL BRACKET

LUSTER EDISON ELECTROLIER

FLUTED   ORNAMENTAL   FLUSH

WOODEN WIRING CONDUITS

TWO WIRE MOULDING   OPEN   CLOSED

WOOD ANGLE MITRE

BRASSWARE, IRONMONGERY AND PORCELAIN FITTINGS

Above: Bells to ring for the servants were sometimes positioned to one side of the fireplace.

The appearance of a house is greatly enhanced by the use of appropriate fittings for doors, windows and services. Changes in decoration and technology since the 19th century have, however, complicated the choice. Old styles of fittings have disappeared from the stores, and new ones have been introduced. Gloss paint and stripped wood have replaced the grained finishes and dark varnishes of the Victorian decorator.

In choosing door furniture – finger-plates, lock-plates, handles, hooks and hinges – you are limited by the fact that brass looks best against unpainted wood, and the standard British oak or ebony handles of the Victorian era really only suit a grained door. Washable gloss paint has removed the need for the finger-plate.

Beware of over-loading a plain door with expensive brassware; door furniture should match the size and importance of the door. In general, brass and bronze door handles are right for public rooms, and need not match; old ones can often be found singly, and the patina of a century's use is far preferable to the anodized glitter of modern matching reproductions. White china handles are an acceptable alternative, and there are many good quality replicas on the market today. Private rooms may be given more modest fittings; back bedrooms often had finger-plates of stamped tin, while kitchen cabinets were finished with plain wooden knobs. Fitting elegant catches to windows may not be consistent with security, and the woodwork may be too weak to take any but the most functional catches.

Electrical fittings should be suited to the background. Unpainted wood deserves brass sockets and light switches; white baseboards or walls look best with plain white plastic fittings.

Right: The lock-plate was re-introduced by the Arts & Crafts Movement; the influence of this school of design made beaten metals an important feature of interior decoration at the turn-of-the-century.

Far right: A commercially produced lock-plate combines both neo-classical and Art Nouveau motifs.

Opposite: This handsome Gothic revival door furniture shows a perfect balance of function and form.

DECORATIVE METALWORK CHINA & GLASSWARE

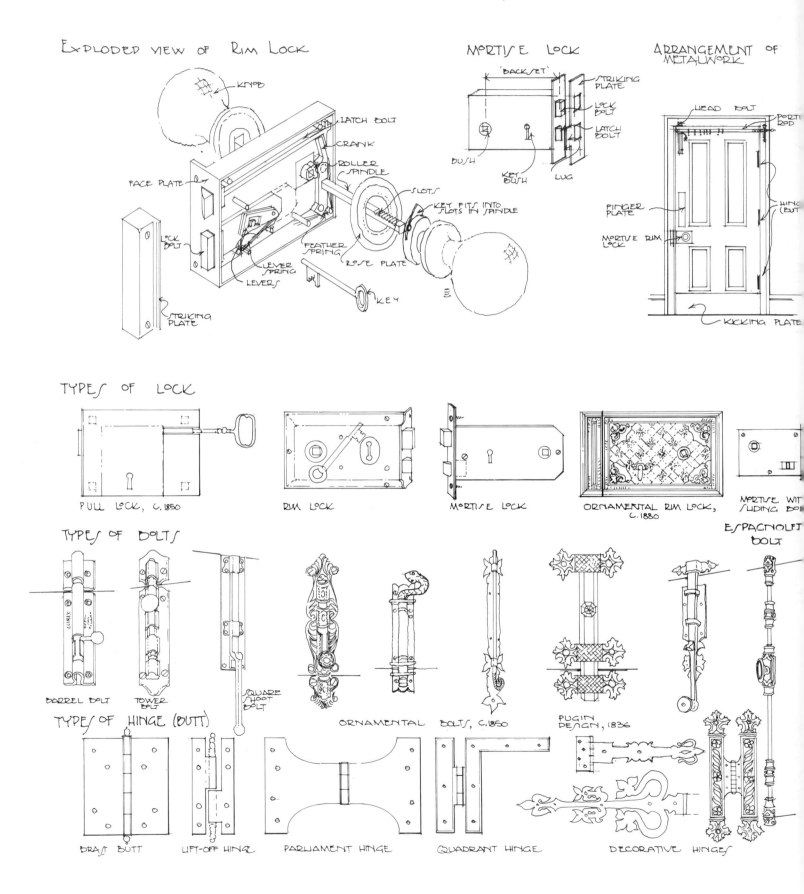

EXPLODED VIEW OF RIM LOCK

KNOB
LATCH BOLT
CRANK
ROLLER SPINDLE
FACE PLATE
SLOTS
KEY FITS INTO SLOTS IN SPINDLE
LOCK BOLT
FEATHER SPRING
ROSE PLATE
LEVER SPRING
LEVERS
KEY
STRIKING PLATE

MORTISE LOCK

'BACKSET'
STRIKING PLATE
LOCK BOLT
LATCH BOLT
BUSH
KEY BUSH
LUG

ARRANGEMENT OF METALWORK

HEAD BOLT
PORTI... ROD
FINGER PLATE
HING... (BUT...)
MORTISE RIM LOCK
KICKING PLATE

TYPES OF LOCK

PULL LOCK, C.1850

RIM LOCK

MORTISE LOCK

ORNAMENTAL RIM LOCK, C.1880

MORTISE WIT... SLIDING BO...

ESPAGNOLETT... BOLT

TYPES OF BOLTS

BARREL BOLT

TOWER BOLT

SQUARE SHOOT BOLT

ORNAMENTAL BOLTS, C.1850

PUGIN DESIGN, 1836

TYPES OF HINGE (BUTT)

BRASS BUTT

LIFT-OFF HINGE

PARLIAMENT HINGE

QUADRANT HINGE

DECORATIVE HINGES

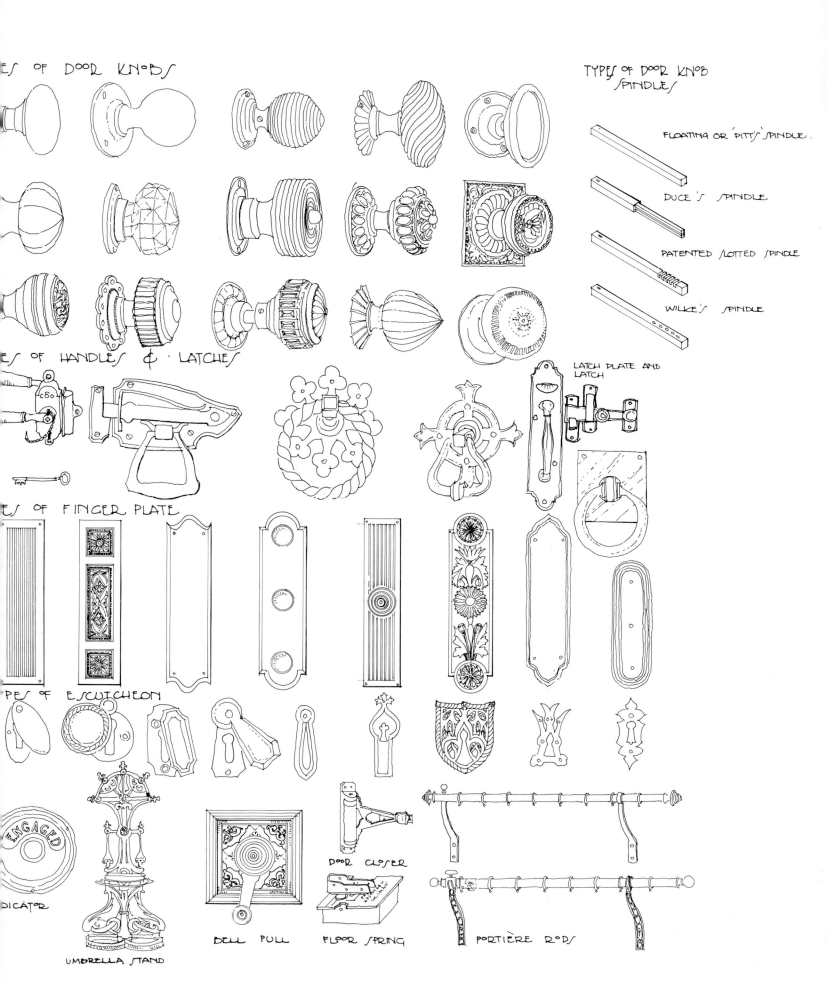

...ES OF DOOR KNOBS

TYPES OF DOOR KNOB
SPINDLES

FLOATING OR 'PITT'S' SPINDLE

DUCE'S SPINDLE

PATENTED /LOTTED SPINDLE

WILKE'S SPINDLE

...ES OF HANDLES & LATCHES

LATCH PLATE AND
LATCH

...ES OF FINGER PLATE

...PES OF ESCUTCHEON

ENGAGED

...DICATOR

UMBRELLA STAND

BELL PULL

DOOR CLOSER

FLOOR SPRING

PORTIÈRE RODS

175

Chapter Four

DECORATING IN VICTORIAN STYLE

W e can recognize a Victorian room by the aspect of comfortableness in its informal arrangements of furniture and in its warm coloring. A cozy domesticity was the hallmark of Victorian middle-class life. A new-found plethora of material possessions was its driving force. The Industrial Revolution both created the wealth to purchase adornments for the home, and also produced the machinery needed to manufacture inexpensively a profusion of new decorative materials in every conceivable style.

Although the façades of American Greek revival houses appeared opulent, their interiors would have been relatively sparsely decorated. Before widespread mechanical manufacture, household items such as chairs and wallpapers were relatively expensive. The elegant simplicity of styles was governed as much by cost as taste.

The main influence on household taste in the first half of the 19th century was the pattern book. These publications carried illustrations of furniture and upholstery which were copied by local cabinet-makers, and as a result they gave a uniformity to American, British, and European taste that had not existed before the late 18th century. In a thorough, Scottish way, John Claudius Loudon's *Encyclopedia of Cottage, Farm, and Villa Architecture and Furniture* (1833) lived up to its encyclopedic boast by illustrating and advising upon every detail of a house from curtains to drains. In the United States its counterpart was found in the books of Andrew Jackson Downing who greatly admired Loudon's work. These two men's informative and frankly improving books were seized upon by the newly affluent who wanted their suburban homes decorated with practical comfort and with a knowing nod towards fashion.

The choice of styles and materials with which to adorn the house was extended throughout the 1840's and 1850's. The great international showcase exhibitions (London 1851, New York 1852, Paris 1855, and so on) displayed the manufactures of the big European and American firms to an eager public. The novelty of the decorative arts produced in Sheffield or Lyons, and their relative cheapness, meant that every middle-class home might become a Great Exhibition in miniature.

Although great artists had designed for some manufacturers

In "Many Happy Returns of the Day" by William Frith, painted in 1856, Charles Dickens presides over a family occasion as might be portrayed in any of his novels. Though a great critic of Victorian order, Dickens's dining room in Tavistock Square, London, shows remarkable conformity to the taste of most of his contemporaries.

and were represented by work shown at the 1851 Exhibition, the majority of decorative arts on display there made it clear that good design and mechanical manufacture had yet to find a happy partnership. New techniques of production, notably in the range of colors made available to manufacturers by aniline dyes and the increasing sophistication of weaving and printing – some wallpaper manufacturers used up to twenty colorways in their designs – fed the High Victorian appetite for novelty, with mixed results. This is most obviously expressed in the vogue for pictorialism in pattern design of the 1850's – naturalistic forms such as flowers were reproduced with profusion in carpets, fabrics and wallpaper.

To Pugin, three-dimensional pictorialism that copied naturalistic forms did not qualify as art or as design. And the furniture of this period, with its heavily upholstered curves, was also condemned by architects and designers who saw no virtue in chairs with hidden metal frames, stuffed and padded. Charles Eastlake's *Hints on Household Taste* (1865) attacked the tawdriness of fashionable furnishings and proposed in its place a robust Gothic. William Morris's reaction to High Victorian taste (or want of it) was to return to the hand-crafted artifact; his insistence on artisan craftsmanship gave direction to the Arts and Crafts Movement and distinguished it from other designers working with commercial manufacturers, even those who sought out pre-industrial forms and decorative arts to find models for new furniture and textile designs.

The word that came to describe the ideas of Eastlake and Morris was "Art." "Art furniture" and "Art wallpaper" and "Artistic" houses

Robert Edis's *Decoration and Furniture of Town Houses* (1881) capitalized on the middle-class vogue for the "Artistic" house. This is the frontispiece, showing his own drawing room.

became as much a social ideal as a decorative vocabulary from the mid-1860's onwards. Outside, the Artistic house was Queen Anne revival; inside there was a heterogeneous range of furniture and fabrics. The furniture would have been modeled on Old English, ancient Greek or traditional Georgian forms; the fabrics were lighter in color than those of popular taste, although during the 1870's the relatively intense effect of the three-part wall (dado-filling-frieze), each band with a different color or pattern, became fashionable. This self-consciously Artistic style of decoration was dubbed the "Aesthetic Movement."

The Aesthetic Movement had its genesis in the tastes of a handful of working artists and architects who liked Japanese prints and blue Chelsea china. The houses of these artists became the fashionable model for the Artistic middle-class home of the 1870's and 1880's. To surround yourself with the paraphernalia of the artist-aesthete was not expensive – London shops sold cheap bamboo furnishings and "genuine old Delft."

Towards the end of the century, when a new generation had grown up with the ideas of the Arts and Crafts Movement, the William Morris-inspired cottage filled with simple, beautiful objects became the social ideal of the middle classes. These cottages with their low-ceilinged living halls, oak settees and large hearths were more likely suburban than rural. Railroads had brought much of Britain within easy reach of the great towns, and the middle classes had come to view the countryside with enthusiasm.

By the turn of the century, architects and designers who had learnt their profession within the Arts and Crafts ethos were beginning to look at Arts and Crafts forms not as social ideals but in terms of design. The radical pruning away of superfluous ornament had given designers a vocabulary of purer forms that they could refine and stylize.

Through all these changes in style, coziness remained the central theme of the Victorian home. A home is a social form of self-expression, and it was somewhere between fashionableness and comfort that the Victorians felt at ease.

A morning room lovingly recreates the clutter and comfort of the High Victorian family room. Although pictorialism in patterns was frowned upon by designers as "false" art, it still remained the dominant popular taste for most of the 1850's and 1860's.

PERIOD DECORATION

LATE REGENCY

Town house, c.1837; first-floor drawing room. Sofa and draperies are standards from an upholsterer's pattern book. Rosewood furniture. *Chaise longue* with buttoned upholstery. Cabinet and folding card table of common Regency type. Fireplace classical, surmounted by gilt mirror contributing to general lightness of the room.

HIGH VICTORIAN

Sitting room, c.1857. Homely comfortableness: piano, family portraits, oil lamps and gas lights. Thick curtains, flock wallpaper, rich colors, glittery gold decoration. Velvet trimming on mantelshelf. Papier-mâché decorated chair. Furniture of no consistent style. Decorative ornaments mainly factory-made.

AESTHETIC

Sitting room, c.1877. Tripartite wall with dado, filling and frieze decorated in different ways. William Morris Fruit and Pomegranate wallpaper. Art furniture: Edis-designed cabinet; vases designed by Christopher Dresser; dining-room chair by Norman Shaw. Japanese fans used as decoration. Bamboo occasional table. Strongly decorated frieze; hand-made china prominent.

ARTS AND CRAFTS

Living hall, *c.*1897. A version of a Cotswolds cottage. Bare wooden floors, ornamental rugs. Ladderwork chair and settle designed by Ernest Gimson. Cabinet based on a design by Lewis F. Day. Walls pale; oak furniture. Antique firedogs and brassware.

ENDS OF THE ERA

Drawing room, *c.*1901. Style influenced by Voysey and Baillie Scott. Furniture has a stylized elegance; wall surfaces are light and have an easy-to-keep-clean simplicity. Arrangement of furniture a sparse neo-Georgian style.

COLOR AND PAINT EFFECTS

The 19th-century painter and decorator was a true craftsman. He served a long apprenticeship, usually seven years of arduous, detailed work involving grinding and mixing of colors, color harmony, the arts of stenciling, lettering, woodgraining, marbling and freehand line drawing as well as the principles of decorative art and elementary perspective. There were no ready-mixed paints so everything was specially mixed on site.

Walls and ceilings which were going to be left plain were painted in distemper, a water-based paint which was the Victorian equivalent of today's latex paint. Distemper was very impractical in many ways as it stained easily and could not be washed without leaving a water mark. It also contained a fair amount of glue size. The Victorians had no effective way of dissolving color or pigment in water-based paint. Instead they used size as a fixing agent. When distemper built up into a skin, it became unstable, and in unrestored Victorian houses white patches of flaking distemper can sometimes be seen, peeling away particularly from ceilings and above picture rails.

If you find that pieces of hardened paint are cracking off while you are trying to paint a wall or ceiling, then you are sure to be painting on distemper. The only way to treat this problem successfully is to soak the wall or ceiling and scrape and wash the distemper off. On the positive side, distemper did have great clarity and

Above: The *trompe l'oeil* scarf hanging over the door adds a touch of humour to an otherwise slightly somber room. The Pompeii Red of the walls was a popular color, and the door has been boldly grained as a rich mahogany to match.

Right: A contemporary adaptation of Victorian techniques has created an elaborately marbled passageway, recalling the popularity of the marbled effect in entry halls and corridors in the 1850's and the 1860's.

Left: The rag-rolled walls contribute to a simple, rustic quality which allows the window to speak for itself and dispenses with the need for curtains.

Above: The salient feature of this room is a painted *trompe l'oeil* frieze which compensates for the absence of an elaborate cornice. The colors of the frieze reflect the restrained palette of the rest of the room, resulting in a calm and harmonious effect.

183

A solid oak door with a paneled doorcase exemplifies the effect emulated in paint and glaze by the trained masters of the woodgraining art.

purity of color. It is still available in an oil-bound form which does not flake.

All woodwork was painted in oil paint, as it is called today, but in the 19th century its chief ingredient was white lead. Great care must therefore be taken when stripping or scraping old paint. If you are interested in finding out the original colors your house was painted in, then simply carefully sand an area to reveal the successive paint layers.

Broadly speaking, until the middle of the 19th century, colors were not dark and somber, as the modern imagination pictures them, but light, soft and used sparingly. To get a feel for early Victorian color schemes it is best to think of the period as an extension of the Regency style, with neo-classical and rococo accents, and pastel colors including pearl whites, delicate pinks and lavenders (see page 178).

In the mid-century colors became deeper and were employed in more complicated combinations. This turn of fashion was influenced by the scientific study of color in the 1840's, undertaken by architects of the Gothic revival, and by the work of Owen Jones who made the first systematic study of Moorish ornament at the Alhambra in Granada. These ideas on color and design were adapted by commercial decorators and used for mass-production wallpapers. The basic idea was to create a complex pattern with one main color and many subsidiary colors, often tonally the same, juxtaposed with some shades of the main color. As a general rule no primary color was used, unless it was tempered to make a deeper or softer shade by the juxtaposition of secondary colors. For example, a poppy red would not be used with a true yellow or a true blue, but with old gold, amber, hyacinth blue or grey blue. Some tertiary colors were employed, such as maroon, purple, olive green and ocher. These were mixed in among the Victorians' wide variety of deep neutral shades such as cream, slate, drab (a mixture of raw umber, ocher and Indian red), buff, sandstone and various greys.

Before painting a room the Victorian decorator would have taken considerable time deciding the best approach; in a new house a substantial delay was inevitable since freshly plastered walls might require up to two years to dry out. The first room to be decorated in the new dark and "masculine" style was the dining room but then quickly followed study, smoking room and drawing room. Bedrooms were thought more feminine and used softer colors.

Great thought would go into getting the correct balance of both color and texture for walls, cornice, ceiling and woodwork. This was especially true when a dado-filling-frieze combination was used, with a different decoration for each band. By the 1840's white was no longer fashionable as a color for a ceiling; instead a tint of the main wall color was used. To provide it with texture a lightly embossed paper was often used. Stenciled borders and friezes became popular in the houses of the rich. Some designers also used stenciling as an overall wall pattern. Stenciled motifs can be simple or highly elaborate, copied from fabric patterns. Some wonderful examples can be found at Knightshayes Court in Devon, England. *Trompe l'oeil* effects were much admired.

With these strongly decorated walls it was necessary to paint the woodwork with a deeply colored woodgrain or to stain the natural wood in a dark color. Staining wood in an ornamental fashion using stencils became very popular, particularly for large doors and for floors around the edge of carpets. Door panels might also be decorated with a single motif such as a flower spray done either as a freehand painting or as a stencil design. Magazines carried stencil patterns on thin tissue paper ready to be traced on to stencil paper and cut out for painting with a stencil brush. Dado-rails and architrave moldings were often painted with small freehand decorations. Marbling, though less common than woodgraining, was also a popular finish.

Woodgraining reached its zenith at the end

of the 19th century. The most popular woods to imitate were oak, mahogany, walnut and satinwood; bird's eye maple and other more exotic woods were copied to a lesser extent. Graining was done chiefly on internal doors and baseboards. The front doors of houses were often grained, usually in walnut or mahogany. The very best woodgraining was done using a water-color glaze, diluted with vinegar and water painted over an oil-bound distemper base; but this is a difficult technique, less often used.

Marbling wood found favor in Britain because real marble is a chilly presence in northern climates; also, real marble had to be imported, and was expensive, whereas marbling cost less and could easily be chosen and adapted to suit a particular scheme of decoration. The most popular finishes were verd-antique, Sienna marble, Breche marble, white, black and gold marble, porphyry and malachite.

A number of special paint effects have recently become highly fashionable. On occasion the results are stunning, but nowadays graining and marbling require large amounts of time and money if they are to be done properly.

Paint combinations are notoriously difficult to match at a later date, and damage hard to repair.

One of the curses of modern decorative schemes is the glaring white paint which rose to such popularity in the 1960's and 1970's. To obtain a more interesting effect, lightly tint any white paint using a little of the base color of the room. The architectural detailing of a Victorian house will inevitably suggest a certain degree of complexity in decoration. You cannot have an elaborate fireplace and elaborate moldings and hope to decorate the room successfully in a stark or simple style. Richness in one area demands richness in the others. Elaborate wall coverings lead naturally to elaborate curtains and so on in a chain of necessary relationships.

A good starting point for a decorating plan may well be the fireplace. The style of the existing fireplace may suggest possibilities, or another may be bought and made the inspiration for a color theme. Curtain treatments, a fine period wallpaper or a beautifully copied stencil frieze are other features from which room plans often flow. An important piece of furniture or picture will tend to dictate its own background.

Right: The sky ceiling of a room designed in an Ionic manner recalls the Victorian fondness for painted ceilings modeled on those of Pompeii. Some homeowners incorporated sky ceilings inside four-poster beds.

Far right: A simple stenciled design has been used to enliven the walls of what would otherwise have been a somewhat cold room. The starting point for this bathroom scheme is an inexpensive translucent patterned paper stuck to the window.

GRAINING AND MARBLING

The basic technique for all graining and marbling is the same. First, a colored eggshell or flat oil base is put down and allowed to dry. This colored base varies according to the wood or marble effect. For woods, it is a light brown, varying from creamy white to a deep dirty pink. For marbles, it is usually white, grey or black. Glaze, which is either a mixture of linseed oil and turpentine or more usually today a proprietary mixture, is then colored and brushed over the base coat. Depending on the effect to be used a number of brushes, rags, combs and feathers can be used to allow the base coat to show through. Some of the more common graining and marbling techniques are described or illustrated on this page.

Marbling and graining must be protected with varnish. Over dark work a polyurethane varnish may be used, but it has a yellowness which will mar delicate effects. An emulsion varnish or specialist oil varnish should be used on pale work.

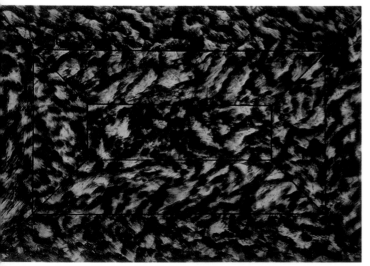

Above: Tortoiseshelling is achieved by laying paint over glaze and varnish. This was not a widespread technique in the Victorian period because the natural material was never in short supply.

SPECIAL PAINT TECHNIQUES

GRAINING

Mahogany Generally a pink base is used. When this is dry, a glaze containing a mixture of burnt Sienna, crimson and burnt umber is painted over in a variety of designs. The "flame" was a popular effect for door panels. Deeper colors were applied in the center with perhaps a few flashes of deeper color at the edges. A wide brush called a mottler was used rather in the manner of an italic pen to imitate the tapering shape of a flame. The design was blended in with a softening brush or overgrainer made either of hog hair or badger hair. The badger brush was initially used mainly for water-color graining, but as it gives a very soft look it gained in popularity and was used on oil-bound glazes as well. Finally, a very thin colored glaze was painted over the panel using both mottlers and overgrainers.

Oak A deep beige made up of white, burnt umber and yellow ocher forms the base color. Over this a glaze of burnt umber and ocher is painted giving darker and lighter streaks. A coarse, long-haired flogging brush and combs with variously spaced teeth are pulled down over the work to show the base color underneath. When the decorator is satisfied with the effect, the whole work is flogged by hitting the brush against the surface all the way up the panel. This process breaks the previously straight lines into short splinters.

Walnut The base is made up of white, raw Sienna and a little raw umber. When a thin glaze of raw Sienna and a little raw umber has been added, a folded rag is taken loosely in the hand and pulled down over the work with a waving but irregular motion. The areas which are not touched by the rag are stippled over with a fitch brush, made of polecat hair, and knots are put in using a number of different short-haired fitches so as to obtain different-sized knots. To obtain this effect, the brush is held in one position, perpendicular to the work, and twisted.

Satinwood An orangey red color can be the base for this wood effect. It is made by adding burnt Sienna and raw Sienna to white eggshell paint. For a deeper color burnt umber may be added. The glaze uses the same colors as the base coat without the white. When it has been painted on, a ragging brush and combs are drawn down in long and slightly wavering movements in one direction, then back again in the opposite direction to soften the work.

MARBLING

Verd-antique A black base is used, then a glaze of chrome green mixed with a little oxide of chromium. The glaze is applied with several long-haired sable brushes held together in one hand and moved jerkily over the whole surface. The effect is softened, allowed to dry and overlaid with some thin whitish veins all running in one direction.

Black and gold marble The base color is again black. Dark grey tints in a dryish mixture of paint without glaze are washed over the whole surface, leaving some black areas, and the work is softened. A mixture of ocher and red is made up and veins are run over the surface. Lastly very fine veins are run from the main veins to split the background into fragments.

Sienna marble The base color is white or off-white. A thin glaze of white and yellow ocher is laid over the whole area and a little vermilion and white are added in parts, making sure there is not too much red. After dabbing the glaze with a small pad of decorator's cloth called stockingette, the whole effect can be softened. To break the monotony of this finish a short-haired fitch is dipped into white spirit and, when the excess has been removed, the spirit is flicked and splashed on to the surface. The wet patches are immediately softened. This process has the effect of revealing large and small spots of the base color.

White marble Over a dry white base is laid a very light glaze with white color in it. Some areas are made slightly darker with a little black and white, to make grey. This same color is used to run in very soft veins. The surface is then padded over with stockingette and softened. A long-haired sable brush is dipped in white spirit, the excess is wiped off and veining marks are made over the surface in one direction. These strokes have the effect of taking off the surface color and revealing the color of the base. With a small sable brush some very fine veins in a light grey may be worked in in some areas.

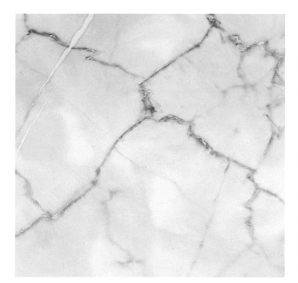

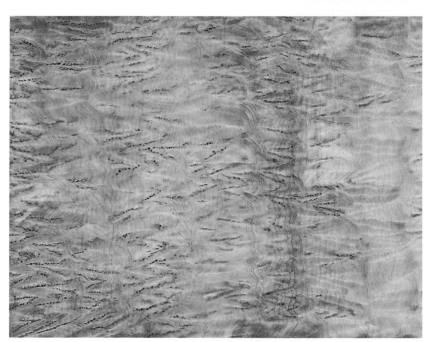

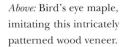

Above: Bird's eye maple, imitating this intricately patterned wood veneer.

Right: Samples of malachite finishes, achieved by combing a surface layer of light green applied on a darker base.

Shown on this page are four examples of sophisticated marbling and graining.

Above left: Sienna marble, see opposite.

Above: Rosa aurora marble, achieved by techniques similar to that of black and gold marble.

WALLPAPERS

Wallpaper production received two giant boosts early in the 19th century. In 1827 the first machine capable of making paper in continuous rolls was imported to America. Then in 1841 a steam-powered machine that could print a pattern on such rolls was perfected. With both the paper making and the printing automated, wallpaper became widely affordable; by the 1840's it had become the preferred way of decorating walls.

At first Americans used paper of a single pattern applied from baseboard to cornice. At the top a narrow, ornamented border might be added; borders might also be used to create vertical panels. This idea was borrowed from the French method of using wallpaper and remained the preferred technique until the mid-1870's. Paper designs imitating architectural details were very popular in America during this period. These included realistic depictions of ashlar stone, wood cornices and molded wall panels. If one could not afford actual wood or stone detailing, the same effect might be had through paper. Scenic papers, showing landscapes or historical themes, were first introduced by the French and were also quite popular; so also were flocked papers. To be avoided were "flashy or gaudy patterns" according to the popular treatise by A. J. Downing. Despite the fact that Downing and other critics throughout the era consistently suggested flat, two-dimensional patterns for walls, consumers continued to buy the more representational three-dimensional designs.

A great change in American wallpaper preferences came with the 1876 Centennial Exhibition in Philadelphia. Here almost ten million people had a chance to see the latest British "Art" papers. Also, the American edition of Eastlake's extremely popular book, *Hints on Household Taste*, had appeared only a few years earlier. This book emphasized many of the patterns that producers displayed at the Centennial Exhibition. These included an entire range of designs inspired by English critics such as Owen Jones. The primary tenet was that "walls should at all times be flat and the very appearance of rotundity avoided." Suddenly French-influenced wallpapers, which ran more to realistic subjects presented in a three-dimensional way, became passé. Stylized or

---

OWEN JONES AND THE GRAMMAR OF ORNAMENT

Owen Jones trained as an architect, but achieved his celebrity as a writer and theorist of color and ornament. After an extended tour of the Continent and Near East, Jones published the beautifully illustrated *Plans, Details and Sections of the Alhambra* (1845) which introduced non-European decoration and design to a wide audience.

In 1850, Jones was appointed as joint architect to the Great Exhibition. He was primarily involved in designing the internal color scheme for Paxton's Crystal Palace.

It was in *The Grammar of Ornament*, published in 1856, that Jones systematized all his ideas and concepts. The encyclopedic scope and the delicately drawn and colored plates guaranteed *The Grammar of Ornament* wide currency as a handbook of design.

Prefaced to the illustration and examination of a wide range of ornament were 37 propositions of "General Principles in the Arrangement of Form and Color." The most famous of these propositions are: "5. Construction should be decorated. Decoration should never be purposely constructed"; and "6. Beauty of form is produced by lines growing out one from the other in gradual undulations: there are no excrescences; nothing could be removed and leave the design equally good or better."

Jones's approach to ornament was that of a professional designer whose roots were in architecture, but whose interests increasingly lay in design for manufactures. In Jones's admirer and follower, Christopher Dresser, the 19th century had its first industrial designer.

Left: Examples of Greek art from Owen Jones's *The Grammar of Ornament* underline his theory that flat-pattern design reflects "the laws which regulate the distribution of form in nature."

Below: This dado paper by Walter Crane belongs to the 1880's, the heyday of the "dado style."

Bottom: The Daffodil wallpaper was designed in 1891 by J.H. Dearle, chief designer of Morris & Co.

189

Above: This wallpaper was designed by Owen Jones some time between 1854 and his death in 1874. After 1854 Jones did most of his work for private clients. His commissions included the redecoration of Fonthill for Alfred Morrison, and Morrison's London house in Carlton House Terrace. Jones also decorated George Eliot's home in Regent's Park.

Right: This is a selection of wallpapers designed for the new Palace of Westminster by A.W.N. Pugin and reprinted from the original blocks during a recent redecoration of Speaker's House. The overall planning of the Houses of Parliament was in the hands of Charles Barry, but Pugin did the lion's share of the design and detailing, chiefly between 1844 and his death in 1852.

geometric representations were preferred, and a new method of papering which divided the wall into three separate areas – dado, filling and frieze – was introduced. A great American love affair with British wallpaper began which lasted until the 1890's.

The end of British wallpaper dominance began, ironically, at another World's Fair, the Columbian Exposition of 1893 in Chicago. This reintroduced French designs, many of which were now in production by American wallpaper companies. These were felt to be more suitable for the new Beaux Arts-influenced house styles that were beginning to gain in popularity. The British papers remained, however, the choice for houses and rooms based on the American version of the Arts and Crafts Movement.

Most of the illustrations in this chapter show British wallpapers, and it is important to remember that the period of their greatest influence in the United States was from the mid-1870's to the mid-1890's – and thereafter only in rooms of Craftsman design.

It is instructive to look at the history of English wallpapers that were so influential at the apex of the American High Victorian movement. Like the United States, England had been influenced by French wallpaper fashions early in the period. During the 1850's and 1860's popular taste ran to pictorial patterns featuring three-dimensional reproductions of plants, flowers and animals. Representational designs included landscapes and panoramic views, with or without figures, and imitations of architectural features such as ashlar walls, cornices, friezes, moldings and columns, statuary in niches, church windows, Gothic doors and pinnacles.

The "impropriety" of pictorialism was criticized by men like A.W.N. Pugin and Owen Jones on two counts: first, a wall is a flat surface and three-dimensional images falsely created an illusion of an uneven, broken surface. Second, direct, almost photographic, copying of nature did not constitute a pattern. The three-dimensional cabbage rose, with or without shadows, violated principles of honesty and taste. Patterns should be formalized, stylized interpretations of nature. These theories were first clearly delineated by Jones in his *Grammar of Ornament* (see page 188). Jones and Pugin both designed wallpapers. Pugin did work for London's Houses of Parliament as well as commercial patterns, many based on a diaper (diamond) motif.

One talented architectural designer soon emerged as the "father of modern wallpaper," William Morris (1834–96) who had a special genius for the discipline of pattern design. Morris designed papers from 1862 until 1896. Whereas the designs of Pugin and Jones had been based on medieval motifs or heraldic devices with comparatively static repeats, Morris introduced flat patterns which were more rhythmical and more representational. It was this "style" with which Americans fell in love at the 1876 Centennial. Interestingly, Morris & Co. wallpapers were more expensively produced by hand, despite available automation. This Craftsman approach allowed Morris's patterns to stay in production even to the present day, since it was possible to continue printing them in small runs (see page 192).

Just as Morris & Co. have come to stand for Arts and Crafts textile design, C.F.A. Voysey

Right: A William Woollams wallpaper of *c.*1870 betrays French influence in the pictorialism of its design.

Below left: One of Voysey's earlier papers includes flowers, foliage and birds characteristic of his style.

Below right: The Bower design is one of the 41 wallpapers created by William Morris from 1862 to 1896. He was also responsible for five ceiling papers.

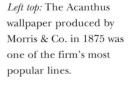

Left top: The Acanthus wallpaper produced by Morris & Co. in 1875 was one of the firm's most popular lines.

Left below: This design for a flocked wallpaper is by A.W.N. Pugin, *c.*1850.

The five wallpapers below are (*from left to right*): a Sunflower design from Watts & Co. of Westminster; a Rose and Coronet design, also from Watts & Co.; a stylized flower design produced for Jeffrey & Co. by Owen Jones; a pink bird design by Watts & Co.; and a modern anaglypta paper.

HAND-PRINTED WALLPAPERS

Hand-printing was and is expensive, but it is a process that keeps alive some of the best Victorian designs. To transfer a design to the wooden printing block, which is generally veneered with a layer of fine-grained pear wood, those parts that are not intended to be printed are cut away.

The printer inks the resulting relief pattern by placing it face down on to a color blanket. With the wallpaper unrolled over his work bench, he registers, or "pitches," the color-laden block over the paper by means of pitch pins at each corner, and lowers it, applying pressure through a foot pedal which operates a system of levers. The amount of pressure varies from one design to another.

Many blocks may be needed to print the whole of the pattern and color range in a single design, and the paper must be allowed to dry between each application. The method is slow and cumbersome, but the modern results are often quite as good as the originals. The re-created Pugin papers in the Palace of Westminster (see page 190) are a fine example of what can be achieved.

represents late Victorian design that stood on the cusp of Art Nouveau and modernism. His designs of the 1890's, when he was a fashionable architect, featured paler colors and took on a lighter and more individual tone. The design is sparser, leaving the lightness of the background to predominate – a precursor of what came to dominate in the early 20th century.

On both sides of the Atlantic, a wallpapering scheme for a Victorian room was typically far more complicated than is usual today. Between baseboard and ceiling, a room could have several different patterns of papers, one in the dado, one for the filling of the wall itself, one for the frieze, and even one for the ceiling.

The dado was traditionally covered in "leather-paper," a thick embossed paper more commonly called anaglypta today. Anaglypta was originally one of several similar patent relief papers; others were Lincrusta and Tynecastle. These papers were a new invention produced in a wide variety of patterns and widths. They were at first made in imitation of the stamped Spanish leather which had been used as wall coverings in the 17th century. Anaglypta papers were similarly colored by painting them a dull brown and laying on a darker brown glaze which was then stippled. Gradually the connection with leather was lost and anaglypta was painted in a variety of colors.

Such embossed papers were very useful because not only were they practical and resistant to damage at the level where scrapes and knocks inevitably occurred, but they created areas of texture and pattern which could be plainly colored to provide a suitable background for furniture. They were frequently used on ceilings and friezes as well as dados.

Anyone trying to remove anaglypta today will see just how robust it is; old paper can be extremely difficult to strip off as the embossed pattern will have filled up from behind with the glue which was used to fasten the paper to the wall. The most effective way to remove anaglypta is to scrape and soak the paper with

methylated spirits and water.

By the 1870's it had become fashionable for the dado to reach a fair way up the wall, and the frieze a good way down, leaving the filling quite narrow. Many artists, such as Walter Crane, designed all-in-one dado-filling-frieze papers. During the 1890's the third division was increasingly dropped, leaving only the two divisions of wall and frieze. However, there might also be ceiling papers with circular repeats which could cover an entire ceiling or be set inside plaster frames. There would generally be decorative borders which ran just below the cornice moldings or above the picture rail.

It is the dominance of a decorated frieze band that most obviously sets a Victorian room apart from rooms of today. Special frieze papers, supplied as strips, were often supplemented by a stenciled frieze.

The first thing to make up your mind about with regard to wallpaper is whether you want it to be merely background or, instead, become a dominant decorative element. That will depend, to some extent, upon whether pictures will be hung on the wall. A simple wallpaper might be used as a background for pictures, while a more exciting frieze paper might be hung above. A rich crimson flock provides a neutral background, as do some of the denser patterned Morris papers.

Although many of the best Victorian papers are still produced in England (Sanderson's took over the printing of Morris & Co. wallpapers in 1930, and has continued to sell them since Morris & Co. went into liquidation in 1940), it is difficult to find the frieze papers that would have accompanied them. Perhaps a doctored wallpaper with stenciled additions could provide the necessary excitement. Many frieze papers were designed to have stenciling applied as highlighting, and you could choose a vertical or horizontal emphasis depending on whether you needed to raise the apparent height of a room or lower it.

The Cray design by Morris & Co. Most of the firm's designs were for textiles and wallpaper.

Lenoble, a painstaking modern reproduction of a mid-19th-century design by Charles Hammond Ltd.

This page: The range and vitality of Victorian pattern design can be seen in these samples. Such designs were often used for both fabrics and wallpapers.

Peacock feather design, from the Silver Studio (Arthur Silver), *c.*1890.

Palmyra, a design originally produced in about 1850, reproduced by Charles Hammond Ltd.

Morris's Artichoke design, *c.*1875.

The design for the Morris & Co. Avon chintz, *c.*1886.

Botanica, a modern reproduction by Osborne & Little.

Another Botanica.

193

CARPETS
AND FLOOR
COVERINGS

By the middle of the 19th century homeowners could obtain a wide variety of floor coverings, ranging from inexpensive matting and oil-cloths to the best Wilton and tapestry carpets, machine-woven in many colors and designs. Factory-produced oil-cloth was made in pieces up to 27 feet (8.2m) wide and 70 feet (21.3m) long and provided a seamless covering suitable for halls and dining rooms; it was frequently used in kitchens. Made from canvas, smoothed and sized and covered with three or four coats of stiff oil paint, and sometimes a top coat of varnish, these cloths were extremely hard-wearing and practical, and could be wiped clean with a damp cloth. Oil-cloths were produced with printed designs imitating tiles, flagstones or wooden floors, or motifs from Persian or Turkish carpets. Some householders made their own floor-cloths and decorated them with stenciled patterns or hand-painted designs.

Matting was recommended for almost any room in the house. Imported from India and the Far East, it came in strips up to 3 feet (0.9m) wide which could be seamed to make a fitted covering for cheap floorboards. In modest homes matting was popular in rooms where the wear was light, such as front parlors and bedrooms. Carpets or rugs were often placed over it, especially to create a warm sitting area in front of a fire; conversely, in summer, matting laid over carpet made a room cooler. When cushioned by the matting, carpeting wore better than when laid directly on wood.

Carpets were a major item of household expenditure; they were expected to last a long time and were looked after with care. Many people laid drugget, an inexpensive cloth of wool, or wool and flax, over the top of better

Above: In this hall designed by C.R. Ashbee small rugs liberally strewn about the floor create an informal room. This was an advantage from the point of view of cleanliness since smaller carpets could be beaten out daily.

carpets. In dining rooms, drugget was often spread under the table and chairs as a crumb-cloth. In less well-off homes, drugget would be the sole floor covering.

Carpeting in the early Victorian period was mainly flat-woven body carpet manufactured in strips between 9 and 54 inches (0.2 and 1.4m) wide. It was similar in appearance to a modern cord, and was reversible. That fact that it could be turned and given a second lease of life made it popular in most middle-class homes.

Pile carpets of various kinds became more readily available after about 1850, and increasingly replaced the flat-woven types in the best rooms. Brussels carpet had a level-looped pile, Wilton a cut pile. Tapestry carpet, which was woven with pre-printed threads, could contain an almost limitless number of colors. Designers pounced on this new-won freedom to indulge the contemporary taste for three-dimensional

Right: The Hammersmith rug was produced by Morris & Co. in the 1880's. Morris followed Pugin's example and finished the rug with a fringe, since knotting the edges was the traditional way of securing the fabric against fraying.

naturalism. Hermann Muthesius, in his *Das Englische Haus*, was not alone in expressing distaste for their "strident flower patterns, their naturalistic animals and landscapes, their imitations of rococo gilt borders and other monstrosities."

By the mid-1870's the fashion for covering the floors of the main rooms with a fitted carpet was disappearing among the wealthy. In *Housewife's Treasury*, Mrs Isabella Beeton wrote, "At the present day in very many houses where tasteful effects are studied, carpets are tabooed to a considerable extent. The old style is now giving place to the far more healthy and cleanly mode of laying down a square of carpet in the center of the room." Stained or polished wooden floors or parquet flooring became popular, with the addition of an oriental rug or two for comfort, or later a carpet to the design of William Morris, C.F.A. Voysey or Walter Crane.

Fitted carpets today come in two forms: the body carpet which was standard throughout Victorian times, and also broadloom carpet. Body carpet is generally sold in 27 or 36 inch (67 or 90cm) widths. Special care is required when laying this so that the seams do not come in the wrong place. One rule is that the seams should run the length of the room and not sideways across it. Broadloom is generally 12 or 15 feet

Above: An English rug of the 1860's sums up the popular taste of the time. Eastlake in his *Hints on Household Taste* ridiculed this kind of English naturalism as an example of "the thousand and one pictorial monstrosities which you see displayed in the windows of Oxford Street and Ludgate Hill," then the two main areas of carpet showrooms in London.

(3.7 or 4.6m) wide and only presents problems if the room to be fitted is wider than the roll.

Fitted carpets in Victorian houses are prone to "tramlines" which develop with the regular use of a vacuum cleaner. Even if a regular felt or underlay is put down, gaps between floorboards allow dust and dirt to be sucked up from underneath the floor. It is best to lay down hardboard if the carpets are light in color. The

sequence is: hardboard, then felt paper, then matting and finally the carpet.

Another option open to the modern homeowner is to adopt the Victorian custom of laying rugs over matting or on wooden floors. Even the traditional oil-cloth is experiencing a modest revival; some interior designers have created elaborate hand-painted oil-cloths for the present-day Victorian sitting room.

Below: Standen in Sussex is one of the few surviving houses designed by Philip Webb. Webb worked closely with Morris & Co., and Standen represents the best existing Morris interior. The carpet was specially made for the house, and designed by J.H. Dearle.

CURTAINS
AND BLINDS

T he Victorians, though anxious to get more light into their houses, were careful to control the impact of direct sunlight. Sun rots fabrics; sunlight, and strong light in general, was considered not kind to complexions. With swagged and curvaceous curtains and deep valances, the effect of large 19th-century windows was often canceled out and the amount of exterior light admitted to a heavily draped room was actually less than in the preceding century.

Male and female commentators agreed that curtains, in Loudon's phrase, gave "an air of comfort to a room." Grand rooms decorated in the perennially fashionable Louis Quatorze style would have had elaborate curtains in keeping with the opulence of the furnishings. The component parts (from ceiling down) were the cornice, the valance, the curtains themselves and the accompanying fringes and ties. The cornice, a boxed-in area which blended into the cornice mold of the room itself, carried the valance, which hid the rod or pole from which the curtain was hung. Valances could also be entwined around the pole with swags and tails, hence dispensing with the cornice board. The curtains themselves often had fringes in contrasting colors and there were ties to loop back the curtains in the daytime. Additional screening from direct light would have been performed by roller blinds or secondary curtains of a translucent material such as lace or muslin, and in the evenings the shutters would be closed.

Loudon deprecated the imported French fashions for their "enormous folds of stuff over poles," which he considered "abominable in

The windows in this room are covered by roller-blinds – a simple treatment, but perfectly adequate in a richly decorated setting.

taste." His encyclopedia gave designs for window draperies of some extravagance, but on the whole he considered the elaborate confections of hangings to be unnecessary and a taste only encouraged by curtain makers who sought a steady income from arranging ever more complex designs. Loudon admitted, all the same, that "window curtains give the mistress of the house an excellent opportunity for exercising her taste in their arrangement." In the 1890's, magazines such as the *Ladies' Home Journal* suggested that one of the marks of being a lady was the arrangement of curtains and draperies in a graceful fashion.

Eastlake, in his *Hints on Household Taste*, called for far simpler treatments, advocating curtains that hung straight down, attached by brass rings to a stout metal rod. In order to stop the draft from the gap between the top of the curtain and the window frame, he proposed a "boxing in of wood," or cornice, and a plain valance.

Curtain material and the style of treatment were chosen to complement the color and status of the room, but in any arrangement the fabric had to fall into attractive folds. The Misses Garrett, in their *Suggestions for House Decoration* (1879), insisted that the "chief beauty of any drapery should be looked for in the folds into which it naturally falls." Damask, silk and lightly glazed chintzes all found ready buyers, but by the mid-century, repp, a ribbed or corded weave, dominated the market. Writers emphasized that curtain material need not be costly so long as it had the right draping qualities; the humbler fabrics, such as cotton, repp or cretonne, were also easier to keep clean, as well as being less prone to retaining smells than richer, denser materials.

Secondary curtains served much as modern sheer curtains. Where there was leaded glass in the top half of windows, half curtains suspended by a rod were ample protection from sun and rude passers-by. Sun blinds, which protected

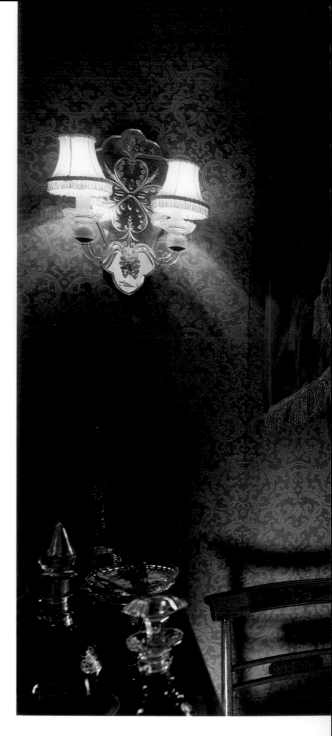

Above: This modest-sized room has been given full-blown curtains with cornice, valance, swags and tails. The actual work of screening the sun is done by roller blinds. Though it can be dangerous to overload a window with grand drapery, in this case a *recherché* window treatment has pulled the room up with it to add an importance belied by its size.

Opposite: In this illustration from J.G. Sowerby's and T. Crane's *At Home Again*, there is a curtain which is half a portière and half an ordinary window curtain. The curtain displays a simplicity modeled after ancient Greek forms which had been one of the *points de départ* of the Aesthetic Movement.

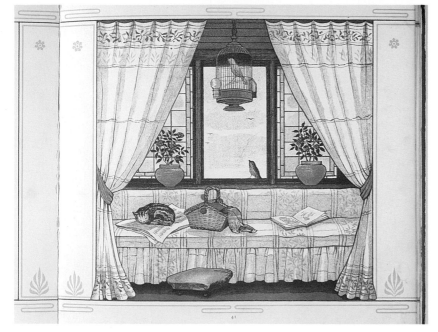

Top: These curtains in the House of Commons were designed by Pugin. Pugin's thesis was that the fringe should be the same color as the curtain, in contrast to the French taste which depended for effect on the use of a variety of fabrics and colors.

Above: Victorian Venetian blinds were wooden and tended to be a trifle heavy and somber. Metal blinds, though lighter in construction, too often have an office-like soullessness, though such a style is the intention in this room.

201

furniture and fabrics from fading, were usually full length. The two standard blinds used were the Venetian and the roller, or Holland blinds. Victorian Venetian blinds were often solidly made with heavy wooden slats and thick ribbon. Roller blinds were frequently treated as transparencies, and painted with landscape scenes or arabesque patterns.

The more showy festoon blinds, made of gathered fabric, could be used as the only window covering, though it was more usual to hang them in conjunction with curtains. As today, they had their admirers and detractors – an architect of the 1890's described them with their "baggy flounces" as "dressy-looking but very cradles for cherishing dust and dirt."

Choosing a style of curtain today will depend on the size and importance of a room. The more ornate, layered French treatments presuppose quite a grand room, or else the curtains will overawe the rest of the decoration. The simpler treatments, such as Eastlake favored, are best seen as background decoration for their impact in a room will be small. Because of the relative cost of good fabrics, it is as well to choose your curtains before making too many firm commitments about decorating the rest of a room.

Where Eastlake's stout metal rod fails us today is in dealing with bay windows. Victorian hardware stores sold knuckle joints which allowed a pole to turn the corners of a bay window. The proportion of window to wall in a bay window rarely allows an individual pole to be mounted along each face of the window with any elegance. Unless you can find a craftsman to create a U-shaped curtain pole, the best solution is probably to use modern plastic fittings and a valance to disguise them. The more extreme solution is to suspend a pole right across the bay window opening and accept that you lose that space for the evening. In some rooms, however, place to hide away toys and papers may be an advantage.

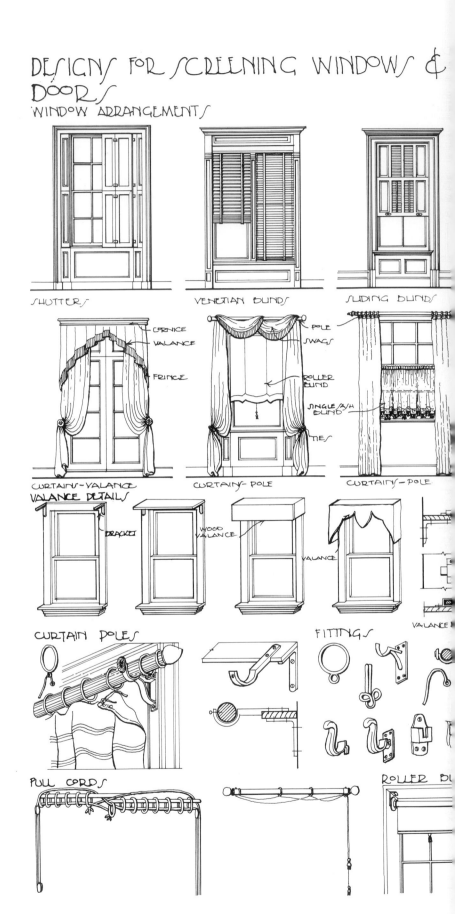

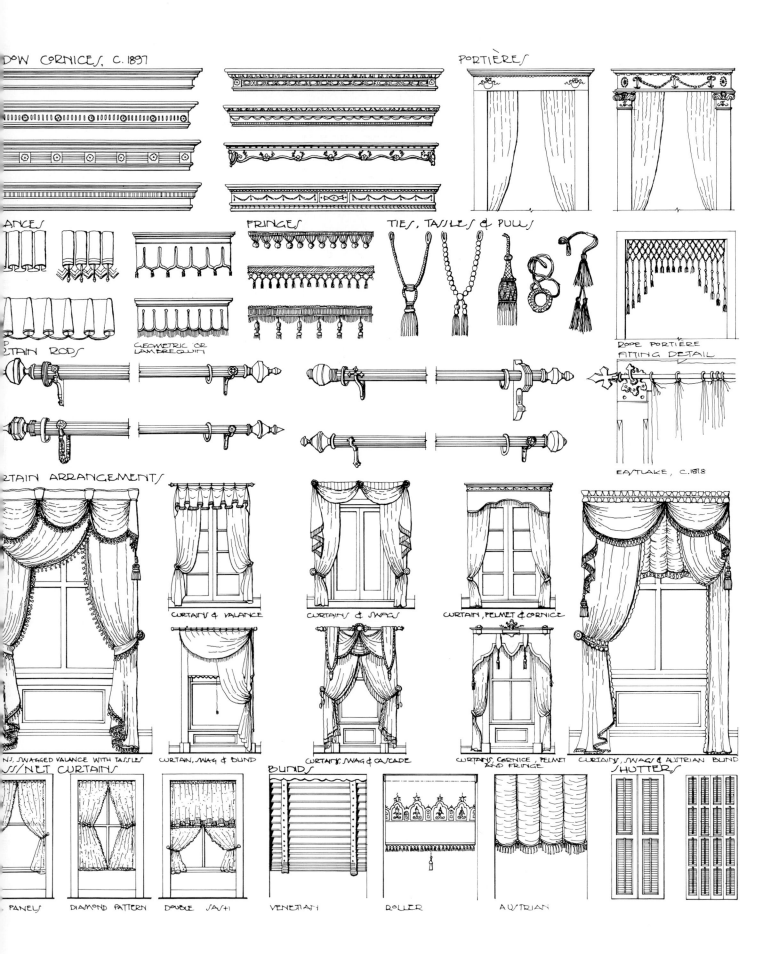

DOW CORNICES, C. 1897

PORTIÈRES

ANCES

FRINGES

TIES, TASSLES & PULLS

ROPE PORTIÈRE
FITTING DETAIL

TAIN RODS

GEOMETRIC OR
LAMBREQUIN

EASTLAKE, C.1878

TAIN ARRANGEMENTS

CURTAINS & VALANCE

CURTAINS & SWAGS

CURTAIN, PELMET & CORNICE

NS, SWAGGED VALANCE WITH TASSLES

CURTAIN, SWAG & BLIND

CURTAINS, SWAG & CASCADE

CURTAINS, CORNICE, PELMET
AND FRINGE

CURTAINS, SWAG & AUSTRIAN BLIND

SS/NET CURTAINS

BLINDS

SHUTTERS

PANELS

DIAMOND PATTERN

DOUBLE SASH

VENETIAN

ROLLER

AUSTRIAN

FURNITURE AND UPHOLSTERY

Even more than heavily carved mahogany and walnut, it is the richly padded curves and deeply sprung chairs and sofas of the mid-century that seem to epitomize Victorian furniture. Upholstery changed dramatically with the invention of the coil spring, which made it possible for the upholsterer to produce the deep-buttoned forms which were at the heart of Victorian notions of comfort.

The new furnishings, their construction hidden under at least two layers of stuffing, demanded much skill and labor on the part of the upholsterer. Underlying all the coverings were the springs, stitched to webbing. Horsehair was used throughout the 19th century for both the first and second layers of stuffings in all high-quality work. Other cheaper materials were hay, seaweed and woodshavings, in fact anything which when placed under "scrim" gave the desired shape. Scrim is a loosely woven but tightly spun linen, which was used to enclose the first stuffing. A second stuffing of horsehair was covered with calico, which stopped the hairs working through the layer of soft cotton wadding placed under the top covering. To complete the effect, a wide range of fabrics was available with new color combinations and patterns, matched by ever more elaborate trimmings, buttons, ruching, cords, tassels and fringes.

Button-back chairs, sofas and *chaises longues* were much in evidence at London's Great Exhibition in 1851, but such feats of High Victorian upholstery never eclipsed earlier styles. In fact, Victorian furniture design is mainly a

Right: For winter, a cozy look may be created by draping a sofa with paisley shawls and a selection of cushions.

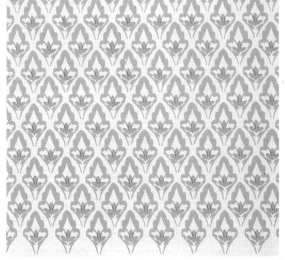

Victorians would have used repp and printed cottons as the standard material for upholstery. Today a linen blend is popular for curtains and chair covers. These are examples of modern fabrics based on 19th-century patterns produced by Bernard Thorp, London.

Top: Chester; a glazed cotton or chintz.

Above: Rainbow Shell; a Bargello style of design in a cotton-polyester tapestry-weave.

Right: Vine Leaves; hand-screen-printed cotton in two variations.

story of revivals – every historical style was copied and developed. As today there was an appetite for antiques. Many pieces, such as the 18th-century wing chair, remained current throughout the Victorian era, and the white and gold painted furniture of the Louis XIV period was ever popular as the *nouveau riche* style.

The Greek revival period favored the American Empire style of furniture which was upholstered in rich silk velvets, damasks and satins or, for dining room and library, in morocco leather. Nearly all upholstery was "French stuffed," with an extra roll of stuffing wrapped in scrim and stitched in place round the front edge of the piece, which gave a fine shaped elegance to Empire furnishings. The better pieces were of solid rosewood or mahogany; the lesser pieces were more often made from softwood, and veneered. These agreeable designs stayed popular and then became part of the revivals of the 1890's.

The best of mid-century Gothic furniture was designed by architects who had learned their art while designing church furnishings; this led to the tendency for Gothic revival furniture to be relatively massive. The Gothic revival and the Arts and Crafts Movement overlap in the figure of Philip Webb who was the chief furniture designer for the firm of Morris & Co. His furniture, especially his tables, were bulky objects.

Later Victorian upholstery can be seen as something of a reaction to the heavily stuffed tastes of mid-century. Designers of the 1870's and 1880's, working within the hand-crafted ideals of the Arts and Crafts Movement or in tandem with commercial manufacturers, began to produce lighter pieces which used English hardwoods, sometimes under the influence of Japanese forms but generally under the banner of Art furniture. Art furniture's significant trait was its antipathy to deep upholstery. By the 1880's there was a change towards neo-Georgian and simpler furniture which was less dependent on springs and stuffing to give it its shape.

STYLES OF VICTORIAN FURNITURE
THE RULING TASTE

The furniture of the Ruling Taste was dominated by the new upholstery and techniques of mechanical manufacture. This usually meant that the structure was hidden under layers of stuffing and heavy padding, further loaded with ruchings, cords and trimmings. The design of these deep-cushioned pieces varied little, but their ornamentation was adapted to new fashions which were largely Paris-led. Foreign hardwoods, such as mahogany and walnut, were commonly used; these were French-polished to render the surface hard and bright.

LADIES' EASY CHAIR

CHESTERFIELD

EASY ARM CHAIR OR FAUTEUIL

PEDESTAL SIDEBOARD

BALLOON-BACK CHAIR

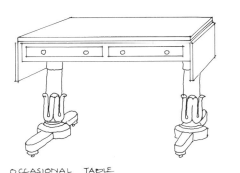

OCCASIONAL TABLE

BALLOON-BACK CHAIR

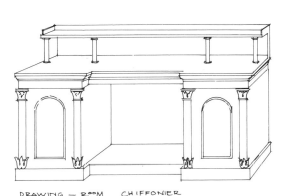

DRAWING-ROOM CHIFFONIER

LOUIS XIV-STYLE C...

ADVANCED AND ARTISTIC TASTE

Victorian architect-designed furniture begins with Pugin, whose motto "form follows function" became the *leitmotif* of furniture designers who came after him. The sham of French upholstery, where structure had no relation to shape, drove designers into the kitchen to find furniture untainted by what was seen as the dishonest upholstery of the Ruling Taste. As well as the kitchen vernacular, architects adapted Gothic, Jacobean and Georgian forms which had an elegance and simplicity in contrast with the curved, soggy comforts of the average Victorian drawing room.

LIBRARY BOOKCASE BY C.L. EASTLAKE. 1878

PUGIN TABLE

LOUNGING CHAIR BY E. GODWIN, 1878

MORRIS & Cᵒ ADJUSTABLE CHAIR, 1866

MORRIS & Cᵒ SUSSEX CHAIR

BUFFET · MORRIS & Cᵒ 1880

MORRIS & Cᵒ TABLE

CENTURY GUILD SETTEE, 1888

VIOLLET-LE-DUC CHAIR

VOYSEY CHAIR

QUEEN ANNE SOFA

MACKINTOSH CHAIR

DRAWING ROOMS

The Victorian drawing room was an essentially feminine room. It was supposed to be pleasant and cheerful, and most of all it was to be comfortable. A drawing room was the main public room of the house – here guests were received and, it was hoped, impressed by the wealth, culture and taste of the household.

The twin aims of comfortable hospitality and social showing off did not always produce a happy effect. Mid-Victorian rooms were notorious for their "showy discomfort." The generation which had been brought up in such rooms rebeled against the contorted and over-stuffed furniture, and created for themselves the lighter and more relaxed Artistic rooms of the 1880's and 1890's. These were modeled on the amusing and individualistic rooms of architects and professional artists, who had become a socially acceptable class.

Of course, even the Artistic room soon filled up with clutter. The Victorian drawing room, or parlor as it was frequently called, resembled a collage which could be endlessly added to. As new fads and crazes came on to the market, these rooms became repositories for the stream of manufactured products, curios from all corners of the world, as well as new art forms such as photography, which all became available at relatively modest prices. And then there were the decorative trimmings – stencil work in the panels of doors, draperies on mantelshelves, on tables and over chairs; decorative woodwork and ornamental plasterwork. The furniture revived almost every historical style, as well as introducing oriental lacquered bamboo and Indian brasswork.

The frame for the display of this eclectic mixture was the "harmonized" color scheme of the room. The Victorians' employment of color is the aspect of their decoration most often overlooked today. There were more and stronger

This drawing room is in many ways an exemplary recreation of a Victorian room – the quaint and amusing clutter is successfully controled by the all-embracing dark reds of the walls and fabric. The effect is deceptively simple, but much skill has been invested to achieve it. The scale and color of each object has been carefully thought out.

colors, but they all related to one dominant effect. Colors were applied in graduated tints of the color used for the filling, the main part of the wall above the dado and below the frieze. The cornice and ceiling would be in lighter tones of the main wall color. The woodwork too was executed in a color that harmonized with the wall treatments. This practice of harmonious decoration had the effect of uniting the room into a visual entity within which all other items of decoration could blend with little disruption.

There was disagreement about dadoes in drawing rooms; since many Victorian drawing rooms were too high for their size, an extra wall

Above: The attraction of this living room, decorated in late Regency style, is the way in which the garden has been effectively brought indoors, as was recommended by Humphry Repton and also by his admirer, Loudon.

Right: A country house decorated in a loosely Loudonesque way employs the intermediate styles of the 1840's. The walls are covered in green damask, and the curtain or *portière* hangs down from a cornice which has been incorporated into the Gothick cornice of the room.

Above: In a cottage sitting room a screen makes a homely family corner, blocking off the sofa from the doorway and its traffic. In large rooms, especially, screens can make a virtue of intimacy while at the same time hiding unfortunate eyesores and stopping drafts.

division was often useful to help reduce the impression of height. Eastlake felt that a room with a single wallpaper running from baseboard to ceiling was the "most dreary method" of decoration. It has the attendant problem that such a room requires a fairly consistent scale and style of furniture. Eastlake recommended a plain dado; but later the dado received every kind of Artistic treatment. Embossed anaglypta or Lincrusta, however, was always a safe option.

Dealing with a drawing room in a Victorian house today requires experimentation with color on a little more daring scale than has been customary since World War II. The 20th century rejected the dense color arrangements of the Victorians and left a legacy of conservative pastels and whites. The varying colors and textures in a true Victorian style can accommodate a far more heterogeneous accumulation of furniture and

Left: This small cottage parlor has an ordered informality and simplicity emphasized by the white walls and ceilings. Cottages in pre-industrial times would have had white-washed interior walls. This bareness was updated and stylized by many Arts and Crafts architects.

Below: The large amount of daylight entering this converted chapel has allowed flowering plants to become the principal decorative feature. The handsome woodwork compensates for the difficult spaces inherent in such an extensive living area.

Opposite: This room is dominated by a French ceramic Art Nouveau fireplace whose colors have been used to create the decorative scheme. The walls are painted and stenciled to give a faded finish, echoed in the upholstery.

Below: The small scale and simple features of this sitting room have been enhanced by an elaborate curtain pole and decorative wall panels created with Victorian frieze papers. Curtains that are looped back during the day will "puddle" when drawn. Here the effect is used to soften the bareness of parquet flooring.

objects than the average modern room scheme. Even modern furniture, if good, can hold its own in Victorian surroundings. The also-rans of modern furniture can at a pinch be softened with drapery, or repainted to blend into the wall. Modernistic pictures, however, can pose insuperable problems, as they are often not compatible with a Victorian room. The restoration of a Victorian drawing room is made less difficult since the wallpapers of the Arts and Craft Movement are still manufactured, as are many Morris & Co. chintzes. These will be expensive, but they do represent examples of the finest pattern designs. The white ceiling is now part of the national psyche, so if wallpapered or densely colored ceilings are not to your taste, a complementary off-white may suffice to harmonize with the walls.

Above: Converted from a malthouse, this cottage has preserved the openness of the original industrial space. The open plan, although creating problems with heating and services, allows the architecture and the character of the malthouse's interior to be retained.

Left: This converted mews has had the ceilings taken away and a large French mantelpiece added to create a witty pastiche of a baronial hall. The fireplace, walls, and galvanized sliding window shutters have all been given a faded, old look so that they work together.

Above: A minimal background has been created by using grey tiles and carpet, with one yellow wall acting as the animating spirit of the room. The danger of hi-tech within the Victorian house is that it can look more like 1950's revival than today.

DINING ROOMS

Prior to the Victorian era, most American houses had no separate room for dining. Meals were served in the kitchen, parlor or wherever space could be found. Only the grandest Georgian or Federal houses were exceptions. During the Victorian era a special room for dining became the rule and was one of the marks of a proper middle-class house-hold. In smaller houses, the drawing room was the front room, and the dining room, separated by double doors, was at the back. In larger houses it was found elsewhere on the ground floor, often close to the rear kitchen and separated by a butler's pantry.

While parlors were considered to be feminine rooms and reflected this in their decor,

Right: The dining room at Flintham, Nottingham-shire, built in 1854, combines echoes of the baronial hall with a high degree of comfort. The Victorian dining room was traditionally the stage upon which a family's largesse could be displayed.

Opposite: The dining room at the Linley Sambournes' home in Kensington, London, is an example of the softer Artistic decoration of rooms which appeared in the 1870's and 1880's. The black marble fireplace, which tended to dominate most dining rooms, has been obliterated by being painted the same colour as the woodwork.

dining rooms were often more masculine. It was not unusual for an American Victorian house to have a parlor with soft pastels and French-influenced furniture, while the dining room was darker, with heavy solid furniture.

Dining rooms were likely to have the typical tripartite wall divided into dado, filling and frieze. Here the dado and dado rail (sometimes called a chair rail) served an important function in protecting the walls from damage by the room's many movable chairs. Late in the century, the dining wall often became two parts, dado and frieze. The dado area extended three-quarters or more up the wall to the frieze, and the dado rail became a plate rail for the display of china.

Furnishings were typically a large dining table, chairs and a massive sideboard which was sometimes built-in. These might have been designed in any of the Victorian era furniture styles – Empire, Gothic, Renaissance revival, Eastlake, Arts and Crafts. Where the wall arrangement allowed pictures, family portraits, fruit cornucopias, hunting and fishing scenes were favorite subjects.

Above: The boxed-in radiator acts as a sideboard in a room that leaves little space for other furniture. Inexpensive folding chairs and simple table dressings provide a sense of lightness in what was originally a rather dark hallway.

Right: Open-plan living presents excellent opportunities for creating a theatrical setting for dining.

220

STUDIES, LIBRARIES AND BILLIARD ROOMS

Portraits of Victorian Man in his study reveal a dark room with solid furniture which stands in contrast to the female equivalent of the sitting room. A study was the place of daily business, with a desk for writing letters, answering invitations and paying bills. It was fitted out with appropriate symbols of male authority: dark oak paneling, pictures with civic and patriotic subject matter, professional certificates and sporting trophies, a coat of arms, perhaps, and other evocative mementos.

In most middle-class homes, the line between study and library was never firmly drawn. A study might contain the bulk of a household's books just as a library had a writing desk as well as the standard central library table.

In the 18th century, books had been expensive and a library was a status symbol. In the 19th century, books and journals multiplied, as did readership. A traditional library was an essential ornament of larger Victorian dwellings. There would have been built-in bookcases of some architectural pretension; pedimented and pilastered in the Classical style, or Gothic with arches and moldings. Free-standing bookcases had obvious advantages for apartments and rental houses. Glazed doors also protected the books from city pollution. One Victorian architect advocated using roller blinds fastened to the tops of bookcases to protect the contents, and it was standard English practice to suspend a tooled or embossed leather valance from each shelf to reduce the dust gathering on the tops of the books.

A room devoted to books becomes expensive when all the bookcases are made to match. Two free-standing bookcases and a wall of built-in shelving will serve the purpose, but will lack the charm of a unified style. To gain the traditional authority of a library, the architecture of the bookcases really does need to be prominent.

If you devote a room today to a study, you will have two main options. With funds, you can create the womb of leather and woodwork favored by Victorians. This is fine for effect, but unless you feel happy working in such dim surroundings, it may be best to produce something closer to a modern office. It will probably be a functional room – private and secure, where mess can remain unmolested until 9 o'clock the next morning. In planning such a room, the starting point is a series of questions: how many books, what kind of shelving, how many filing cabinets, what machinery – computer, printer, fax machine and so on – in short, what must the room accommodate? For the office-with-study, custom-built shelves, counters and cabinets will probably serve best.

Opposite: This 1890 room in the home of B.B. Comegys, President of the Philadelphia National Bank, shows the study as a masculine retreat filled with a display of cultural and historical artifacts. Part museum, part office-at-home, the effect is obviously meant to impress the visitor and signal the occupant's wide range of interests and learning.

Opposite below: In this writing room the wallpaper is hardly conducive to serious thought, which suggests that it was not intended for everyday use. Country houses generally had such a room where guests could write their letters.

Left: The library of Horstead Place, Sussex, was outfitted in the mid-19th century by a local carpenter. Bookcases were always carefully sited away from external walls to prevent damp penetrating from outside, and placed where they would offer the best sound-proofing.

These fixtures can be sympathetically incorporated into the style of the room by painting or graining, as also can the filing cabinets.

When siting your bookcases you should pay attention to sound-proofing, not simply to blot out television and music-system noise from outside, but also to muffle the sounds of telephones and machines from inside. A built-in bookcase will help cut down noise passing through a wall, and heavy carpets and underfelt have a useful deadening effect.

In the late 19th century many libraries were combined with other, more sociable, uses and this type of library became a popular room. In some houses the library served as a family room where stories could be read aloud to the children. In others it became a retreat for smoking and for after-dinner brandy. Or it housed a billiard table, a pertinent indicator of the intellectual ambitions of the middle and upper classes.

In country houses and middle-class villas, a separate billiard room was a desirable feature. It was usually a ground-floor room at the back of the house where a strong floor could be provided to take the weight of the table. The grander type of billiard room had high wood paneling on the walls, and was decorated in a masculine style, with some concession to women in a large inglenook or raised platform with comfortable upholstered leather seats. The wooden floor was left bare except for wide runners round the table.

Traces of billiard rooms sometimes survive in the form of tell-tale relics such as cue fittings on the walls. Today, a billiard room may have limited appeal. To accommodate a full-size billiard table you need a large room of 18 feet by 24 feet (5.5m x 7.3m) giving a minimum of 6 feet (1.8m) around the table. The bulk and weight of the table limits which floors will accommodate it.

Open-plan living of the 1960's had obvious antecedents in the 1950's office, with its rejection of private space. If this plan is used for a private house which is to incorporate a work space, as here, it will only be satisfactory if the household and the vicinity of the desk have low noise levels.

Left: This example of the late Victorian country house billiard room was designed by Webb for Standen in Sussex. Billiards was the big, male social pursuit of the late 19th century, and billiard rooms were usually given a clubland feel. Many middle-class villas and town houses had them, not only to entertain the males of the household but also to attract potential husbands to the house.

Above: A newly built library has been designed with traditional features such as tailor-made bookcases, glass-fronted cabinets and fully paneled walls, and some modern facilities as well, including concealed lighting. The grills of the lower cupboards are screened with fabric that matches the curtains over the Gothic arched windows of the room.

Chapter Five

KITCHENS AND
BATHROOMS

T he greatest changes in modern use of Victorian houses have
occurred in kitchens and bathrooms, and in everything to
do with washing and sanitary arrangements; few Victorian
homes even had anything we would recognize today as a bathroom.

Compared with advances in transport, engineering and
manufacturing, progress in kitchen and bathroom design in the
19th century seems surprisingly sluggish. "A New Design for Kitchen
Range," first patented by Thomas Robinson in 1780, remained the
basic pattern for cookers for over a century: a cast-iron, coal- or
wood-burning hearth, with the fire becoming increasingly enclosed
as improvements were introduced. Gas stoves were shown at
London's Great Exhibition of 1851, but they were not in general
use until the end of the century. The reason for this lack of progress
is probably social; the availability of servants meant that many
housewives could avoid the kitchen, which remained the jealously
guarded sanctuary of the cook.

The kitchen in most early 19th-century houses was either in
the basement or, in rural areas, in a completely separate structure.
As new stoves decreased the probability of fire, kitchens were
increasingly housed in an addition at the back of the house –
although, in homes that had servants, efforts were made to keep
its activities separate from the rest of the house.

Nineteenth-century kitchens were bare and functional rooms;
whatever coziness they possessed derived from the cooking range,
and from the simple china-lined dresser and wall shelving for
utensils. Otherwise the furniture was serviceable rather than
comfortable, with perhaps a rush-seated Windsor chair for Cook
to sit on after working hours. The sink would have been in
enameled cast iron, with a teak or marble drainboard and, perhaps,
a wooden plate rack hung above. There was no working countertop
as understood today; all preparation was carried out on a central
work table, scrubbed daily, and with the working cutlery stored in
drawers underneath. Hot water was obtained either from kettles
or pans suspended above the open range or from a cast-iron boiler
situated on one side of the fireplace. On the other side was the oven,
which was used for baking only, as the heat was too uneven and
variable for roasting. Roasting was carried out on spits in front of
the fire, with the melting fat collected in trays below. Cooking stoves

The great kitchen at
Lanhydrock in Cornwall,
fitted out in the 1880's,
contains all the elements
one associates with a
Victorian kitchen – the low
scrubbed table in the
middle, the dresser with its
open shelves, and ranks of
copper pans and jelly
molds. Although not built
for elegance, it has its own
beauty in its utilitarian
simplicity.

A modern kitchen/dining room combines the traditional look of the Victorian kitchen with the eating requirements of the present day. No money has been spent on upper cupboards. Instead, there are open shelves where everything can be seen, and the white stove does not look out of place next to the pine cabinet because the room is primarily functional.

with flat hot plates on top, as on modern models, worked through a system of flues and dampers which passed hot air under the plates and around the oven before being taken up the chimney.

The scullery, which in large houses was exclusively set aside for washing up, became in late Victorian Britain attached to smaller suburban houses as well, where it was always positioned next to the kitchen. In the United States, a "butler's pantry" was the most typical secondary kitchen room. This was positioned between the kitchen and the dining room and supplied with both counter space for serving and ample cabinets for dish storage. It had the additional virtue of providing a buffer between the dining room and the odors and heat of the kitchen. Back porches were the usual location for iceboxes and arrangements were made so the ice could be delivered and put in place without disturbing the household.

Bathrooms as we understand them now were not widely installed until the end of the century. For most of the century bathing was carried out in large portable tubs, preferably placed in front of an open fire. These varied from shallow trays to stand in while sponging oneself down to hip baths with a high sloping back. The bather lay half in, half out, with knees inevitably protruding. There were also full-size reclining baths, though these were rarer. Servants provided the hot water in buckets, and removed the soapy waste afterwards in the same way. It was also their task to empty chamber pots from bedrooms every morning. In middle-class homes all washing took place in bedrooms, or in tubs placed before the kitchen range in poorer homes. The familiar marble wash stand, with its matched set of china bowl and pitcher, gave good service for decades. A significant advance came about with the development of tall water towers allowing enough pressure for municipal water supplies to be piped to flow throughout each house. With the introduction of the first formidable-looking hot

The exuberance of this decorated porcelain basin, with its blue transfer motifs, is matched by the ornate paper, mirror and fittings in a rich, High Victorian style, providing a good example of the use of pattern on pattern.

In one of the bathrooms at Castle Drogo, built by Edwin Lutyens from 1910 onwards, the basin is a plumbed-in version of the traditional marble wash stand set upon an oak plinth, a satisfying marriage of end-of-the-period elegance and hygiene.

water heaters, the built-in bath with its own supply of hot water made its appearance.

Piped running water was also the inspiration for the rapid improvement of the "water closet" in the years after 1875; prior to this, most households had depended on "outhouses," privies in an outbuilding, and chamber pots for indoor relief.

Now rooms began to be set aside for bathrooms. At first, these were often converted dressing rooms adjoining a bedroom and were usually provided with a fireplace and furnished with chairs and other comfortable accessories. Thus they were sometimes pleasantly large by modern standards. Later, when custom-built bathrooms began to be installed in new houses from the 1880's onwards, they were comparatively small, reflecting the priority given to the activities performed in them. Also, by this time, a concern for hygiene began to stress tiled surfaces and exposed pipes as easy to clean, rather than the more furnished look of the earlier bathrooms, now thought to promote the harboring of germs.

KITCHENS

Right: The comfortable, rustic feel of this kitchen comes from a subtle use of Victorian elements. The sea green of the stove has been picked up in the newly made dresser.

Below: In a kitchen of the 1890's, pride of place goes to the black-leaded, cast-iron range with its two ovens, semi-enclosed fire-grate, hot plates and warming compartment. Such ranges required a constant and very hot fire, and are estimated to have consumed more than a dozen scuttles of coal a day.

It is almost impossible to create anything like a faithful replica of a Victorian kitchen without compromising modern standards of convenience and comfort. One option is to evoke the Victorian past through fittings and decoration, but we must remember that whatever we do in this direction will be largely an effect rather than faithful reproduction. The other option is not to take this path at all but to go for a highly modern treatment; very often, the kitchen is in a part of the house not provided with elaborate moldings or architectural details, so modern fixtures will not look out of place.

Today, of course, we have the modern cooking stove in place of the range, the refrigerator instead of an icebox, and perhaps an automatic dishwasher to replace the work of a single large sink. This means that if we do wish to echo Victorian features, it will have to be

230

through the use of wallpaper, moldings, paneling and tiles, fixtures such as old-fashioned faucets and spigots, and – most atmospheric of all – a Victorian dresser (see page 235). If the kitchen is to be used for eating, the traditional table (particularly one with drawers) may be too low for comfort; but a new wooden table need not look out of place, and its working surface will probably be at a better height. Open shelves and simple wooden floor units will also be appropriate. A work top in wood, or quarry tiles supported on a wooden framework with open shelves below, will look better than many of the modern "antique" or "country" units now advertised, which are fitted with elaborately paneled doors, and are correspondingly expensive.

Many excellent modern kitchens have been assembled out of assorted Victorian pieces of more or less junk furniture. If the woods do not match, then the whole assembly can be painted, perhaps in the traditional colors of chocolate or apple green.

In a new kitchen it is important to choose your appliances first, decide where they should be placed, and ensure that they are all adequately supplied with electricity and plumbing. Then build the storage units and work surfaces around them. The kitchen will be one of the most complex rooms in the house in terms of pipework and electrical power supply; any lack of forethought in the planning of these services will inevitably prove costly and painful to rectify at a later stage.

There is rarely much of a role in the kitchen for the avid restorer; the changing function of this room since the Victorian period has meant the removal of most authentic features. Few ranges survive, except in some rural buildings, but where they do exist they are well worth retaining, if only for occasional use. The same is true for bits of cabinet work or moldings which may remain.

Below: Here, a modern gas hob has been built into the chimney breast, and is given a traditional look by the copper hood and a simple white tiled surround which is very effective.

Right: These built-in cabinets have been designed to match the Gothic windows, themselves restorations since previously an ugly picture window had been knocked through the façade.

Two matching dressers show what can be done with a very simple design, using tongue-and-groove boarding, a finely detailed architrave at the top and open shelves at the bottom.

The kitchen of an unmodernized tenement flat in Glasgow provides an excellent reference for a modest, turn-of-the-century family kitchen, down to the built-in coal box behind the table. Dun colors predominate, and *trompe-l'oeil* wallpaper masquerades as wood paneling and tiles.

In the kitchen of Cragside, in Northumberland, built in 1870, ornament has been reduced to a minimum, resulting in an impression of austere efficiency.

DRESSERS

In the Victorian kitchen, apart from the obligatory range, the only item of built-in furniture would probably have been the dresser. Particularly common in Britain, a dresser is a piece of furniture with shelves for dishes; it may either be open or have doors, often of glass. It is also called a china cabinet or cupboard in the United States. Though very often stripped today, it would have been painted in Victorian times, with cup hooks along the shelves and with narrow grooves or strips of wood along each shelf to hold the plates displayed there in an upright position. The bottom part would hold drawers and deep cupboards or large open shelves for a breadbin and other bulky objects.

It is often a good idea to leave out a wall of built-in cabinets and have one great big dresser, either found or custom-built, with china and other objects displayed in the original way. A simple version can be made from an old double sideboard with new shelves of the same length fitted above, held in position by a plain vertical frame. If the kitchen is small and modernistic, do not be tempted to put in a dresser just to soften the starkness of it. Stick with the modern idiom.

Above: The traditional glass-fronted cabinet of the butler's pantry provides the inspiration for a simple kitchen design with no expensive fripperies and a dark paint color which really works.

Opposite: A thoroughly practical and elegant kitchen has been created under a sloped glass roof in this modern addition. The traditional touches in the foreground furnish a link with the elaborate period treatment of the other rooms of the house.

Right: A modern fitted kitchen unit plays upon Victorian themes and has been painted to give some semblance of age, but the blue and white crockery looks as though it is hardly ever used.

Far right: This stylish window treatment provides a wonderful example of how to draw on the past and simplify, but still achieve a very Victorian feeling.

236

CUPBOARDS AND SHELVES

Many people today want built-in cabinets, yet the Victorians, like hard-working chefs in modern restaurants, almost always went for more easily accessible open shelving, where utensils in daily use could be kept within easy reach.

If authentic Victorian kitchen furniture is beyond your means – or not to your taste – you may be able to adapt other pieces of furniture to achieve the desired effect. Old-looking lower cupboards are easier to find than upper ones, and it maybe preferable to replace high-level cupboards with open shelves around the kitchen, stocked with uniform and handsome storage jars and interesting bottles. Everything is on display in a neat, attractive and accessible fashion. But for those who still resist this approach, there is something to be said for the "pantry look," based on the traditional butler's pantry, with glass-fronted cabinets at eye level and simple paneled cupboards below.

An alternative is to build cabinets to your own design, achieving some degree of Victorian atmosphere by copying architectural details from elsewhere in the house. If you live in a Victorian Gothic house, for instance, you can put a Gothic arch molding on the front of the kitchen cupboards or echo the moldings on the doors of the house. This will mean that a modern Victorian kitchen might contain a large element of pastiche that can be both effective and enjoyable.

If the house you have bought has fitted kitchen cabinets which you dislike, a simple way to change them is to remove the doors and get a carpenter to make up paneled or boarded wooden doors to the same size. The replacements can then be attached with the same hinges as the old doors and the shell of the cupboards can remain in place, totally obscured by the new wooden doors. You could complete the decorative scheme by constructing a matching wainscot along those sections of the walls not covered by cupboards.

On the other hand, if you are going to install a modern built-in kitchen the task is relatively easy and needs little comment. But there remains one important caveat; don't be tempted to redo the kitchen in such a way that the feeling of the Victorian architecture or the proportion and scale of the room are lost. It is not necessary to lower ceilings and remove cornices. It is better to place a minimal hi-tech kitchen around the walls of a frankly Victorian room rather than try to streamline every nook and cranny. Or, as some designers propose, you can take this idea one step further by placing all your modern kitchen equipment in a carefully designed island in the middle of the room.

Above: The tongue-and-groove back to these shelves, as well as the display of china, are entirely in keeping with the period, although their use as a backdrop to a kitchen sink certainly is not. None the less, this is a delightful and inventive solution.

Above right: This is modern living with a Victorian veneer. The cooking hob and sink unit have been set into an old sideboard, bringing the kitchen into the dining room rather than the more usual reverse.

Right: The open style of this sink area follows in the Victorian tradition, while a miscellaneous collection of Victorian tiles helps to bring interest to what would otherwise be an insignificant corner.

SINKS AND SURROUNDS

Other than using the traditional deep butler's sink – usually made of a heavy white enameled finish over cast iron – there is little you can do to introduce a proper sense of authenticity to the sink in a modern kitchen. Modern stainless steel sinks are probably a necessary compromise, but you might like to consider those that are finished in colors rather than shiny metal.

There is no need to put the kitchen sink underneath a window. This is a throw-back to a former age when the washing up would take half the day, and this placement can entirely spoil a kitchen plan. A lot of modern kitchens do not have full-sized drainboards on the assumption that a dishwasher will be used for most kitchen and dining ware, but in practice this often proves to be a mistake. Drainboards still have their uses; teak ones may be the most sympathetic. Old-fashioned faucets, or at least old-fashioned-looking ones, are available in brass and can give the sink area a Victorian feeling.

Tiles – used in the splashboard to the sink and elsewhere – are particularly effective in giving a Victorian look to a kitchen. Unfortunately a complete set is one of the hardest things to find. Although there are reproduction Victorian tiles on the market, most of them look like reproductions. One trick is to buy old tiles and not attempt to match them. Just select a number of single tiles which you like the look of and put them up together on the wall in a pattern or a random display.

When arranging the electrical sockets at work-top level, try to take the tiling grid into consideration. There is nothing more irritating than to find, after buying some old Victorian tiles, that there is a socket which cuts into the corners of four of them. It is worth laying the tiles out on a template and giving the drawing to the electrician before he starts wiring.

Above: The kitchen of Cragside is splendid in its austerity. Modern purists would have to go this far to be authentic.

Right: The elements of this modern kitchen are virtually identical to the above, and the same era is evoked, yet this design manages to marry practicality with affection and warmth.

S U R F A C E S   A N D   L I G H T I N G

Opposite: The hand-painted motifs on the doors bring a note of individuality to an otherwise stark room, and are authentic, but they are badly worn and will be difficult to restore. The sink is well lit, and the idea of mounting plate racks above it is both traditional and efficient, provided that the supporting framework is left open at the bottom to let moisture drain through.

The units in this kitchen are built into surrounds inspired by a traditional hearth and the surfaces and shelves of a dairy or wine cellar. The fluorescent lighting works well under the chimney breast, but is harsh and uninviting when used unshaded above the window.

Apart from the central kitchen table, Victorian kitchens had no work surfaces. We definitely require them today and to many minds a hardwood finish, such as teak or any of its close cousins, unquestionably looks best. Tiled work surfaces look good when new but are difficult to keep clean; the grouting and edging soon begin to look unhygienic. Slate is a fine looking alternative, and not too expensive if it does not require intricate cutting.

Vertical wooden surfaces in a kitchen, including doors, cupboards, and paneling, are the most used of any in a house and need hard-wearing finishes. Stripped wooden furniture and bare wooden surfaces may achieve a nostalgic effect, but they are quite impractical as well as unhistorical. The Victorians themselves were great enthusiasts for paint and varnish, but beware of special paint finishes. Graining, stippling and other effects do not last well, and should perhaps be avoided in kitchens. For a nostalgic look, tongue-and-groove boarding is recommended, all painted in one color. Recessed paneling is more expensive to do, but looks good, especially if it matches the style of the original doors of the house.

For kitchen floors you need have no hesitation in using tiles, provided that there is a sound concrete base on which to lay them. They could be Victorian tessellated tiles, or ordinary quarry tiles. But putting tiles on top of a wooden floor can be risky. Wooden boards move, and then tiles crack. They are only likely to be successful if you remove the wooden boards, infill between the joists with wire mesh, put a concrete cement bed into that, and finally tile on top. But even then, there may still be movement in the floor because of the flexing of the joists.

After tiles, consider a cork floor, which has the advantage of being less hard on the feet. The Victorians, however, preferred linoleum above all other finishes in their kitchens and traditional linos still have their place. But they are becoming increasingly hard to find. Linoleum tiles in a suitable color could also be used.

As we have already noted, lighting must be either functional or decorative. By all means have a brass or white-painted wrought-iron lamp in the middle of the room as a decoration, but that is all it should be – you will also need more efficient lighting to carry out kitchen jobs. Use shadow-free task lighting, either in the form of track lighting or strip lighting fixed underneath the cupboards and shining down on work surfaces. There is also much to be said for low voltage spot lighting. But if you are using recessed downlights, do not forget that by cutting into the ceiling to position them you will have removed one layer of insulation protecting the rooms upstairs from the smells and noises of the kitchen. Additional insulation must be provided.

Preparation of food requires bright task lighting, but when the family wants to eat in the kitchen a far lower level is appropriate. This makes it convenient to have two separate lighting circuits, each with its own switch and dimmer. If the kitchen opens on to another room, you can have some decorative light on in the kitchen without needing to have everything lit up.

Far left: The use of roughly hewn stone and decorative lighting makes this walk-in pantry very inviting – both practical and a delight to the eye.

Left: Victorian paneled doors have been adapted here to slide open and provide a wide entrance to a modern utility room.

BATHROOMS

To create a modern version of the Victorian bathroom we have to dream a little; the image that comes to mind is one of space, warmth, and the luxury of enjoying a bath surrounded by pictures, carpets and elegant furnishings.

This is the bathroom of the transitional period when the first fitted and plumbed baths were installed into dressing rooms and spare bedrooms and still recalled the days of the hip bath before the open fire.

Even the later, hygienic bathrooms of the turn of the century, all tiles and functionalism, provide a valid model for an attractive modern scheme, reminiscent perhaps of spa hotel or athletic club.

Above: The custom-built furniture of the Cragside bathhouse combines a forward looking stylishness with the late 19th-century concern for a functional and hygienic environment in the bathroom.

Right: This thorough and lavish evocation of the early Victorian bathroom has entirely modern plumbing. Large roll-top baths, full of water, are extremely heavy, so it is essential to check that the floor is adequately supported.

A design with white tiles, and green top molding demonstrates the merits of using a simple setting to highlight fittings of good quality.

This richly decorated modern bathroom recalls a High Victorian ornamentation more readily associated with libraries or churches than with plumbing.

BASINS AND LAVATORIES

For most Victorians, the place of ablution was the wash stand which, until the introduction of internal piping, belonged in the bedroom or dressing room. Wash stands usually took the form of a wooden dresser with a polished marble top, upon which was placed a variety of china basins and pitchers, dishes for soap, shaving equipment, tooth brushes, and perhaps a brass can, filled by hand, to supply hot water. When piped water arrived, the same style of wash stand simply had running water added via taps. But this hybrid form was soon superseded by the all-ceramic pedestal basin – familiar to us today – which was considered easier to clean and thus more hygienic.

The word lavatory would, in the Victorian period, have indicated a wash basin. It only developed as a euphemism for the water closet after the 1880's when the water closet began to be found more and more as an internal fixture, usually placed in the same room as the wash basin. Prior to this, indoor water closets had suffered from the poor state of the sewerage system outside and tended to smell bad because of the sewers to which they were attached. By the middle of the 19th century it was considered essential for houses to have a fixed sanitary arrangement of some kind – be it an earth closet, an ash pit, a primitive water closet, or just a seat over a cesspit. It usually seemed more agreeable to keep it out of doors.

The turning point came about 1875, the year that marked the arrival of the first commercially successful "wash-out" water closet. It represented a significant advance on the design which had held sway, with only minor improvements, since the 1770's and which used levers to operate a flap in the bottom of the pan. The new water closets dispensed with the flap and depended on the rush of water from an overhead tank to flush waste matter through to the sewerage system. Further improvements in the last quarter of the 19th century took advantage of piped-in water to fill overhead storage tanks, as well as improvements in the public sewers. These quickly brought the technology of the WC to a level which was wholly acceptable indoors, and is still current today.

Many late 19th-century water closets were elaborately decorated on the outside with raised scrollwork, or even colored both inside and out with transfer-printed foliage or landscapes. The seat was invariably made of wood and usually suspended over the bowl on two cast-iron wall brackets. Boxes for paper, in matching wood or decorated china, were sold as part of the suite: rolls of lavatory paper were available from the 1880's. A high cast-iron water tank was operated by a chain with a porcelain handle, sometimes inscribed with the word "pull" for those unsure of the technique. Low-level tanks, which reduced the disagreeable noise of rushing water, became possible after the 1880's through the introduction of the "syphonic" system, pioneered in the United States, which improved the effectiveness of the flush by creating a temporary difference in pressure in the S-bend. But even this improvement was not persuasive to all – many Victorian houses remained without an inside lavatory until the 1950's.

Left: The quality of this vanity unit is well matched by the William Morris-style wallpaper. The lavatory is disguised, in mid-Victorian fashion.

Below: Traditional white and blue give prominence to the elegant brass cross-topped tap.

Above: A traditional design owes its strength to the bold use of the horizontal line along the tiled dado.

Right: This transfer-printed Victorian lavatory would look more in keeping on a wooden floor.

BATHS AND SHOWERS

Below: Completed within a comparatively modest budget, this arrangement well evokes the transitional era of Victorian bathrooms, when dressing rooms or bedrooms were converted to house baths supplied by piped water.

To most Victorians, having a bath meant immersing the middle of the body in a hip bath. Hip baths had to be filled – and emptied – by hand, so when a pressurized public water supply enabled homeowners to pipe water through the house, a genuine labor-saving improvement could be celebrated, and the fixed bath as we know it today had arrived.

This arrangement only made sense, however, if the water could be heated. Various precarious solutions were tried, including primitive circulatory systems emanating from the kitchen range, boilers fitted into the bedroom fireplace, and burners which applied gas flames directly to the base of the bath. The breakthrough was the introduction of the gas water heater in the late 1860's. The pace of development was none the less slow and it was

only at the end of the era that the great Victorian bath – the vitreous enameled, cast-iron roll-top with ball-and-claw feet – became widespread.

The heyday of the Victorian shower arrived with the fixed bath. Showers had always had a following, even when they were little more than a tank of water suspended over a tin bath, enclosed by a tent-like curtain; the tank was filled by hand or by a pressure pump, and spilled its contents like a watering can at the pull of a chain. Now one end of the bath could be used for a fixed shower stand. Separate shower stalls were also installed and these often also included horizontal jets of water, with a set of taps labeled "shower," "jet," "spray" and "plunge," as well as "hot" and "cold." But these were the playthings of the well-to-do; the majority continued to make do with the hip bath.

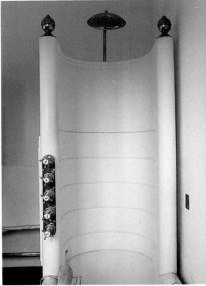

Top: Authentic Victorian bathroom elements have been set in an uncompromisingly modern context, which serves to highlight their craftsmanship.

Above: In this treatment of a Victorian bath the panels are extended to form an elegant partition. The boxing-in of sanitary arrangements was the subject of controversy; many believed free-standing fixtures to be more hygienic.

Top: The shower-cum-bath is a classic child of Victorian invention. Water for the shower came from the rose overhead and from holes in the horizontal bands in the side of the shower stand.

Above: What this shower at Cragside lacks in pressure, it makes up for in volume. A chain operates a simple valve to produce a stream of cold water.

247

VICTORIAN AND MODERN

"A well-equipped bathroom will contain a bath, shower bath, wash basin, hip bath, bidet, heated towel rail, mirror, clothes hooks, a shelf for towels and a receptacle for used towels," was the assessment of one turn-of-the-century critic – demonstrating that although the bathroom was late in coming, when it did come, it came virtually complete.

In deciding on how to design your bathroom, remember that there were two main schools of thought in the 19th century. The earlier approach was to enclose or box in fixtures giving a "furnished" appearance to the bathroom. By the 1890's, critics were applauding the hygienic advantages of a bare-bones, tiled bathroom with free-standing fixtures.

Most of the elements of the Victorian bathroom are now available in reproduction (see Appendix, page 308 for suppliers), particularly hardware, wash basins and lavatories. Genuine antique fittings are often cheaper than their counterparts in reproduction, but they may be terribly inefficient, and the dimensions of the pipework and washers are likely to be non-standard. If you want a very large cast-iron roll-top bath, you will probably have to buy an antique one, which, if properly re-enameled, will cost a great deal. Reproductions are made to the shorter standard length only, but they are considerably cheaper to buy.

There is no reason why a new bathroom, using inexpensive modern fittings, cannot be arranged to fit comfortably into a Victorian house. The bath, for example, could be boxed in by simple paneling with the baseboard detail of the rest of the bathroom running along the bottom. Furnishings and decoration can be used to supply the keynotes; the early Victorian bathroom contained much more free-standing furniture than ours, and chairs, wooden towel rail, pictures and photographs on the walls, matched by a wooden lavatory seat, will create a convincing result.

The Victorians were troubled by condensation, which became an issue after the introduction of very hot water supplied from a hot water heater. In order to avoid the damage to decorations caused by dampness and to increase cleanliness and hygiene, they often covered both the floor and walls with tiles. Anaglypta or Lincrusta wallpaper, heavily encased in an oil-based paint, provided a cheaper and more effective solution. For the floor, linoleum was popular, with cork mats to stand on.

Today, with mixer taps, ventilating fans and central heating to raise the ambient air temperature, we need concern ourselves less with condensation and can turn our attention to decorative effect. Tiles provide a long-lasting surface for areas exposed to splashing. If the tiling is going high, it may be convenient to leave out an area above the basin for a mirror. Elsewhere modern water-resistant wallpapers can be used. Painted anaglypta beneath a dado-rail can provide a true note of authenticity.

Small hexagonal tiles are now easily available for bathroom floors. Alternatively, a Victorian effect can be achieved by covering the floorboards with plywood and laying dark cork tiles on the surface. Polished wood or simple flooring materials like jute matting can also be effective. However, try to avoid wall-to-wall carpet in the bathroom. Rag rugs were used by the Victorians – as convenient and washable then as they are today.

For bathroom lighting a combination of the traditional and the modern is probably the happy medium – recessed low voltage spots and cornice lighting, for example, so that you can see properly in the mirror if you need to, and decorative lighting for effect.

Of course a bathroom in a Victorian house does not necessarily have to have a Victorian look. A modern bathroom can be both efficient and pleasing, and may be preferred.

Left: The clean, uncluttered lines of a modern bathroom may be the most appropriate solution in a very restricted space, leaving decorative touches to evoke the period of the rest of the house. Here the basin has been fitted into the space that would normally have been taken up by the window sill.

Above: The references to the Victorian world here are subtly implied – a round-topped window set in an asymmetric configuration, with frosted glass bordered by tinted glass, and lead tracery.

249

BATHROOMS, BATHROOM FIXTURES & FITTINGS

TYPES OF BATHS

FREE STANDING

MARBLED

LIONS CLAW

ENCLOSED PANELED

PATTERNED ENAMEL

TYPES OF WASH-BASIN

TRADITIONAL WASH/TAND

PLUMBED IN LAVATORY

BASIN ON CAST IRON SUPPORTS

CORNER BASIN

PEDESTAL BASIN

CABRIOLE LAVATORY

TYPES OF WATERCLOSETS

PEDESTAL WASH-DOWN CLOSET

PEDESTAL WASH-OUT

THE LAMBETH 1875

RAISED ACANTHUS 1895

SWING LAVATORY

PEDESTAL LION CLOSET

PULL CHAIN

WASH DOWN SUITE 1898

ART NOUVEAU, 1907

TYPES OF SHOWERS

TYPES OF FAWCETS

ACCESSORIES

PAPER HOLDERS

TOWEL ROLLER

JUG & BOWL

TOWEL RACK

Above left: Unusual fittings like these brass taps deserve the special attention that they receive from a restrained setting.

Above middle: A modern mixer unit shows the influence of its Victorian predecessors in its cross-topped taps and understated curves.

Above: Nickel bathroom fittings are attractive for their honest functionalism, but are rarely available in reproduction. This set is in a bathroom at Cragside.

Opposite: A note of solid authenticity with a redeeming touch of humor is struck by the shower-like pendant lampshades.

251

THE PRIVATE ROOMS

Beyond the first-floor drawing room, the Victorian house was an intensely private place, hidden from public view and rarely entered by visitors. If we lack a vivid mental picture of this intimate world of bedroom and boudoir, dressing room and nursery, this is perhaps due to the reticence of Victorian novelists and illustrators on this subject; not for them the bedroom romps of a Fielding or a Hogarth. Fortunately, the stalwart domestic economists of the day were more enlightening, and popular periodicals such as *Godey's Lady's Book*, *Harper's Bazaar*, *Good Housekeeping* and the *Ladies' Home Journal* have left us with a good record of Victorian taste in the private rooms.

When trying to imagine what everyday life was like in a family house of the time, the most obvious thing to bear in mind is the large number of people occupying even the smallest houses. Families were huge by present standards, with six to nine children quite the norm. As the children grew up and left home, space became free for aging grandparents, bachelor uncles, spinster aunts, cousins on hard times and a host of other relatives in need of sanctuary. In houses where the kitchen was still located in a basement, the family lived in the privileged center of a sandwich, with the servants living and sleeping above and below them. In poorer homes, spare rooms might be rented to lodgers and basic board provided. There was clearly far less room for personal privacy than today; indeed, privacy was then a luxury enjoyed only by the very rich. From comfortable detached homes down to the smallest row houses, bedrooms were shared and most rooms were in use for much of the day.

Away from the public rooms, the ostentation we associate with the period was reduced to a minimum, becoming virtually non-existent in the servants' sleeping quarters. The simplicity that marked such fixtures as cornices, moldings, architraves, baseboards and fireplaces was echoed in the decorative scheme; the rich paintwork and wallpapers favored in the main rooms gave way to pretty pastel shades and a general air of cheerful cleanliness.

In larger British houses, a husband and wife often had separate bedrooms with a connecting door. Each room would have had its own dressing room, and adjoining the lady's bedroom would have been her private sitting room or boudoir. This was the feminine

Opposite: In the grandest houses, the opulence of the public areas extended to the main bedrooms. Sumptuous red drapes are here combined with *chinoiserie* paneling to create an air of refined exoticism. Where space was no object, a sofa and occasional table were often placed at the foot of the bed.

equivalent of the study, a private retreat where she could read, write letters or a journal, and practice music. Although the use of separate rooms was advocated in America, it was less often implemented. In France, the boudoir was one of the most ornate rooms in the house; English taste inclined towards a more sober and businesslike room. Lady Barker, an adventurous, much-traveled English woman with a taste for the Arts and Crafts Movement and the Queen Anne revival, thought of such rooms as "one's own little private den" where a woman could be "busy and comfortable." The dado, where present, could be covered in leather-paper or deal paneling painted light blue or pink; for the upper part of the wall, a William Morris wallpaper might be used. The furnishings could include a desk, an armchair, a piano, shelves for a small collection of favorite books and a few treasured ornaments.

In the bedrooms, walls were covered with pale shades of distemper or light, delicately patterned wallpaper, both of which could be renewed frequently. There was a widely prevailing distaste for strong patterns in bedrooms; some believed that they "might be likely to fix themselves upon the tired brain, suggesting all kinds of weird forms." Ella Rodman Church, in *How To Furnish a House,* considered delicate pink, pale green and dainty buff suitably restful, while some periodicals promoted light tints for south-facing rooms and darker values for north-facing ones. Bright greens were avoided since the pigments used to produce them contained arsenic. Walls could also be covered in a pastel-colored chintz, stretched tightly over panels which could be easily removed for cleaning.

Hygiene was a major concern. Webster and Parkes, writing in Britain in 1844, believed that bedrooms should be "neat and plain, and everything capable of collecting dust should be avoided as much as possible," and this advice was echoed by almost every subsequent British and American writer on the topic. Furniture was supposed to be simple, easy to clean and kept to a minimum. Plain varnished boards with a few scattered rugs were preferred for the floor; carpets were permissible provided they were not fitted, and could be taken up and cleaned frequently. Window blinds were considered more hygienic than curtains, although festoons of chintz or cretonne, which could be removed and washed easily, were also recommended.

The Victorians believed that frequent air changes were necessary for refreshing sleep. The practice of making bedrooms low-ceilinged to allow for a grandly proportioned drawing room below was widely deplored. It was frequently stressed that every bedroom should have a fireplace to encourage a through draft; windows should be left open when the weather and the health of the occupant permitted; alternatively, various ingenious patent ventilators might be installed.

The growing taste for fresh air and horror of dust traps had a

Left: This 1883 illustration shows a typical nursery of the period, equipped with a simple fireplace and a little hanging bookshelf on the wall. The floor is covered with linoleum or matting.

Right: A cosy but dignified interior has been created through a stylish combination of decoration and furnishings: the lightly patterned wallpaper; a lace counterpane on the bed; a folding screen covering the door; and the elegant desk in a pleasant, sunny window.

255

great effect on the type of beds in use. When Queen Victoria came to the throne in 1837, those who could afford it still had a bed that could be curtained off completely, either a four-poster (or "full tester"), a French bedstead with a central support for the drapes, or a tent bed with an arched frame (see pages 266–67). A hangover from the days when houses were built without corridors, and people had to pass through one room to reach the next, such beds provided some privacy and warmth . By the middle of the century, however, partial curtaining of the bed was being recommended as a healthier alternative. The "half tester" – with hangings around the head only – gained in popularity. By the last quarter of the century, critics such as Eastlake were recommending simple wood or iron bedsteads with no hangings at all.

If this preoccupation with bedroom hygiene strikes a modern reader as somewhat excessive, it must be remembered that there were pressing reasons for it. Victorians gave birth to their children at home, so the bedroom frequently had to act as a maternity ward. In an age when infectious diseases such as typhoid and cholera were widespread, it also had to function as a sick-room. Moreover, since separate bathrooms did not become standard until the end of the century, most washing went on here too, with maids bringing up hot water and emptying the waste in slop buckets. The fact that so many home economists felt the need to stress – in terms often bordering on stridency – that bedrooms should be light, cheerful and clean suggests that the reality was often very different.

Despite these strictures, there was more flexibility in the way bedrooms were arranged and used than is generally recognized today. For the sons and daughters of the house, and those living in smaller homes, the bedroom often had to double as a private sitting room. This may have a surprisingly modern ring to anyone brought up on the idea that a Victorian bedroom was a desolate, fusty place containing only a bedstead, a wash stand, a chest of drawers and a looming, ugly wardrobe. Many young people used sofa beds and closed wash stands to disguise the fact that anyone ever slept there, and plain wooden bookshelves, Japanese chests, South American ceramics, palm plants and gypsy tables were all pressed into service under the influence of the Arts and Crafts Movement. The cheerful bohemianism of this late Victorian approach may well appeal to modern homeowners, particularly in houses and apartments where space is limited.

Although many Victorian homeowners liked to dignify their home by setting aside as many rooms as possible for specific purposes, in practice they had to be more flexible. A dressing room next to the main bedroom might be allocated to a child for a few years, reverting to its original function later on. Children of both sexes shared nursery rooms in infancy, but soon moved into segregated bedrooms reserved for either boys or girls.

In very large houses, there might be a night nursery for the children to sleep in as well as a day nursery for play. The decoration of the nursery followed much the same principles as it does today – bright, cheerful wallpapers and hardwearing, washable surfaces. Nurseries sometimes occupied the attic space, where swings could be hung from the exposed rafters.

As the last of one generation grew out of the nursery, the children of the older brothers and sisters would move straight in, providing a comfortable sense of continuity. In British houses there was almost always an adjacent room for the nanny, who enjoyed a special status in Victorian families, below a governess or tutor in big houses, but above the cook and the other servants. She would always have a room of her own, even if small, and would not socialize with the other staff.

A low-ceilinged cottage room has become an attractive and comfortable bedroom with a genuine period feel. The small fireplace and the fitted cupboard with its tongue-and-groove ledge door have been treated with respect; the iron and brass bedstead is of a type that became popular in the last quarter of the 19th century.

BEDROOMS AND NURSERIES

Below: Although the four-poster bed became less popular in the later 19th century, it was occasionally revived for its medievalist effect. Here, in the Acanthus Room at Wightwick Manor, embroidered linen drapes in the Arts and Crafts style are set against the William Morris wallpaper that gives the room its name.

The furnishing of bedrooms is an intensely personal matter, today just as in Victorian times, and tastes have changed less in this part of the house than in any other. Bedrooms were always the most simply furnished rooms, and Victorian papers, fabrics and curtain treatments can still be most attractive to us today. Modern homeowners may well prefer the cheerful sobriety of early and late Victorian styles, and will probably want less furniture than the mid-

Victorians, but with careful selection even some of the ornate High Victorian pieces can make a suitable starting point round which to build a decorative scheme.

Apart from the bed, the largest piece of furniture was the wardrobe. For mid-Victorians, the most popular design was a massive double wardrobe with a central mirror. Big heavy wardrobes have long been unfashionable, and (continued on page 262)

Left: A charming attic bedroom with a simple fireplace and overmantel has been given a touch of period elegance by the gilt-framed portrait.

Above: The dark varnished furniture of this High Victorian bedroom draws on Renaissance and classical styles. The somber gravity of the bedstead and the double-fronted wardrobe would be oppressive were it not for the light walls of the room.

Left: The simplicity of the late Victorian bedroom lent itself to warm climates. The pink gauze drapery of this Australian bedroom is actually a mosquito net.

Below: High Victorian taste finds its full expression in this bedroom at the Speaker's House, Westminster, London. The half tester bed, the rich drapes and the oak paneling and doors all betray a Tudor influence.

Left: The false bookcase concealing the door of this London bedroom, and the corona of drapes over the bed, evoke the French Second Empire.

Above: The Victorian taste for matching drapes in light cotton fabrics lends itself to a modern reinterpretation, as has been done here.

(continued from page 258)
can be picked up cheaply. Stripped of dirty, blistered varnish, they can look surprisingly good in the right setting. For those who find wardrobes unappealing, a Victorian alternative can be found in Cassell's *Household Guide*, which recommends hanging one's clothes from a brass pole across the chimney recess, with pretty chintz curtains across the front. This idea could work well in an old-fashioned cottage with deep recesses on either side of the fireplace.

The wash stand was an essential part of the Victorian bedroom, the top often made of marble and the splashback tiled; pitchers, soap dishes and wash bowls were usually decorated

Above: Draperies can provide useful sound-proofing for bedrooms, as well as creating an atmosphere of warmth and comfort.

Right: Good lace is expensive, and is usually employed sparingly as a decorative trimming. These ivory lace pillows, counterpane and bed drapes would have represented considerable luxury in Victorian times, as today.

with flower motifs; the free-standing furniture could also include the dressing table – on which combs and brushes were displayed along with candlesticks, bowls and bottles and tiny trays – an easy chair or two around the fireplace and, if there was room, a sofa at the foot of the bed. As drapes around the bed went out of fashion, screens were used to exclude drafts and ensure privacy. The wide variety of finishes included Dutch leather, floral paper and Indian and Japanese designs. There might also be a small table for books and papers.

Many of these pieces find a natural place in the modern bedroom. Bedside tables do not have to match; an antique table or reproduction military chest on one side of the bed can be paired quite easily with a simpler table on the other side, covered with a cloth and skirt. Before buying bedside tables, measure the height of the bed from the floor. It will probably be much lower than you imagine. Screens are not often used today, but they have great potential for altering the contours of a room or hiding an ugly but necessary piece of furniture. It is not difficult to find them in markets, and they can easily be re-covered with an attractive period paper.

Many traditional ideas may also be used in nurseries, which can be among the most attractive rooms in a house. In a nursery, however, safety comes before everything else. The windows should be child-proofed, even if it means using bars or grills. The next essential is cleanliness and comfort. The floor should be both easy to mop and easy on the knees. In less well-off Victorian households, linoleum was often laid in upstairs rooms. Cork or vinyl tiles are good modern alternatives, and may be covered with big, easily washed cotton rugs. Hearth rugs in Victorian times were designed with special patterns for children; Voysey

The best nursery cabinets are deep and wide, allowing plastic baskets or toy hampers to be stored.

produced several with scenes from fairy tales. Most artists who designed wallpapers did special ones for children, and Walter Crane's nursery-rhyme wallpapers were popular from the 1870's. Children's book illustrators such as Cecil Aldin and John Hassall designed friezes. These traditions are now experiencing a revival. A sink will always be useful in a nursery, and an armchair for adults adds an aspect of the parlor.

The built-in compartmentalized closets that came into vogue in the 1880's were promoted as being less liable to harbor dust than free-standing furniture. Such closets, however, are expensive to build and do not offer the best way to see your clothes. They often have small cabinets at the top which can be reached only by standing on a chair. If I must use built-in closets, I put in big sliding doors that can be decorated to match the walls of the room. I generally start a fitted closet with what is called a potboard – a shelf just off the floor – and build it up from there. The space between the potboard and the floor is then finished with baseboard. This follows my principle of running Victorian-style details around almost all new fixtures, so that they become an integral part of the room.

But wherever possible, I avoid prefitted closets and adopt a walk-in closet, which is sometimes large enough to equal a dressing room. Having found or created a suitable space the size of a very small room, I start my design at the bottom with a potboard, trimmed with baseboard mold. Then I allow space for two clothes rails, one above the other, for hanging ordinary-length dresses, skirts, suits and jackets; coats and long dresses will have to go elsewhere. Above the upper rail is a shelf, open to the ceiling, where suitcases, hat boxes and other tall items can be stored within reach. The hanging space may be divided vertically to provide deep drawers and shelves along some of its length. To conceal the clothes, I use a method that closely follows the Cassell's *Household Guide,* and run a simple cotton curtain all round.

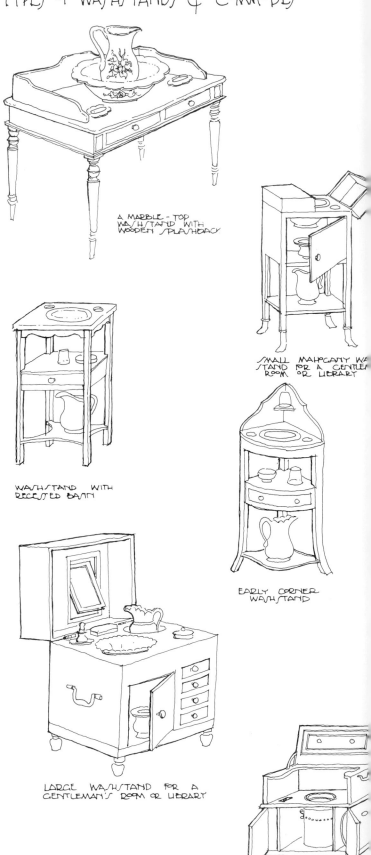

BED ROOM FURNITURE
TYPES OF WASHSTANDS & COMMODES

A MARBLE - TOP WASHSTAND WITH WOODEN SPLASHBACK

SMALL MAHOGANY WASHSTAND FOR A GENTLEMAN'S ROOM OR LIBRARY

WASHSTAND WITH RECESSED BASIN

EARLY CORNER WASHSTAND

LARGE WASHSTAND FOR A GENTLEMAN'S ROOM OR LIBRARY

AN EARLY COMMODE

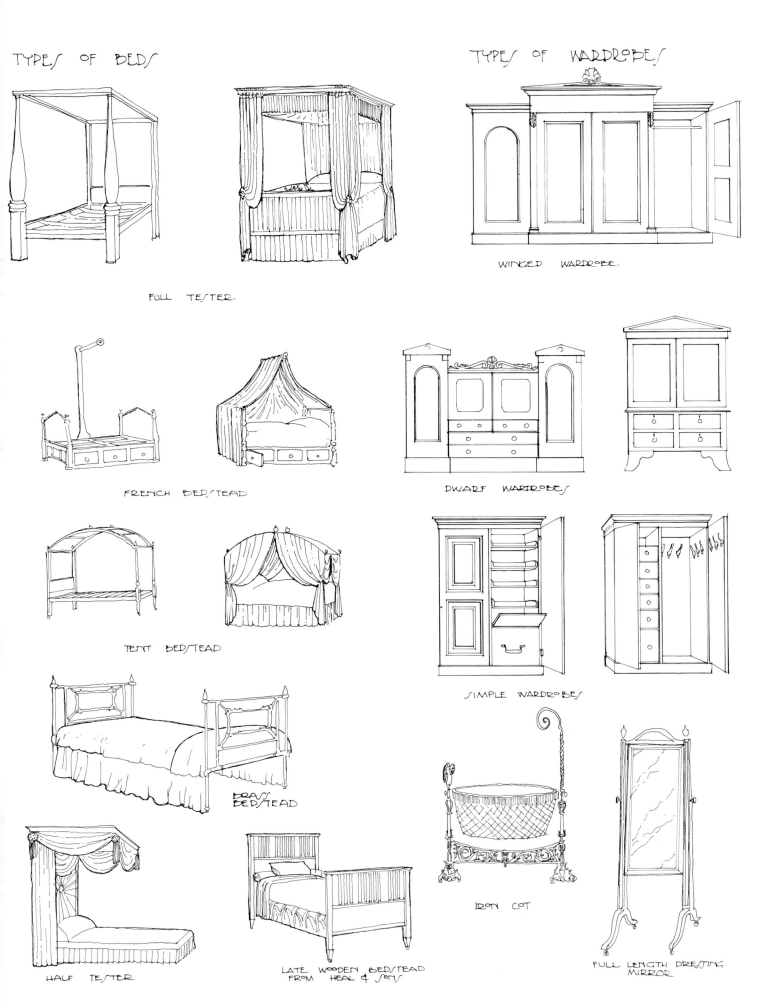

TYPES OF BEDS

TYPES OF WARDROBES

WINGED WARDROBE

FULL TESTER

FRENCH BEDSTEAD

DWARF WARDROBES

TENT BEDSTEAD

SIMPLE WARDROBES

BRASS BEDSTEAD

HALF TESTER

LATE WOODEN BEDSTEAD FROM HEAL & SONS

IRON COT

FULL LENGTH DRESSING MIRROR

C h a p t e r   S e v e n

GARDENS

The survival of gardens in anything like their original form is even more precarious than that of houses. Where a Victorian house may have endured through a century and then been spoiled by the addition of an inappropriate dormer, it is at least possible to make out the lines of the original. In the case of gardens, a few months of vigorous reshaping and replanting will obliterate almost all evidence of what was there before. Conservatories, summer houses, pavilions, pergolas and garden seats are also more at risk than houses. They are exposed to weather and vulnerable as seasonal accessories, forgotten and abandoned during the winter. Were it not for these processes of decay, we would have far more evidence today of the various metamorphoses that gardening underwent in the Victorian period.

The key change was that gardening ceased to be an occupation pursued only by the rich for their pleasure and the poor for their survival, becoming instead a popular pastime for almost anyone with a little plot of land to cultivate. This popularity reflected not just changes in the distribution of wealth resulting from the Industrial Revolution, but also the much greater variety of plants available, new species having been discovered and brought to England and the United States from all over the world.

It is difficult today, with our immense catalog of readily available species, to realize how restricted was the range of plants in the typical American and British garden right up to the beginning of the 19th century. Many of the everyday landscape plants we are likely to take for granted as indigenous species were in fact introduced from abroad during this period. Dahlias arrived in England in 1788, followed over the next decades by tea roses, hydrangeas, salvias, camellias, hybrid rhododendrons, gardenias, chrysanthemums and fuchsias, among countless others. From England, these many new varieties were quickly imported into the United States. The aspidistra, an indoor plant which was to make steady headway under the Victorians and then entrench itself as an essential adjunct to early 20th-century living, first arrived from the East in 1824. So-called "old roses" were propagated about this time, mainly by the French, and were in turn "improved" to coarser varieties bred for longer flowering at the expense of color and scent.

Britain's Royal Botanic Gardens at Kew in London played a vital role in this process and foreshadowed developments in many other horticultural institutes. When Victoria came to the throne, Kew already had a reputation as a center for scientific botanical study.

Opposite: The late Victorian garden was characterized by the balance between romantic informality on the one hand and the regimented geometry of bedding designs on the other. This garden at Peckover House, in Cambridgeshire, England, with its geraniums, rose pergola, sundial, classical urn and palm tree, shows a harmonious combination of eclectic interests typical of the era.

The garden of a house in Mayborough, Queensland, shows the same use of lawn and borders that typified the Victorian garden all over the globe. The invention of the lawn mower put the tidy management of lawn within the reach of all homeowners.

In 1838 John Lindley completed a report recommending that it be maintained as the Royal Botanic Gardens. So in the 1840's it was given a new lease of life; thousands of horticultural specimens, gathered from all over the world by botanists and travelers, were sent home for classification and cultivation.

Through the work of the growing ranks of commercial nurserymen a huge new range of plants entered the popular consciousness, primarily by means of a completely new group of gardening books and magazines made possible by improved printing processes. In this way, the new American and British middle classes were kept abreast of landscape fashion. The most important of the early British garden magazine editors was John Claudius Loudon (1783–1843), a Scotsman who had come to England in 1803. He set up a school of agriculture in Oxfordshire, then in 1822 produced *An Encyclopaedia of Gardening*. This was followed by *The Gardener's Magazine*, published from 1826 and carried on even after Loudon's death by his talented and industrious wife Jane. Loudon recognized his broad audience and addressed himself to the new middle class. The word "gardenesque" was coined to describe his approach, a combination of small-scale layout necessitated by the smaller tracts of land owned by Loudon's average reader with the more grand and picturesque style promoted by the 18th-century gardeners. These earlier landscape designers, such as Capability Brown, had simply shown off the beauty of vast natural landscapes; Loudon's new smaller gardens showed off the skill of the gardener, combining both the formal and the romantic. He recommended an enormous number and variety of plants, yet these were to be contained in formal French-style parterres which he thought would suit even the smaller garden, with *allées* flanked by statuary and stopped with classical features such as urns or closed arches.

In the United States, a young landscape designer, Andrew Jackson Downing (1815-1852), was so impressed by Loudon's works that he wrote his own version titled *A Treatise on the Theory and Practice of Landscape Gardening*. First published in 1841, this book was widely read by Americans for the next twenty years. Downing stressed the relationship between a house and the landscape, urging that the house be built on the best site, with a curved entry road leading to it and a lawn surrounding the house. Downing also divided trees into two broad groups, round-headed and pointed. The former he felt were beautiful and could stand alone, while the latter were more appropriate when echoing the lines of the house or as part of a grouping. Yet for all his appreciation of the natural landscape, Downing still advocated parterres – formal, geometrically

Horticultural techniques advanced swiftly in the 19th century with the aid of industrial technology. Here crown glass fixed into a cast-iron frame forms a very rigid cloche to force plants and protect them from the frost.

patterned areas for flowers. In the Loudon tradition, he also published a magazine called *The Horticulturist* for several years.

The intricate geometric layouts of flowering beds that Loudon and Downing recommended were made possible by the availability of cheap labor. During the Victorian period and well into the 20th century almost all middle-class detached houses had at least part-time gardeners.

The Victorians were ever on the lookout for new mechanical devices. One of the most notable of these was the lawn mower, patented in 1832. Up to this time, cutting the grass called for intensive hand-labor, using scythes, sickles and shears, or cropping by domestic animals. Now every home could have its smooth lawn and, as a bonus, the new machine was advertised as providing

"In the Garden" by George Bernard O'Neill (1828-1917) displays a fashionable sentimentality, but also demonstrates the way in which a natural, informal garden design of lawn, trees and shrubs could be accented by formal touches in topiary and brickwork.

beneficial exercise for the country gentleman. No doubt, too, the possession of such a contraption would have provided one of the earliest suburban status symbols and the presence of a broad expanse of front lawn, still so popular today, proclaimed to the world that the owner could afford not only the land, but also the labor and devices necessary to trim it.

The proper relationship between formal and informal planning provided the main topic for debate among those concerned with Victorian garden design. W.A. Nesfield (1793–1881), a British ex-army engineer, carried out vast "Italian" layouts at numerous English great houses. His earlier profession seemed to be echoed in layouts that were militarily correct and regimentally precise. Yet, within his strict lines, his parterres depended on extravagant use of color. Nesfield was one of several specialist gardeners who helped to popularize "bedding out," the practice of planting entire decorative beds with annual flowers which were changed and replaced several times a year. This fashion gained a lasting popularity, which even today can be seen in municipal gardens all over the world. Contemporary accounts show that sometimes the plants of an entire parterre would be changed overnight by an army of gardeners, the last one fleeing just before dawn in order to spare the sensibilities of any early-rising guest who might chance to glance out of his bedroom window. But soon parterres and bedding out began to be viewed as restrictive and opposed to nature. In 1908 the *Ladies' Home Journal* told its American audience that "the Gardeners of our Public Parks have much to answer for. Very soon their annual hideous work will show forth. Beds of hyacinths and tulips of precise geometric exactness in the form of zones, of circles, stars, triangles, squares and ellipses will blossom forth, and thousands will admire and exclaim. And, worst of all, they will go and do likewise on a smaller scale in their own gardens... and a hopeful anchor of 'Dusty Miller,' edged with clam shells, will be cast against a terrace like a railroad station embankment; stereotyped beds of screaming geraniums will cut up a lawn....And if we are spared the owner's initials in party-colors, we are fortunate!... How far from nature do we depart when we so insult the flowers, the grass and our neighbors!...With a people in such crying need of gardening as we Americans are, it is really nothing short of criminal that such excrescences are allowed on the green lawns of our parks – [the parterres are] veritable pimples in the face of Nature."

The journal, in printing these sentiments, was echoing the thoughts of an opposing view of gardening which finally took root in the 1870's and 1880's as a strong movement associated with the Queen Anne style of architecture which sought an "old-fashioned" look to the garden. This was a reaction to the tight formality of bedding out. Instead of the brash, low-lying, newly naturalized

The cramped and shaded spaces created by rear additions – a typical feature of Victorian houses after the kitchen was connected to the first floor – pose a challenge for the gardener. The use of dark-leaved plants (which have higher chlorophyll content and so need less light) provides an effective solution here, brightened by the summer display of Bouncing Bet, geraniums and fuchsias.

This modern piece of eclecticism brings life to a blank brick wall with a molded concrete plaque and a Victorian firegrate used as a plant holder – touches that successfully evoke the era.

plants used by the parterre designers, Queen Anne gardeners favored romantic, informal drifts of tall flowering plants – sunflowers, hollyhocks, tiger lilies, and abundant climbing plants such as morning glory and passion flower – many of which belonged in William Morris's catalog of desirable "medieval" plants. A balancing element of formality could none the less be provided by low hedges of clipped box and topiary.

The dispute of formality versus informality, old versus new, found its mediator in the most important British garden journalist of the middle Victorian years, William Robinson, an Irishman who came to work in the gardens of Regent's Park, London, in 1861 and took charge of the herbaceous section. For Robinson the purpose of gardening was not so much to create a formal composition in which flowers played their part, such as in a parterre, but to create a layout which would show off plants to their best advantage. Developing a passion for English wild flowers, he sought to incorporate them into traditional flower borders, mixed in with such foreign introductions as he thought would not destroy their essentially English character. Robinson can be said to have established the "English Garden" as it is understood today. He found, in traditional cottage gardens, a perfect synthesis of the practical and the charming and he went further, advocating "wild gardens" where exotic plants could be cultivated as if in the wild. In 1871, Robinson published a magazine called *The Garden* and later his *Garden Illustrated* for the owners of smaller gardens. Both publications were highly influential.

The best evidence of how the small garden was laid out and planted a hundred years ago lies in the illustrations of pattern books and gardening magazines, in photographs (though these are only in black and white), and in the backgrounds of paintings of the period, and it is to these early sources that one should first turn in beginning to re-create a Victorian garden. Just as today the influence of *House and Garden* or the current television expert can be seen in our own gardens, so the various 19th-century fashions were reflected in the smaller gardens of the time. Parterres shrank to a mere terrace of brick or crazy paving, and bedding out was confined to a semi-formal border separating the terrace from the lawn beyond, with a pair of miniature mass-produced urns to mark the centre. Perhaps the winding path, a feature so readily associated with the romantic garden, survived further down the plot, leading to a wild garden in the form of a shrubbery.

In these respects, the smaller Victorian garden may justly be accused of confusions of scale, for the average suburban plot can only take so much design and many Victorian gardens must have presented a confusing array of ornament, shape and color.

The classical sculpture and the conservatory recall two major themes of the Victorian attitude towards gardens and garden design. The grouping of the two here displays the marble in exceptionally sympathetic light.

The cottage-garden effect in front of this late 19th-century house is achieved by a mixed planting using a broad and vibrant palette. The straight path indicates a workmanlike attitude towards the garden: tall borders such as these would provide a decorative screen in front of the less presentable vegetable patch.

RAILINGS AND GARDEN WALLS

Opposite: Any danger of monotony in this brick wall is relieved by the polychromatic brickwork and the ornamental, figurative sculpture.

Below: Brick walls form a sympathetic backdrop to a garden, offering warmth and protection for plants. Here the effect is embellished by unusual semi-circular shapes, in the lee of which grow robust perennials.

Bottom: An old majolica water caddy provides the pleasurable surprise of the "found object" set against a weathered brick wall.

Garden walls, railings and fences are very much a feature of the Victorian house, and particularly illustrate the way in which inexpensive land and homesteading produced a nation of small landowners across the United States. These new owners wanted to create boundaries both to define their territory and to provide privacy.

In many American neighborhoods front lawns were not fenced, but were left open to public view, with only the rear garden enclosed for privacy. Often the main side gates and fence were quite elaborate as they could be viewed from the street, while the borders of the rear garden itself were likely to receive more modest treatment. In other neighborhoods, such as the Garden District in New Orleans, open ironwork fences were used around the entire property, to provide an illusion of separation and privacy.

Brick walls were very expensive and most Victorian gardens were bounded by simple fences made of wood or, less commonly, iron. Most of this was of a kind familiar today: overlapping boards in panels supported by intermediate posts. But lighter, more open styles – such as criss-crossed split post, comb-like picket fencing, or even cast-iron panels – were more widespread than they are today with our greater concerns for security. Another popular solution was the combination of a low brick or concrete wall topped by fencing.

The use of hedges as fencing increased with the growing number of plants introduced from overseas which could be used for this purpose.

Right: An elegant and beautifully preserved cast-iron gate sets the scene for the enticing mature garden which lies beyond.

GAZEBOS AND SUMMER HOUSES

The Victorians brought to garden architecture a lightness of touch which was often absent in the solemnity of the house itself.

Early Victorian Britain saw a continuation of 18th-century temples and garden houses, though often without comparable style or sense of landscaping. These temples and summer buildings echoed the classical themes from the immediate past. Many later Victorian garden buildings were more consciously rustic, with a preference for burred wood, bark, unsawn branches and thatch. Sometimes these were erected in the branches of a tree with simple stairs or a ladder for access, providing wonderful rooms for children. Other garden buildings incorporated dovecots, holding doves bred for their prettiness on lawn and gravel walk rather than for the pot as hitherto. Unfortunately, these rustic structures were particularly vulnerable to time and weather and most have now disappeared. Americans were most entranced with gazebos and pergolas, most commonly made with latticework and covered with vines.

The British Victorians loved ruins, and a number of Gothic-style garden houses were built or re-assembled from ancient stones during this era. Few grottoes or hermits' caves were built, however. Such frivolity, common during the 18th century, would have been morally distasteful to the Victorians. Nor were they great folly builders. Much of their inventiveness was channeled into domestic building, and structures we might today consider follies were considered at the time as serious architectural essays.

The Victorians were in their most playful mood when it came to garden architecture. There is great enchantment in their arbors and summer houses, their pergolas and verandahs, and above all in the detail of such rustic wood, trellis, lattice and ironwork as has survived.

Below: The open structure of this elaborate pergola is designed to support a profusion of climbing plants which will eventually create a "room" roofed and walled in leaves and flowers – a living summer house.

Below right: This is a delightful example of the spatial effects of *trompe-l'oeil,* in this case achieved by carefully constructed trellis work laid on to a flat wall, bringing a garden image into a covered space.

One of the functions of a summer house or gazebo is to provide a space and atmosphere that is quite different from the interior of a house. This summer house is constructed of untrimmed wood and thatch to produce an intensely rustic look, which nicely complements the informal woodland garden.

This summer house derives all its character from the set of Gothic arches, demonstrating that the Gothic style works remarkably well in small buildings.

CONSERVATORIES

The history of protecting plants indoors through harsh winters goes back almost two thousand years; in Pompeii translucent sheets of marble were used in frames. However, the development of the greenhouse as we would recognize it today began in Renaissance times when new glass-making technology coincided with the introduction of exotic plants from warmer climates.

One of the earliest and most fashionable of these was the orange, known to have arrived in Europe by the 14th century. By the 15th and 16th centuries sophisticated ways of keeping orange trees alive in winter had been devised. In southern European climates, subject only to occasional frost, the trees could be covered outside but the process was laborious and risky. Further north, the trees were grown in mov-

able tubs; during the summer months they would decorate the terraces and take in the sun, but during the winter they would be wheeled into garden rooms and summer houses specially boarded up for the purpose. So the earliest winter gardens were born.

It was not until about 1700 that glass manufacturing first produced flat panes big enough for the double-hung sash windows which gradually replaced the old leaded lights and bottle glass. The first glasshouses appear in illustrations at this time. They consisted of sloping windows facing towards the south (great attention was paid to obtaining the best angle for maximum penetration of sunlight) and backed against brick or stone walls. The wall stored up warmth during the day and released the heat at night. In appearance, both these glasshouses and the

Left: A hipped roofed conservatory has extended the living space of this row house considerably. Although modern, it has been carefully detailed; a decorated ridge and the elegant tracery in the fanlights lighten the effect of an otherwise predictably geometric design.

Above: The design of the tracery in this modern, custom-built conservatory takes its inspiration from the Gothic elements of the house to which it is attached, with the further embellishment of traditional roof crestings. This is a very solid piece of work, built to last.

The roof space over an addition can provide an interesting site for a perched conservatory, with access from an upper floor. This kind of alteration, however, demands a fairly cavalier attitude about the silhouette of the house.

early orangeries resembled classical buildings with rather large windows.

Around 1800, as panes of glass could be produced in larger sizes and more cheaply, the greenhouse proper was born, with a ridged roof and pitch glazing on two sides. The southern orientation was no longer a critical factor. Gradually glasshouses and orangeries began to look like the greenhouse of today. Stoves were replaced by hot-water heating in pipes and improvements were made to ventilation. By the time Victoria came to the throne, a number of huge glass structures were built and these culminated in the Crystal Palace, built in London by Sir Joseph Paxton for the Great Exhibition of 1851 in London.

At a more domestic level, the first English conservatories, bright greenhouse-like garden rooms attached to the house proper, were designed in about 1800. By the 1830's the conservatory began to enjoy extraordinary popularity as an adjunct even to quite modest British houses, and a prefabricated product was offered via catalogs.

American Victorians never developed quite the same general enthusiasm for conservatories. Downing's books, some of the most popular of the period, did not feature conservatories in their floor plans. Even Calvert Vaux's *Villas and Cottages*, with its collection of plans for great houses, showed only a few which included either a conservatory or "plant cabinet".

A typical conservatory of the middle period might consist of a low brick wall all round, with window glazing up to the level of the eaves. The roof would usually be of straight glass (curved glass was more expensive) and decorated with iron crestings and elaborate gable boards. Iron trusses and cast-iron columns provided intermediate support in larger examples. All were detailed with simplified Classical or Gothic moldings.

Conservatory floors were composed simply of iron grilles or of tiles with grilles over the drainage and heating outlets. Furniture, because of the all-pervading moisture, was gener-

ally in iron and came with loose cushions if any. Indian and other furniture inspired by British colonies in the tropics also provided sensible and attractive seating. This gave rise to the wicker and rattan furniture that is still so popular for garden rooms today.

This same colonial heritage also brought the verandah or porch, another overseas exotic now so much a part of the American architectural tradition. Indeed the origin of porches seems very much tied to the warmer English colonies, particularly the West Indies, Australia and America. In the southern United States porches soon dominated and almost every home built during the Victorian era had a full-width or even a wrap-around porch. Whereas originally the word porch meant only the area at the entry door and additional outdoor spaces were called verandahs, today the word porch commonly refers to all. Frequently these porches served as American versions of the conservatory – indoor/outdoor rooms, where plants were grown and hanging baskets hung, that could be used for entertaining or family living. Only in the hard of winter did the plants need to be pulled inside.

While attached conservatories never achieved anything like their popularity in Britain, at the turn of the century "sunrooms" became quite fashionable in the United States. By the 1920's front porches had been eclipsed by side porches and by sunrooms that were most often placed on the side of the main house block. These were surrounded by windows, usually double-hung, and had floors, and sometimes even walls, covered with tiles.

As in Victorian times, ready-made conservatories are again available today, many in a quasi-Victorian style which adopts some of the more obvious and coarser detailing of the period. A custom-designed conservatory using good quality wood and clear glass will generally prove to be the better choice.

This is an old conservatory designed for the sole purpose of cultivating plants. None the less, care has been taken to see that it merges with the overall architectural style of the house, using the kind of detail that is so often omitted today for the sake of economy.

Below: The front porch offers an intermediate living space between the house and the outside, artificially protected from the elements. In warm climates the American porch provides a counterpart to the conservatory, and there has always been some cross-fertilization of ideas in the decorative styles of both.

281

FURNISHING THE GARDEN

The furnishing of the Victorian garden was distinguished from previous eras in two notable ways. First, the new cult of outdoor activities – from fresh-air teas to lawn sports such as croquet and tennis – inspired the manufacture of movable chairs specifically designed for entertaining in the garden. Second, almost anyone with a plot of land devoted to ornamental gardening (as opposed to supplementing the diet) had in the mind's eye gardens on a grand scale; the challenge was to reproduce at least the atmosphere of these in a suburban back yard, and to this end statuary, urns and decorative vases became widely popular.

Garden statues and ornaments had originally been hand-carved or painstakingly molded in lead or in terracotta. Towards the end of the 18th century the invention of Coade Stone (see pages 24–25) provided a means, albeit still comparatively expensive, to reproduce such ornaments on a large scale. When cheaper substitutes became available in the first half of the 19th century, manufacturers were inspired to produce an extraordinary variety and range.

Outside furniture tends to be massive if it is to be left permanently in place or airily light if it has to be taken indoors during every rain shower. Until the 19th century it was generally made of either stone or wood. Iron began to be used for exterior furniture around the beginning of the 19th century.

The Regency period introduced some delightful terrace furniture made of a cast-iron frame with wirework infilling, a fashion which lasted well into the century. The well known "fern leaf" and "ivy" designs have a sense of fun which is lacking in their indoor contemporaries. Some cast-iron seats incorporated painted wooden slats for the seating area and so formed the pattern for park and municipal outdoor furniture for the next few decades. With the Queen Anne revival

(continued on page 286)

Opposite: Sculpture, sparingly used, provides an important break in the rhythm of a garden, and hence a focus for reflection. Such items should be chosen carefully – they are not just casual fillers.

Far left: A monumental plant holder has been created here by recruiting an elegant "found" piece of architectural sculpture to support a molded concrete pot.

Left: During the Victorian period classical reference, as in this lead urn, was more widespread in the garden than in interior decoration.

The Victorian era was the Indian summer of the angel and the cherub. This fine marble carving of a sleeping cherub, placed casually in a rough-hewn basin, brings a delightful element of surprise.

Below: The statue at the axis of this herb garden is the focus of the formal layout, bringing a sense of balance to the very informal planting.

Below right: The Egyptian theme of the sphinx in this garden is reinforced rather ingeniously by the pyramidal forms of the topiary.

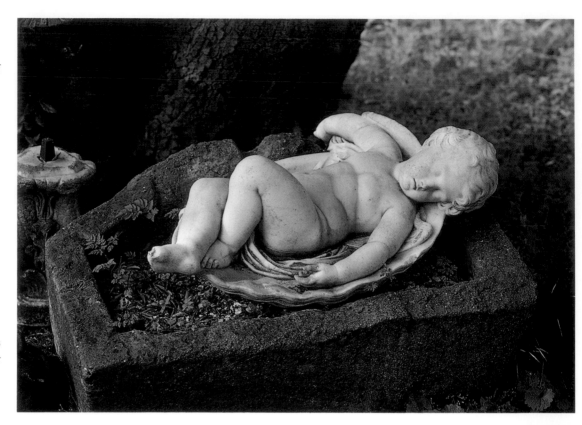

Arches at the entrance of the garden help to emphasize the feeling of passing from one distinct space into another, as well as to frame a first impression. This arch brings a touch of chinoiserie to an informal layout of lawn and borders.

Far left: The weathered look of the cherub has an agreeable correspondence with the silver-leaved senecio and the darker foliage to the rear.

Left: This garden, lying in the shadow of a large house, shows an effective combination of Victorian elements: ironwork, topiary in a formal layout around a statue, offset by the informal shapes of the trees.

285

(continued from page 282)
and the Arts and Crafts Movement, wood returned to favor as a material to be used on its own, sometimes in Gothic designs, sometimes in oriental and sometimes in the new Craftsman mode.

Some 19th-century molds for iron furniture have survived and excellent originals – one can hardly call them reproductions – are still obtainable today. On the cheaper side, a current favorite is the imitation of cast iron in cast aluminum. Not only do these pieces appear obviously thin to the eye, but somehow their very lightness when moved is disconcerting.

Outside lighting in Victorian times was mostly achieved by lanterns, traditionally of iron and glass. Japanese stone lanterns came in around the turn of the century along with more ephemeral variants in wood and paper, lit by candles. Authenticity today presents difficulties; the wiring up of old lamp posts for garden use is unlikely to be acceptable to purists. Reproduction fittings frequently only succeed in looking cutesy – too brassy or too curly. Tin lanterns which take candles are available; if these are thought too expensive, reproductions can be made up quite easily by a competent metal worker from sheet steel, after which they can be galvanized or simply painted with good-quality paint, preferably matte. Outside as well as in, reproduction fittings are generally best when they follow simple designs.

Right: The rustic effect of this seat of split wood is typical of the robust style of much Victorian garden furniture, here concealed in an intimate corner beneath a rose-covered arbor.

Far right: This is a fine example of the intricate patternwork of Victorian cast iron, painted in an appropriately subdued matte blue.

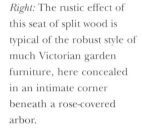

Left: Defying time and the elements, stone seats are one-offs: no modern method can reproduce them at a viable cost.

Above: A simple wooden settee of Chinese-influenced geometric design has been invitingly hidden away.

Above left: This stone urn has seen better days, but is delightfully planted with a limited palette of yellow and white.

Above: The lavish ironwork of the huge Victorian urn and the seat behind it is complemented by its sugary selection of flowering plants and the clean lines of the box hedges.

Above and above right: Old clay chimney pots can have a new life in the garden – ideal for the informal, kitchen-garden style of layout.

Left: Containers can be quite nondescript if adequately covered by plant material.

Right: A terracotta pedestal container has been planted for winter using evergreens, and including the orange-fruiting Jerusalem Cherry.

287

In this converted malt-house, an airy bathroom has been created where wooden bins of barley once stood. By adopting an open-plan design, the owner has been able to preserve the original structure of the building and the characteristic tongue-and-groove boarding of its walls and ceilings.

TECHNICAL ADVICE

Chapter Eight

KEEPING FAITH WITH THE PAST

Many Victorian houses have lost much of their original charm and character during ill-considered alterations made by succeeding generations of owners. It is only too easy to destroy the visual appeal of a Victorian house by installing an aluminum-framed, "picture" window, but not all modifications have to clash: a well-designed addition may enhance the original architecture. The key to a successful alteration or repair, no matter how small, is to follow the original.

All Victorian houses will have inevitably suffered the ravages of the climate on the outside and general wear and tear on the on the inside. In the average mid- to late-Victorian house, the original roof will probably have reached the end of its useful life. The brickwork may have deteriorated. The rain-water gutters and downpipes, if not regularly maintained, are likely to leak. Damaged plasterwork will need attention. Windows, doors, porches, verandahs and conservatories may have reached the stage where replacement is more cost effective than patching and mending.

Once the moment of replacement arrives, the decision has to be made whether to match the original exactly or substitute a cheaper, off-the-shelf alternative. Correct reinstatement can be expensive, but this minor act of homage to the past adds to the value of a property and helps to improve the neighborhood to the advantage of everyone, including future homeowners. The ownership of an old house does not confer unlimited property rights. Legal restrictions are imposed by building and planning regulations, and moral restrictions are increasingly recognized and accepted; as homeowners, we not only inherit the work of past generations, we are trustees for posterity, and we ought to discharge that duty at the same time as securing our own comfort. A respect for Victorian architecture should encourage us to make the outlay necessary to preserve it in recognizable form.

Sometimes major alterations are necessary. It is always a shame to subdivide an old house, but the owner may have no alternative. Even in the heyday of Victorian development, conversion became a practical necessity if the speculator had wrongly judged an area and his houses failed to find good families. The first sign of a neighborhood going down was the sign in the window saying "Rooms to rent". Multi-occupation, or what we call a boarding house, was the simplest form of conversion – a change of use with the minimum change of facilities.

The recent rise in home ownership to historically unprecedented proportions has brought with it both new standards of convenience and new dangers to the fabric of old houses: plasterboard partitions, flush doors at the bottom of stairs, cramped front lobbies and truncated moldings where new rooms meet old. In this chapter I have provided guidelines for sympathetic conversions: if the job has to be done, let it be done as well as possible. A little care taken over detailing and finish will pay for itself handsomely in pleasure and capital appreciation. The same principles will also serve the owner of a badly converted house who wants to repair the damage and improve the appearance of the property.

Some conversions do not affect more than one part of the house – making a separate apartment in the basement, for example, or combining two rooms into one. Other projects that are more disruptive require sensitive handling, including the conversion of complete houses, attic conversion and additions. Finally in areas of high property values where single-family houses are hard to find and prohibitively

expensive, the prospective homeowner may be able to buy only a corner of a once-grand house: a side-entrance hall perhaps, with an awkward opening cut through what was once the servants' quarters; a couple of large rooms requiring conversion into reception room, bedroom, kitchen and bathroom; a maisonette on two floors where a new internal staircase is needed. In such cases, an understanding of architectural detail and a bit of flair with paint, wallpaper and finishing touches can produce aesthetically satisfying results.

Before starting any work that will affect the structure or appearance of a house, seek professional advice from an architect.

ASSESSING THE CONDITION

For anyone about to restore, repair or modernize a Victorian house, the first task is to assess its condition. The full professional inspection of a house undertaken on behalf of buyers, either for their own information or as a condition of a mortgage, can be a powerful diagnostic tool. Its aim is to establish what faults a house may have and what remedial action is necessary. Neither potential home-buyers nor existing owners will be able to manage anything of this scope or intensity without employing a professional inspector. The pages that follow identify key areas where faults commonly occur both inside and out. They are not intended in any sense as a substitute for a professional inspection.

Roofs and chimney stacks
Unlike most other external features of a house, the roof is very difficult to examine closely. An old roof can appear sound when viewed from the ground but can in fact hide many small but significant problems. Most faults stem from poor maintenance and shoddy craftsmanship and materials or sometimes just from age. Reroofing can create its own problems. Roof timbers designed to support a covering of slates may buckle under the extra weight of modern concrete tiles. Badly laid loft insulation can cut down on ventilation from the eaves causing condensation, rot and damp to occur. Where slates or tiles meet the chimney stack, the usual lead or copper flashing may have been replaced by

a cheaper mortar filling.

External walls
The Victorians generally used lime mortar for greater plasticity, allowing walls to shift and settle slightly without cracking. In the absence of building regulations, there was no common practice governing depth of foundations or even the inclusion of a damp proof course, masonry walls being generally dry only if the site on which the house stood was well drained. Original damp proof courses in British Victorian houses are often a layer of overlapping slates lying horizontally across the width of the wall, one or two bricks above the ground.

Settling and bulging walls are a major problem and unless tackled immediately can lead to

serious damage. They necessitate the services of a professional builder or structural engineer.

Drainage
The Victorian rain-water gutter was generally made of cast iron and emptied by way of a swan-neck, rain-water head and downpipe to a gulley or drain. Sewage is disposed of direct to an underground sewer by means of a stack. Waste water from sink or bath can be fed directly into the stack but when rain-water is discharged into the sewer it is not uncommon to see bath or sink outflow feeding into the rain-water head.

If walls remain damp over several years, due to a faulty drainage system, structural problems can arise. There may be frost penetration of bricks and the resulting dampness

and condensation within the house can lead to dry rot, wet rot and flaking plaster. A cracked underground drain may cause part of the foundation to become waterlogged, resulting in localized shifting. A blocked or broken sewer is obviously a health hazard.

External woodwork
Surprising quantities of Victorian woodwork still survive. Top quality pine, oak, deal and other woods were used. These woods were well seasoned and mature, their resinous sap acting as a water-repellent preservative. They compare extremely favorably with the timbers used today which are often unseasoned kiln-dried woods, requiring treatment with artificial preservatives. Original woodwork should be kept wherever possible.

THE EXTERNAL INSPECTION

1 Slates and tiles missing or slipped

Cracks, also worrying, are almost impossible to spot from ground level.

2 Ridge tiles

Missing or not firmly bedded in.

3 Moss

This indicates that water is not running off the roof as it should. Tiled roofs may have deposits of soot or wind-blown dust trapped beneath the tiles, encouraging moss to develop. Trapped water may be sucked up under the tiles by capillary action.

4 Delaminated or painted slates

Slates lose their outer layers due to frost penetration, and water can consequently find its way into the roof. Painted slates indicate a problem that has only been temporarily cured.

5 Mortar fillet to a party wall

Mortar is not as flexible as lead flashing and may become dislodged over time.

6 Hollows that collect water

Victorian flat roofs were often covered in lead or zinc sheets connected by rolled joints (where the two edges overlap and are rolled up together). Zinc goes brittle with age and is susceptible to hairline cracks. Any water that does not run straight off the roof may seep through it.

7 Patches and signs of temporary repair

The only effective way to stop water coming through a flat roof is to replace it completely.

8 Leaning chimney stack

Most stacks need repointing, being more exposed to the action of wind, rain and frost than any other part of the house. A stack that has been left unpointed for many years may develop a slight lean as the mortar between the brick courses decays and turns to powder.

9 Old flashing around the stack

Examine from the top of a ladder. If flashing has never been replaced, it will be brittle and liable to leak. Points of weakness are the gutter at the back of some chimneys and corroded soakers – overlapping protective zinc or lead plates tucked up around the chimney stack where it meets the roof.

10 Wall plates

A sign that a bulging wall has been tied. If the house is sited on land liable to sinking, for example on a hill or in a mining area, the problem may recur.

11 Bulging walls

Easily overlooked except by a very observant eye. The best way to detect a bowing wall is to compare it visually with a strong perpendicular line such as a drainpipe or the wall of an adjoining house.

DEFECTIVE RAIN-WATER GOODS
1. Hopper
2. Rain-water downpipe has broken above bracket causing damp in wall behind
3. Rain-water gutter has broken away from the bracket

DETAIL OF WINDOW SILL DRIP
1. Timber sill
2. Water drip
3. Window-frame
4. Brick wall

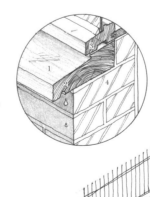

FLASHING TO CHIMNEY
1. Brick parapet on party wall
2. Mortar fillet
3. Lead flashing and soaker
4. Ridge tile
5. Haunching

POINTING
1. Flush (correct)
2. Weathered or struck (incorrect)
3. Bucket handle (acceptable)
4. Recessed (acceptable)

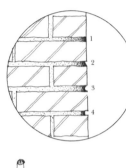

DAMP PROOFING
1. Old slate damp proof course
2. Holes bored for the injection of a damp proof course
3. Ventilation to void under suspended wooden floor

12 Cracks in brickwork and arches or lintels out of alignment
Fallen arches or broken lintels are often caused when structural woodwork, that is, those sills, lintels, joists, etc., that support brickwork, have warped or rotted. The most common place to find shifting is under a bay window.

13 Damp walls
These are often difficult for the amateur to spot, particularly in a damp climate. It is wise to hire a damp specialist to take accurate readings with a meter.

14 Damp proof course (DPC)
Scrape away mortar between the courses of bricks nearest the ground and try to look for evidence of a slate damp proof course. Earth from the garden may have piled up above the damp proof course, concealing it and conducting moisture up the wall. Even if a slate damp proof course appears intact, slight settlement could have caused cracking in some of the slates, with water rising up the wall through capillary action. A series of holes filled with mortar indicate that a chemical DPC has been injected into the walls.

15 Blocked air bricks or vents
Air bricks are essential for underfloor ventilation. They combine with a damp proof course to keep walls dry. Sometimes Victorian builders put in too few. Often earth and leaves have been allowed to obstruct the passage of air. Houses that have a floor below ground level tend to have "periscope vents" which serve the same purpose as air bricks.

16 Bad pointing
When a wall has been repointed, all too often there has been no attempt to reproduce the same lime/mortar mix as the original pointing. Mortar the wrong color and strength will not merely look ugly, it can also split away from the brickwork in frosty weather, taking part of the brick's surface with it (this is called spalling).

17 Painted walls
A brick wall keeps dry by "breathing" and when a wall has been painted or covered with stone cladding, moisture will be unable to escape from the porous brickwork. A painted or clad wall with rising damp will far more easily transfer moisture to the inside of a house.

18 Cut bricks
Attempts to clean up the brickwork of a housefront by abrading the surface of the bricks with a cutting tool or abrasive disc will remove the outer layer of the brick, making it more porous and more susceptible to damp and frost damage.

19 Additions
Where an addition has been made to a house, its foundations may have settled causing the old and new brickwork to part company with each other. Sometimes cracks are obvious but occasionally they are tiny hairline fissures. Remedial work need not be drastic.

20 Damp patches beneath guttering
Since holes and cracks are usually found inside the rear of eave gutters, damp patches may be the only visible sign of damage.

21 Uneven or sagging guttering
Weak joints, broken gutter clips or brackets may cause the gutter to sag and prevent water from draining properly. In rainy weather a sagging gutter will overflow.

22 Damp patches behind downpipes
Cracks or holes caused by corrosion or frost damage often occur where cast-iron pipes have been fixed so close to the wall that painting them is impossible.

23 Absence of water seal in rain-water gulley
If no water is visible at the bottom of a gulley, this means the stoneware trap at the head of the gulley is cracked, allowing water to seep into the ground around the foundations.

24 Bad-smelling main drain
The inspection chamber under the manhole cover may be inadequately rendered or the drain-pipes themselves may have cracked.

25 Disorganized pipework
Technically not a problem, but changes in plumbing over the years may have led to an unsightly tangle of exterior pipes. Pipework can be rationalized by feeding pipes directly into the stack. Seek the advice of a qualified builder or plumber.

26 Uneven surface on window sills and bottom rails of sashes
These are the most likely places for wet rot to occur since they are the most exposed. The surest way of finding rot is to prod the wood with an awl or small screwdriver. Uneven paintwork may indicate shoddy filling of rotted wood. Unless areas of rot have been cut back to the solid wood and then treated with a preservative, the rot fungus will continue to spread.

27 Flaking paintwork
This indicates shoddy or old work that has to be stripped off and at least three fresh coats applied to the bare timber. A primer, undercoat and, if possible, more than one top coat should be applied in sequence.

28 Replacement doors and windows
Many of the replacement doors and windows installed in Victorian houses between 1950 and 1980 now seem a matter of regret. Window conversions can also be reversed if the original outer frame has been left in place. Most old sash windows can be renovated and their life extended by a generation.

293

THE INTERNAL INSPECTION

Plumbing

The Victorians used lead piping throughout the house. The advantage was that joints could be easily soldered. The low melting point of lead also allows plumbers to "sweat in" copper pipes to connect with contemporary fittings.

By the late Victorian period, domestic hot water was provided by coal-fired water heaters located in the kitchen. Their galvanized iron pipes were often adapted when central water heaters were added later. Besides being large and ugly, galvanized iron pipes connected to copper piping are an invitation to leaks because of chemical reactions at the joint.

Modern balanced-flue water heaters can be sited in almost any area either upstairs or down. The placement often hinges on finding a location where the connecting pipework causes the least inconvenience.

The vogue for antique bathroom fittings has arrived too late to save all but a few genuine articles. Many so-called antique taps and bathroom fittings were made in the 1930s and have had their chromium plating removed.

Electricity

A small number of houses built at the end of the Victorian era were wired for electricity and sometimes vulcanized, fabric-covered wiring, or even lead-sheathed cable, may be found when making repairs or alterations. Such wiring is potentially lethal. It is unwise to tamper unnecessarily with the electric wiring and wise, if in any doubt, to call in a qualified electrician.

Turn-of-the-century light fixtures are highly collectable and will add to the atmosphere of a house if put back into use. They must be converted for modern wiring.

Gas

Many Victorian houses were lit by gas (see page 168), evidence of which is often found when lifting floorboards or looking in the attic. Whereas much of the electric wiring was carried in thin metal conduits, small bore gas piping used much thicker metal. Sometimes gas pipes were chased into the plaster of walls, ending in wooden roses which originally supported swan-necked light fittings. Old gas fittings of this kind can easily be adapted as electric light fittings, but they must be rewired. Brass bayonet bulb holders can then be inserted in place of the original gas mantle and a period or reproduction glass lamp shade fitted (see page 168).

LATH AND PLASTER
1. Brace studding
2. Stud
3. Wooden laths
4. Plaster
5. Cornice

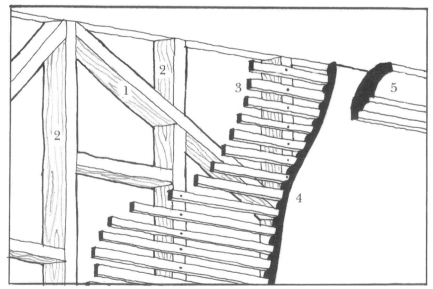

flaking or unsound plaster. This possibility should be investigated and, if necessary, put right before replastering. Dampness can usually be prevented by rendering a bare wall with a mortar mix of one part of cement to six parts of sand before the finishing coats of plaster are applied. If the plaster is undamaged, a slightly damp wall can be prepared for papering by hanging it with pitch paper – one side of which is coated with bitumen. Tin or aluminum strips, glued and rolled on to a wall before paper is applied, can also be used to isolate dampness. It is worth remembering that the plasterwork of Victorian builders was seldom exact so the final finish should not be mirror smooth.

Plaster

The Victorians rendered their walls with a lime/horsehair plaster mix applied to bare bricks or laths. Only when wallpaper is completely stripped off can the state of the plaster beneath be seen and judged. When several layers of heavy wallpaper have been allowed to build up, stripping the paper can pull the surface skim coat of plaster off the wall. Cracks or bulges point to unsound areas of plaster which can be easily dislodged with a sharp hand tool such as a stripping knife. When investigating unsound plaster, it is best to adopt a radical approach; rather than repair isolated patches with filler, it is just as easy, and cheaper in the long run, to put a skim coat over a large area. Dampness can cause

Ceilings

Original Victorian ceilings are of lath-and-plaster construction. They are usually papered over and this helps to prevent cracking. But a combination of settlement and age has left many city ceilings a little shaky.

In cases of cracking, ceiling paper should be carefully stripped off and cracks cleaned out and filled with a flexible commercial filling compound. Alternatively, a strip of thin gauze scrim will hold fresh finish plaster over the cracks, preventing them from opening up again. Once the cracks have been dealt with, the ceiling can be repapered.

Where water has found its way through a ceiling from burst pipes or an overflowed tub, areas of plaster may separate from the laths. If the sag is extreme, it is best to remove both plaster and laths, and nail extra thick plasterboard to the joists before redecorating. If the sag is only slight, then it may be possible to contain both laths and plaster by lining the ceiling with sheets of plasterboard, securely nailed in place with long galvanized clouts.

Staircases

The staircase of the standard row house was made of timber. The underside of the staircase should be well ventilated to prevent dry rot and the pillars (newel posts) that support the handrails should be securely anchored to the floor joists.

Wood rot

Wet rot in the main attacks external timbers; internal outbreaks tend to be localized and easily eradicated. Dry rot, on the other hand, can cause a great deal of damage within the house. This makes it the principal antagonist.

Dry rot – *Merulius lachrymans* – is a fungal growth which, despite its common name, thrives in warm, damp conditions. Tiny spores of the fungus settle on moist wood and rapidly develop into a fruiting body which feeds off the wood, breaking it down. As the fungus takes hold, it sends out filaments which spread the rot to nearby wood. It needs, or attacks, damp, warm, unventilated timber. One reason why dry rot is so deadly is that these filaments can travel across concrete, bricks or even steel joists in their search for damp timber. It is so virulent that it can penetrate a 3ft (1m) thick wall in days. Eradication is particularly difficult since it involves the destruction or sterilization of all building materials that have come into contact with it.

Dry rot is thought to have been introduced into Victorian houses by domestic coal. Wooden pit props in damp mines were a breeding ground for the fungus and spores were present in coal which was stored in such damp spots as cellars or under the stairs. Today's dry rot spores are probably wind-borne or have been lying dormant in timbers, awaiting the right conditions for growth. The fact that outbreaks are sometimes only local when they do occur in Victorian houses stands as a tribute to the enduring quality of the timber used. Most of this was cut down when fully mature and consisted of dense, close-ringed heartwood which has a natural resistance to fungal attack. Today's pine, mostly sapwood, is much more vulnerable.

Dry rot can develop unseen behind baseboards, under floorboards and in roof spaces and it is often only detected when it has already caused a great deal of damage. It has a damp musty smell and affected wood breaks up into small cubes. For obvious reasons, it should be treated as quickly as possible. To prevent dry rot, keep potentially damp areas, like the attic, cellar and bathroom, well ventilated and cure plumbing leaks as soon as they are detected.

Treatment of dry rot

Although many people prefer to use specialist firms because of the offer of a guarantee, a good builder will also be able to tackle dry rot effectively and often without undue expense. The builder may himself use a specialist firm if large areas have to be sprayed with a fungicide. In either case, the technique is to cut back timbers and expose affected brickwork or masonry beyond the limit of fungal growth. The exposed brickwork will then be treated with a flame gun or blowlamp before being sprayed or brushed with a fungicide worked well into the mortar joints in the brickwork. Alternatively, after treatment with a flame gun, the affected area should be left exposed until it has fully dried out. Dry rot dies after exposure to oxygen, and it is cheaper and safer to ensure that exposure than to use chemicals that are highly toxic, dangerous and ecologically unsound.

All timbers removed from the site should be burned promptly as there is a danger of spores spreading. However if dry rot has infected carved or decorated woodwork, perhaps on a staircase or built-in cupboard, there may be an alternative to destroying it. Timber can be removed carefully and sterilized in a drying kiln before being pressure-impregnated with a preservative.

Treatment of wet rot

Wet rot is another fungus that attacks damp timber, particularly door and window-frames. It often develops underneath cracked paintwork and it can go undetected for some time. Affected timber is invariably discolored and spongy when wet, powdery when dry. Wet rot is not as serious as dry rot because it is usually confined to a small localized area. The cause of the damp should be cured before cutting away the damaged timber. The wood can then be painted with a preservative before being patched up with filler and being redecorated.

Woodworm

The presence of woodworm or wood beetle is indicated by large numbers of small holes in wood. These are caused not by the beetle itself but by its larvae which develop from eggs laid on the timber. The larvae eat their way through wood, creating bore holes. Finally, they emerge as fully-grown beetles through larger flight holes. Structural timbers should be inspected regularly for any tell-tale signs. Flight holes appear in the summer months and will show up bright in contrast to the dull or dusty surface of the timber. In the United States, termites are insects which even more actively damage wood. Left untreated, affected timber can be weakened, disfigured and ultimately ruined.

Victorians had no effective treatment for the wood beetle and paid it as little attention as possible. Today, eradication of both beetle and termites is usually achieved by pressure spraying or fumigation with an insecticide.

STRUCTURAL ALTERATIONS

Sometimes the original design of a Victorian house does not satisfy current demands. For example a dingy room at the back of the house may feel claustrophobic, or a modest house may become too small for a growing family. There are several options available to people who want to open up, adapt or expand their existing living space, but having said that, tampering with the structure of a house could alter its appearance and nature forever and should not be taken lightly. Major alterations may have to comply with the local building codes or have permission of the local Landmark Commission. Because of the legal and technical difficulties, it usually pays to call in professional advice before the first brick is laid or the first blow struck with a hammer.

Planning permission

In most cities and towns in the United States zoning restrictions exist to control the siting and appearance of buildings and additions. The regulations vary from town to town. For example buildings in a large city or suburb are generally under tighter restrictions than those in smaller and more remote locations.

In addition, some buildings are designated landmarks or are listed by the town or state government as being of historical interest. These usually require planning permission before alterations are made. In certain cities and towns, there are also designated historic districts where permission must be sought if the appearance of the building is to be altered.

Building codes

Almost any structural alteration to a building in the United States must comply with the building codes which are enforced to safeguard health, safety and the stability of a building. Before starting any major work on a house, therefore, check that your plans comply with the codes.

Preservation guidelines

The United States National Park Service has prepared two essential preservation resources which should be consulted before deciding whether and how to make structural alterations. The first is The Secretary of the Interior's Standards for the Treatment of Historic Properties available at http://www.nps.gov/history/hps/tps/standards_guidelines.htm. These contain a uniform set of historic preservation standards followed by Landmark Commissions through the United States and enshrine valuable preservation principles.

The second is a set of several dozen Preservation Briefs that treat a multitude of topics such as roofs, paint, ceramic tiles, exterior additions, conserving energy, flat plaster repair, identifying character-defining features, exterior additions and controlling moisture. These are available at http://www.nps.gov/history/hps/tps/briefs/presbhom.htm.

Hiring a specialist

A preservation architect should be called in by anyone who intends to change the structure of a house. A worthwhile architect, sought out through your State Historic Preservation Office or through local preservation groups, will not only draw up detailed plans but will also be responsible for obtaining any necessary permissions.

Contractors and sub-contractors work best when they have specific plans to follow, preferably drawn up by a restoration specialist. When it comes to a Victorian property, it is wise to consult somebody who is familiar with the style. Many architects hire contractors on the homeowner's behalf; this is a good idea because the architect and contractors will probably have worked together in the past on similar projects and any work carried out will be the responsibility of the architect.

TWO ROOMS INTO ONE

"Knocking through" is the process of opening up a wall between two rooms, often the wall between a ground floor front room and a back room. This creates a larger single space and is the most important and most common alteration made to Victorian houses by modern residents. The advantages and disadvantages of this alteration have been discussed in Chapter 3.

Internal walls

The interior walls or partitions in a Victorian house are sometimes load-bearing which means that they act as supports for the timber floor or ceiling joists above and also contribute to the structure and solidity of the external walls. Additionally, they may act as a support for staircases. However, not all internal walls are load-bearing and it is never easy to tell those that are from those that are not. This is where an expert's opinion is essential; opening up a non load-bearing wall is comparatively simple;

removing a load-bearing wall is dangerous and must be left strictly to the professionals.

When demolishing or opening up a load-bearing wall, an RSJ (rolled steel joist) or UB (universal beam) will have to be positioned above the opening to take the weight of the floors above and supply the rigidity that would otherwise be lost. The first step towards this end is to demolish the wall section by section, temporarily inserting adjustable steel bars to bear the load. When the opening is the right size, brick or timber piers are built to support either end of the RSJ or UB. When the new joist or beam is finally inserted, the most critical maneuvers are complete.

Walls

The scars left to the walls after knocking through can be finished off by replastering and, if appropriate, a new double-door frame, complete with architrave mold, can be installed.

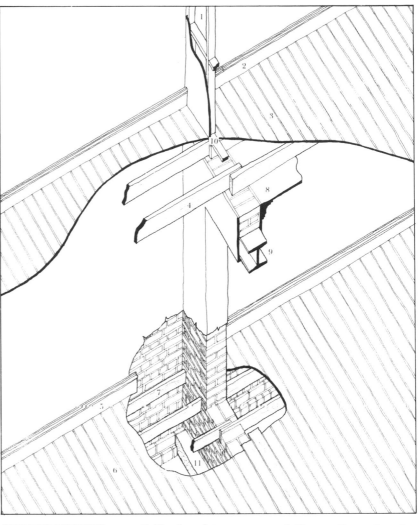

OPENING BETWEEN
ROOMS
1. Stud wall
with plasterboard
2. Baseboard to second
floor

3. Floorboards to
second floor
4. Second-floor joists
5. Baseboard to first floor
6. Floorboards to first floor
7. First-floor joists

8. Plaster ceiling and cornice
9. New RSJ to support
second-floor joists
10. New floorboards in
location of former wall
11. Foundation to new pier

Cornices

In Victorian houses, the point at which the wall meets the ceiling is usually modified by a cove, molding or length of decorated plaster cornice (see page 128). These are always worth preserving.

When combining a pair of rooms with high ceilings and cornices, it may be better to stop the opening below the line of the picture rail to avoid damage to the cornice above. However, this option is not realistic

where low ceilings are involved and where the entire wall has to be removed. In such cases, the cornices in both rooms will have to be removed to allow the steel beam to be positioned.

If cornices have to be removed or end up damaged, a new molding can be taken from a piece of cornice left in situ and lengths of fibrous plaster cornice made up off-site by a specialist firm (for a list of companies specializing in this field, see page 309).

Baseboards

One side-benefit of knocking through is that surplus baseboards will be left over from the base of the dividing wall in both of the rooms. Some of this can be reused for other locations, so before the wall is demolished, carefully remove all the baseboards with a crow-bar.

Refitting baseboards is not easy. For a start the ends have to be mitred to make neat joints and the wood itself may be brittle and difficult to secure.

Floorboards

Once the wall has been demolished, floorboards will have to be laid across the space previously occupied by the dividing wall. If the floorboards in the two main rooms have been stripped, it is obviously sensible to put in old floorboards in the new floor area. Architectural salvage companies may be able to supply old flooring. When attaching the new boards, make sure the new supports beneath them are well secured to existing

joists and that they bring the new boards to the exact level of the existing floor (see above).

Relocation of utilities

The demolition of a dividing wall will probably entail the relocation of electric plugs as well. The upheaval caused by such a major building project will in any case provide the homeowner with an ideal opportunity to resite plugs or to install wall lights or even a completely new wiring system.

CONVERSIONS

Basement conversions

Some older Victorian houses were built with cellars or basements where the ceilings are too low for them to be used for anything but storerooms. Prone to dampness and poorly ventilated, these rooms are often uninhabitable. They are, however, natural candidates for improvement. It is often possible to lower the floor and and improve the lighting at front and rear by installing, say, windows at the front and french windows at the rear. The space gained could provide not just extra living room but even a self-contained apartment with its own kitchen and bathroom facilities.

The building work involved, however, is complex and can prove expensive. Professional advice is definitely required. The floor will generally need to be lowered below that of the existing foundations of the house. This means either strengthening the foundations or underpinning the whole house. Water levels can also cause problems, as can drains that run underneath little more than compacted earth,

and a newly excavated cellar will almost certainly have to be made waterproof (walls as well as floor). This is best left to a reputable contractor.

As an alternative, a basement can be brought into the main body of the house by opening it from the top to create an unusual living area, full of height and the sensation of space. Where two ground-floor reception rooms have been knocked into one, the floor of the rear room can simply be removed, with access provided to the basement floor by a spiral staircase. The opening must be made safe with balusters and handrail, creating the effect of a balcony within the drawing room. This adventurous and radical plan is unlikely to provide extra space but could offer a new perspective and sense of volume.

Creating new rooms

It is sometimes possible to achieve a more economic and effective use of space by moving or adding walls – easy enough if they are mere partitions, not load-bearing. A run of three

ROOM CONVERSIONS

BEFORE:	AFTER:
1. Kitchen	1. Day room
2. Dining room	2. Kitchen
3. Lounge	3. Hall
4. Hall	4. Living room
5. Parlor	

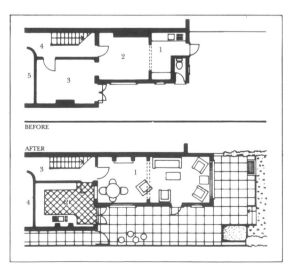

BEFORE:	AFTER:
1. Kitchen	1. Day room 2. Dining room
2. Dining room 3.Bathroom.	3. Shower/WC 4. Utility room.

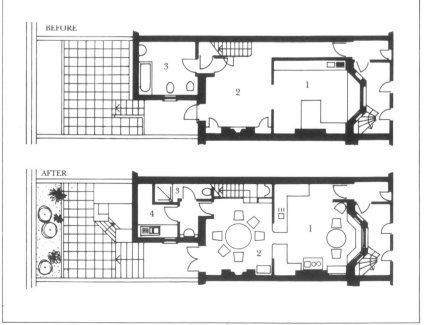

bedrooms could be converted into a suite of two bedrooms and two bathrooms. If there are only two bedrooms, both rather large, the wall dividing them could be removed and its place taken by two stud walls, 6 feet (2m) apart. This would create two slightly smaller bedrooms with a long, narrow slip between them, which could be split into two separate tiny rooms, with doorway access from each bedroom. One of these could become a walk-in wardrobe with fitted shelves and rails (for example see page 266), while the other might become a small en-suite bathroom or shower room.

Similarly, an average-sized room can be made into a grand room by moving the back wall further back, and making the resulting thinner room behind into a kitchen or bathroom. An extra sense of spaciousness can be achieved by styling the entrance to the kitchen so that it looks like a set of partition doors leading to another reception room.

Attic conversions

One of the simplest ways to gain space in a house is to convert the attic, generally into bedroom, study or storeroom. When considering an attic conversion in a Victorian house, great attention needs to be given to making sure that changes respect the intentions of the original architecture and the general quality of the streetscape. All too easily, a row of fine houses can be spoiled by a single, insensitively designed dormer window conversion. This really is a case where the modern owner is honor-bound to try to keep faith with the past, regardless of the latitude extended by the responsible authorities.

External considerations

The use of skylights allows the profile of an existing roof to be retained where this is important to do so. If dormers have to be added to give ceiling height and views, then these should be in keeping with the style of the building, and preferably in the rear.

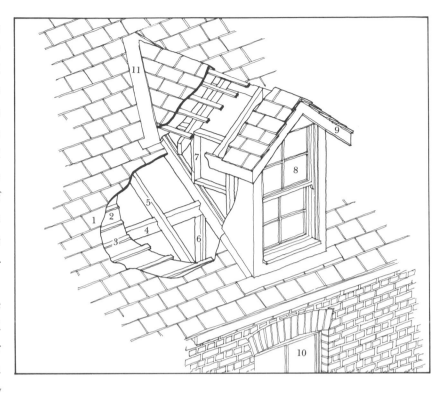

On dormer roofs, or on any part of the main roof that has to be rebuilt, care should be taken to obtain a cladding material which matches that of the original roof. Second-hand slates may sometimes be available, but they need careful checking. New slates are now very expensive. A cheaper but effective substitute is found in the many modern types of resin-bonded composition slates or fiber cement slates. On tiled roofs, second-hand stock is again a suitable answer, with the local builder's merchant a likely source or, failing that, an architectural salvage company. Modern tiles can also be found to match the color of old tiles darkened by soot and grime, but it is often impossible to match for size. In the case of a new dormer, however, size may not be as important as color because new tiles will not be laid side by side with old ones.

Many 19th-century houses in the USA and some in Britain were roofed with cedar shingles. When working with these, it is advisable to check the condition of the whole roof. Original shingle roofs are steeply pitched to throw off water but isolated damage or missing shingles lead to rain-water penetration and the rapid spread of rot. Even so, this type of roofing is extremely long-

DORMER WINDOW
1. Slates
2. Sarking felt
3. Roof boards
4. Purlin to main roof
5. Rafter to main roof supported on purlin and external wall
6. Additional studs to support end of purlin
7. Studwork to side of dormer
8. Double-hung sash window
9. Bargeboard
10. Existing window with brick arch
11. Valley gutter

lasting: the life expectancy of a shingle roof can be more than 50 years.

Wood shingles present more of a fire hazard than other forms of roofing, but they can be treated with a chemical fire retardant. Newly laid shingles will gradually age to the silver-grey color of the old roof so long as colored stains are not applied.

Internal considerations

Victorian roofs were built on site by skilled carpenters. The roof timbers were supported by posts, tie-beams and purlins which occupy attic space and sometimes prevent it being used as a room. Where this is the case, the essential timber framing has to be moved and replaced by new structural beams capable of supporting the weight of the roof. Usually this means adding large wooden beams from which stud frames are built up to support the roof timbers and any dormers that are added.

When a floor has to be laid in a converted attic space the existing ceiling joists may not be of sufficient size to support it. Thicker, stronger joists might have to be laid alongside existing timbers and their ends supported from new cross-members - either steel girders bolted together in sections or floor beams brought in through an open section of the roof. The dimensions of the new flooring joists will depend on the distance they are spaced apart as well as on the floor area to be supported. Architectural standards available at local libraries contain tables of joist sizes, spacing and floor loadings.

The ceiling height in new rooms is an important consideration. Building codes may require a minimum ceiling height over at least half the total floor area. In other areas, the amount of headroom required is left to the discretion of the local Building Inspector. Even so, it is wise to try for as much height as possible.

Although access to attic storage space may be via a ladder or disappearing stair, access to an attic conversion is best provided by a permanent

staircase. From a design and space-saving perspective, this should generally be sited over the well of the existing staircase. Ideally, it should follow the same detailing as the staircase below, although it does not matter too much if treatment alters as the stairs ascend. Many Victorian staircases have elaborate turned banister spindles, but modern equivalents may be of simpler design. It would be reasonable to alternate plain and turned balusters. In the end, the homeowner should seek a balance between cost and authenticity.

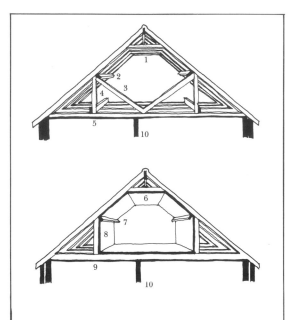

ATTIC CONVERSION
1. Collar
2. Purlin
3. Purlin struts
4. Vertical struts
5. Ceiling joists
6. Attic ceiling
7. Retained or strengthened purlins
8. Plaster walls on additional struts
9. Additional deeper joists
10. Spine wall

Fire regulations governing the installation of staircases are troublesome in terms of design, even though very important for safety. Local fire regulations vary but it is likely that all doors opening on to the stairwell may be required to be fireproofed, including existing ones, and each door may have to be self-closing. It is often necessary to increase the fire resistance of the floor and ceiling with floor grade chipboard or tongue-and-groove boarding.

In the event of a fire, a person could easily be trapped in an attic bedroom with no means of escape. Fire regulations may require the provision of an escape route, for example via an exterior stair. Where a route is provided, some of the other restrictions may well be relaxed.

Utilities

Attic conversions require electric circuits for power and light. They also necessitate re-arranging the plumbing within the original roofspace. Many attic conversions are intended as extra bedrooms and it is often desirable to provide a bathroom or, at the least, a wash basin. Have a plumber determine if there will be adequate hot water and water pressure from the hot water heater below, or if an additional heater must be added.

If the central heating is extended to the attic, then a larger central heating system will probably be necessary. A space heater or heat pump is often better for a single room and much cheaper to add than altering the central heating.

Converting into apartments

Converting a basement or attic into a self-contained apartment is comparatively simple when compared to dividing up a large Victorian house into a number of separate living spaces. Apart from the building and demolition work involved, stringent local regulations often have the final say on how the final design should or should not look. It is essential to have an architect draft up detailed drawings before any work commences.

APARTMENT CONVERSION
BEFORE: 1. Bedroom, 2. Bedroom, 3. Bathroom, 4. Bedroom.
AFTER: 1. Living/dining room/kitchen, 2. Bedroom, 3. Bathroom.

APARTMENT CONVERSION
BEFORE: 1. Hall, 2. Parlor, 3. Store, 4. Store, 5. Lobby, 6. Scullery, 7. WC.
AFTER: 1. Entry hall, 2. Hall, 3. Bedroom, 4. Bathroom, 5. Kitchen, 6. Living/dining room.

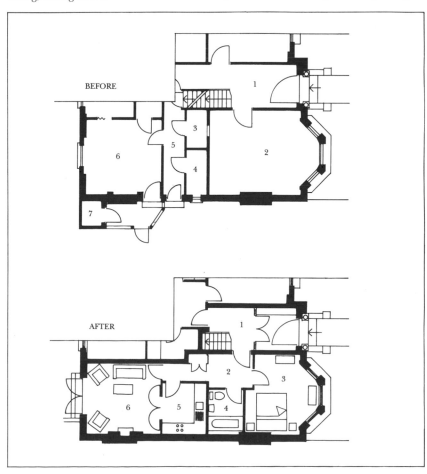

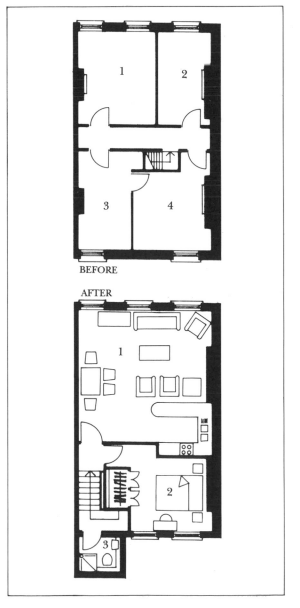

ADDITIONS

Later Victorian row houses were often built with additions at the rear, for kitchen, pantry, bathroom or servant's room. A grander addition might comprise a self-contained service wing. It is possible to build over an existing addition, but a number of questions have to be resolved and planning permission sought, before any work commences with an architect. For example, can the lower addition take the extra load? How will the new addition be insulated? Will it connect with the stairs and corridors of the existing house? Similarly, an addition over a garage may require under-floor insulation. There is also the vital issue of matching the addition to the existing house. If strengthening of the original addition is required, the work could involve underpinning. But where ground-floor doors and windows are being resited it may be simplest to knock down the original structure and start again. Alternatively, the use of single-skin walls of thermalite blocks, topped with a flat roof, may make it possible to construct a second story in keeping with a minimum load.

A single-story addition at the back of a house poses questions of a different kind. An architect should specify the type and size of the foundations needed to support the new structure and details should be given on how they are to be tied in to the existing foundation. Drains and inspection chambers are frequently found at the back of old houses and they have to be either relocated or provision made for them inside the new building.

A flat roof weighs much less than a pitched slate or tile roof, but is visually appropriate to a limited range of buildings; cheaper flat roofs have a short life of 10 to 15 years.

The walls of most new additions are of brick veneer construction with a space between the inner and outer walls; this provides improved insulation, but the brickwork bonding must follow the original pattern.

When adding an addition, care must be taken to match visible brickwork and roof cladding. Use of recycled building materials is advisable. If the roof of the main house is in a state of disrepair, the construction of an addition could be a good time to replace all the roofing of the house so that the pitched roof of the new addition matches the main roof.

New additions need to follow detailing of existing doors, windows and lintels, cornices, etc. – these should be covered by the architect's design. Make sure to get the proportions right, especially the size of the windows. If they are too small, they will make the new part of the house look inferior to the old. If they are too big, they will swamp the original architecture.

Conservatories

Conservatories are by far the cheapest means of adding to a house. They are capable of giving the greatest pleasure but do substantially alter the atmosphere of the room to which they are added, making it feel, paradoxically, a good deal

NEIGHBORLY ADDITION
1. New rear addition
2. Adapted dormer window
3. New clerestory window
4. New windows
5. New french windows
6. Original windows

Right:
ENGLISH BOND
BRICKWORK
1. Stretcher
2. Header
3. Queen closer

Far right:
FLEMISH BOND
BRICKWORK
1. Stretcher
2. Header
3. Queen closer

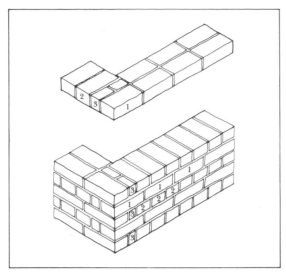

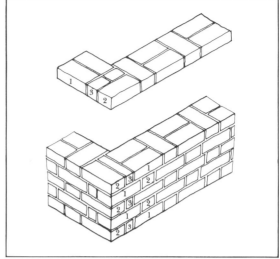

more indoors, and affecting the amount and quality of natural light in it.

Many pre-fabricated Victorian-style conservatories are available, and manufacturers will assemble them on site to specifications. These often look acceptable but, if funds will stretch, it is worth looking into the possibility of a custom-made conservatory. It should be double-glazed and well ventilated in order to prevent condensation and remain cool in summer.

HEATING AND INSULATION

CENTRAL HEATING
Victorian central heating systems were often vast and inefficient but they led to one of the most practicable types of central heating for Victorian homes – a "wet" system involving circulation of hot water through pipes and radiators. The modern, "dry" alternative of ducted air is normally installed when a house is built, and only becomes an option in an old building when it is being reconstructed.

Those moving into Victorian houses still devoid of central heating have the advantage that they will be able to install a heating system that meets their known requirements and if applicable, one that can meet possible future demands such as an attic conversion or an addition.

Before installing a brand new system or upgrading an existing one, it is a wise precaution to call in a heating engineer who will be able to calculate what is required.

Gas-fired central heating
On grounds of cost and flexibility, gas is often the preferred fuel, assuming it is available; houses outside large towns and cities are not always near a gas line. Most modern gas-fired boilers have "balanced" flues which enable air to be sucked in and burnt gases expelled through the same aperture in the wall. These flues are compact and comparatively neat, but there are limitations as to where the flue can be sited – for example, it must not go underneath a window – and local building codes may prevent it from being positioned in areas where it could be an eyesore. It is always best to consult a surveyor or architect before installation.

However, these boilers may be too small for larger houses, where a floor-standing model is required. This can be sited in a fireplace, and the flue can be ducted up the chimney. To prevent acid residues from destroying the inside of the chimney. the stack has to be lined with non-corrosive material and a special cowl placed on top.

Oil-fired and electric central heating
When gas is not available, oil is often a good alternative. It has one major disadvantage – the need for delivery truck access to the oil-storage tank which is an indispensable part of the system. The tank itself must be concealed where possible outside the house.

Oil-fired boilers are available in wall-mounted or floor-standing models. The former can be sited against any external wall, while the latter may require a chimney lined with protective ducting. Oil-fired systems are efficient and reliable. Electric heating is often more expensive, but is simple, neat and easily available. Electric systems are similarly reliable and have the advantage of being able to be sited almost anywhere in the house.

Pipe runs and radiators

The Victorians made a virtue of their central heating systems, siting large and elaborately decorated radiators in prominent positions. Some people living in Victorian houses may wish to echo this Victorian fashion (see p.113), at least in rooms where an imposing effect is wanted. However, most homeowners prefer their central heating to be more discreet.

The Victorians were perfectly prepared to run their horizontal pipes along the top of baseboards. In general the modern homeowner will want to run them under the floor. This poses few problems in the case of a suspended wooden floor, but it may be necessary to stick to the baseboard position in some instances – for example, to avoid damage to tiles or where there is a solid concrete floor. It is worth remembering how cold both outside walls and solid floors can be in winter, particularly if a house is left unoccupied. Any pipework laid against these surfaces should be insulated.

Vertical pipes running from ground level to upper floors also need to be concealed. Many late Victorian houses were built with fitted cupboards in the kitchen, on landings or in bedrooms, and pipes can run inside them. Otherwise, pipes will have to be boxed in or chased into the plaster with insulated metal trunking. Boxing in offers an opportunity for elaboration into a column, complete with capital, if the general style of the house will accept it.

The siting of radiators calls for efficiency as much as for discretion. In living areas, wall-mounted radiators are best placed under windows, close to the point of maximum heat loss. The cool air from the window is lifted and flows across the room more efficiently. In bedrooms, where slightly cooler temperatures may be desired, an internal wall is often more economical; some cool airflow from the windows will be felt, however. It is best to avoid siting a radiator against a panelled window recess – not only will the paneling be concealed but it could get charred as well.

Heat loss from a radiator on an external wall can be cut down by putting reflective foil behind the radiator. Hiding a radiator in a perforated box may seem attractive but the heat output will be reduced.

There will probably be awkward spots where radiators are hard to site due to lack of wall space. Instead, a hot water convector can be installed at baseboard level or even above a door. Convectors are particularly useful in kitchens or bathrooms where work surfaces or fitted units take up most of the wall space.

ENERGY CONSERVATION

Whether a house is heated by gas, oil, electricity or coal fires, a heating system will be more efficient if heat loss can be minimized. Of all forms of heating, an open coal fire is the least efficient; around 80 per cent of the heat is lost up the chimney. Even so, a coal fire is still the best source of radiant heat, felt intensely at close quarters.

Drafts

The Victorians stoically accepted drafts as a fact of life. Rather than cure them, they went to great lengths to avoid them. The sitting room and the bedrooms often contained screens, and doors were hung with thick velvet or chenille *portières*, suspended from a brass rail which was hinged to open with the door.

Today, there are a number of products available to help the energy-conscious homeowner. Drafts around external doors can be prevented by a self-adhesive foam draft-excluder or, more attractively, brass weather-stripping. A threshold seal consisting of a tightly packed brush held by an aluminum or nylon strip can be fixed to the bottom of the door.

A more radical, and more effective, solution to cure front-door drafts is to add a storm door and storm windows. The design of storm windows is of great importance, as they alter the exterior appearance of a house. Some homeowners avoid this by installing removable interior panels which serve much the same purpose as exterior windows and leave the exterior appearance of the house untouched.

Fireplaces can be a major source of heat loss even when unlit. Warm air in the room simply disappears up the flue. Victorian builders fitted metal registers into fireplaces in upper bedrooms and when not in use airflow could be blocked off from the chimney by closing the register.

Unused fireplaces are often removed, most commonly to save bedroom wall space and at the same time to cut down on drafts. This can be a very messy operation as soot and rubble will be lodged behind the grate. When bricking up and

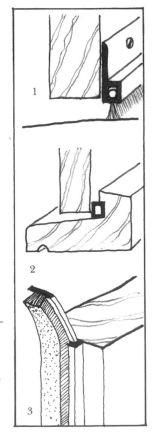

DRAFT EXCLUDERS
1. Brush draft excluder
2. Vinyl-sheathed urethane foam seal
3. Plant-on seal with removable brush

plastering over the opening, it is important to provide space for an air vent at the bottom and it is equally important to leave the top of the chimney uncapped. Any fireplace that has been completely closed off will cause condensation in the flue and this could leach out through the walls causing problems of damp, flaking

plaster and dry rot.

Floorboards at first-floor level can also be a source of drafts. Suspended floors are ventilated from beneath through airbricks. But if the floorboards are not close fitting, and in the absence of a floor covering and subfloor, a first-floor room can become distinctly breezy. As a

remedy, the floorboards can be relaid closer together. As an alternative, the cracks can be filled with a commercial filling compound or home-made *papier mâché*, a cheap but effective filler.

The war against drafts, however, should have limits. Gas and coal fires need oxygen to burn and must have some draft,

however small. Particularly in Britain, fires are made to draw better by providing grills on either side of the hearth which can be opened when the fire is lit, allowing air to be drawn up from the crawl space beneath the floor rather than across the room. When the fire is out, the grills may be closed. Antique furniture benefits

from the moisturizing effect of drafts. Central heating is the enemy here, drying out the air and then, in consequence, old timber. This causes splitting and warping. In rooms where sealing has been too effective, well watered plants and radiator humidifiers will help restore the moisture balance.

Attic insulation

Because it involves no structural alteration but merely the laying down between the joists of a material such as fiberglass roll or expanded polystyrene granules, attic insulation is the cheapest and most cost-effective form of household insulation to install.

There are a number of rules to observe when insulating an attic. When laying fiberglass, for instance, it is best not to take it all the way to the edge of the eaves but instead to leave a space of at least 6 inches (15cm). Most old roofs are

ventilated from below the eaves and reduced ventilation here could lead to condensation, dampness and rot. Because heat is prevented from passing upwards through the ceiling, an insulated attic will be much colder than before. This makes it essential to further insulate all pipes and water tanks in the attic. It is best not to lay insulation under water tanks, however, allowing them to receive some heat from below.

If the attic has been converted for use as a habitable room, then insulation should have been incorporated in the

building materials used. The attic's ceiling and walls will probably have been constructed from thermal plasterboard incorporating a foil vapour barrier to ensure timbers on the other side stay dry. In addition, the space between the roof timbers should have been packed with insulating material.

Wall insulation

Thermally insulated sheetrock can help minimize heat loss through walls provided they are dry. This type of wall cladding is frequently used on new additions to Victorian houses. Its use is

problematic, however, in rooms where there are original plaster cornices and baseboards. Here it is much easier to coat the walls with a wafer-thin layer from a roll of polystyrene. This will double as a lining paper, evening out pitted or bumpy plaster and providing an easy base for wallpapering.

Floor insulation

Floor insulation is a great deal more radical than merely sealing the floor boards against drafts but luckily it is rarely essential. The job can entail taking up the boards and fitting expanded polystyrene

blocks between the exposed joists. Battens are nailed along the sides of the joists allowing the polystyrene to sit flush with the top of the joists. As in roof insulation, it is important that no gaps be left where stagnant air might encourage condensation and the development of dry rot.

Double glazing

Since only ten per cent of a house's heat loss is by way of windows, double glazing is scarcely the remedy for high fuel bills that salesmen's rhetoric often claims. In addition the appearance of many Victorian houses has been ruined by inappropriate aluminum frames. Some companies have begun to offer windows that retain the original lines of the sashes or glazing bars; and sometimes they can be

fitted into existing Victorian frames.

Quotations for factory-made windows should be compared with the cost of employing a local joinery firm to make new wooden sashes suitable for double glazing.

Secondary glazing

When window frames and sashes are in good repair, it is worth considering secondary glazing – the fitting of another set of windows inside or even

outside the existing frames. The greater distance between outer and inner panes makes secondary glazing particularly effective in reducing noise but the drawback is the lack of a vacuum seal between the two layers of glass; unless some form of ventilation is provided, condensation may develop.

The frames or clips that support the new panes of glass can look out of sorts with a Victorian interior.

Other solutions

The Victorians themselves had a range of simple forms of insulation which are still perfectly practical today.

Almost all of their early houses were fitted with folding pine internal shutters. These were usually made in the form of two or even three doors, hinged in the middle. When not in use they were folded back into recesses in the wall. Some still survive unrecognized

under so many layers of paint that they appear to be a form of panelling. Rescued and unfolded, they are a delightful feature of a room.

The Victorians also made use of heavy, lined curtains to cut heat loss at night. On large windows these can hang right to the ground (see p.198). Deep ruffled valances above the curtain rail help prevent heat loss from the top of windows.

ADAPTING VICTORIAN FIXTURES AND FITTINGS

In both Britain and the United States, particularly during the 1950's and 1960's, many original fixtures and fittings were removed from Victorian houses and replaced by substitutes which now appear unsuitable, if not cheap and ugly. Detail gave way to flat, easily cleaned surfaces. Fireplaces were removed and thrown away. Balusters were hidden beneath hardboard paneling and the moldings on doors were hacked away or covered over with hardboard.

The many companies now specializing in reproduction or original fittings (see page 309) are an enormous help in reversing this trend.

The first step is to know what is missing. If in doubt about the nature of the original fittings, check for references in this book. Neighbors are a useful resource, since often another house of the same period on the same street will still have many of its original fixtures.

Reproduction fittings need to be scrutinized with care. Some are a weak pastiche of Victorian style, made in inferior materials and likely to look out of place. Others can be extremely effective. For homeowners with a scavenging instinct and a sharp eye for a bargain, it is still possible to buy original Victoriana at a price not very much higher than reproduction pieces.

Doors

Replacement Victorian or Victorian-style doors will be required in badly modernized houses.

The first step is to measure the frame into which the new door is to be inserted. Victorian joinery was made up on site and doors can vary by as much as 6 inches (150mm). Old doors will need to be stripped, either to reveal the original wood, or as preparation for repainting. Generally, the caustic soda bath should be avoided – it dries out the timber, causing the wood to bleach and crack; and it also wreaks havoc with glued joints which shrink and weaken the door's structure. Some companies offer a less drastic stripping service. If a door does come back bleached, it is possible to restore the natural shine and color of the wood by repeated application of teak oil.

For home-stripping – a foul, messy, astringent and time-consuming affair – use a hot air gun. Remove the remaining vestiges of paint with wire wool pads soaked in a strong chemical paint stripper and always remember to wear rubber gloves.

Restoring light fittings

Any antique light fittings encountered are likely to be of turn-of-the-century origin. Several early companies manufactured fixed and pendant light fixtures, and also magnificent brass or silvered electroliers. These were often balanced by a counterweight which allowed them to be moved up or down by tiny pulleys.

An original light fitting bought in an antique shop will probably have been rewired in the process of restoration, and only require reconnection. Sometimes, however, it is possible to come across dusty old light fittings in markets and junk shops; these will need cleaning, polishing and re-wiring, best done professionally.

Brass fittings

With luck, a door salvaged from a demolition site or builder's yard will have all its fittings – hinges, finger plates, knobs and lock. A hunt around antique shops and junk yards is often worthwhile, but as a last resort, reproduction brass fittings are sold coated with varnish; in time this will wear off and a genuine patina will follow.

Trying to find an original Victorian door lock that works is a labor of love and in most cases a modern mortise lock is a better bet, especially on a front or back door.

Restoring a tarnished brass fitting requires elbow grease, 000 gauge wire wool and brass polish. Rub the fitting gently with wire wool dipped in the polish, remembering that brass is a comparatively soft metal and easily scratched. Avoid using chemicals at all costs as these can cause the metal to oxidize.

Antique faucets and fittings can prove difficult to adapt. Victorian plumbers used to hand-cut the threads of pipe connections, so if part of a fitting is missing it will normally be impossible to find an exact replacement. In addition, 19th-century fittings were made for varying pipe sizes. It is important to ensure that a Victorian fitting comes with a length of its original piping, to which a suitably sized copper pipe can then be joined. The alternative to joining different gauges of pipe is to adapt the fitting itself, which is a job for an engineer.

China fittings

Original china fittings – door knobs, lavatory chain pulls and fingerplates – are hard to find because they are easily broken. Again, reproductions are readily available although it is worth seeking out those that follow the Victorian style faithfully.

Windows

Victorian windows are virtually impossible to find outside the confines of a house. The best option for anyone seeking a realistic look-alike is to contact a specialist joinery company.

Fireplaces

The British Clean Air Act of

1958 enforced the use of smokeless fuels and led to the devastation of the old Victorian fireplace, which was either removed or boarded up. In the northern U.S. the demise of the fireplace was due more to the great popularity of central heating which began during the Victorian era. However it gradually became clear that fireplaces have symbolic functions for which there is no good substitute and nowadays, fireplaces are being restored (see p.146).

If the chimney breast has not been removed, then somewhere inside the old hearth will probably have survived. The wall covering and plaster on the lower part of the chimney breast should be opened up and it will then be possible to see where the original hearth has been bricked up. The top of the opening was finished with a brick arch supported by an iron strip called a water bar.

Remove the bricks or breeze blocks under this arch and dispose of rubble. There will probably be a small pile of more ancient rubble right at the back of the hearth and this should be left. Its purpose was to sit behind the cast-iron fireplace, making sure it did not move and helping to cut down heat loss.

Measure the size of the opening and begin the search for a similarly sized cast-iron firechamber. These complete fireplace units, called register grates, were far more common in Britain than the U.S. The back plate of the replacement firechamber should overlap the sides and top of the hearth opening to prevent smoke escaping (see Chapter 3).

Typical British cast-iron firechambers were molded and cast in separate parts that bolt together. The fire-basket is bolted to the back plate; the bars to the grate bolt from behind; the riddle and chimney plate are adjustable and loose fitting to allow cleaning. The firechamber is held in position by the mantelpiece which is nailed or screwed to the wall.

Before fitting the firechamber, check that the chimney flue is in good condition and that it has not been capped. The firechamber should stand flush with the chimney breast, with the original pile of rubble found in the hearth now placed between the firebasket and the chimney.

Whereas British register plate firechambers were constructed totally of iron, tiled firechambers had firebrick cheeks and a fireback held in place by a metal band bolted across the back of the grate. The inset tiled panels were held from the back by a bolt-on metal frame. This was filled with plaster to hold the tiles themselves in place. Reasonable care must be taken when handling either kind of firechamber – cast iron is brittle and decorative tiles are hard to match or replace.

In America, cast-iron stoves can sometimes be bought cheaply, and used in a fireplace. Decorative tiles may be placed in the area just inside the mantelpiece. Tiles are not always of standard size so use care in purchasing and fitting them. Often a number of matching tiles were used with two middle tiles of different design, providing a "feature." When fitting a new set of tiles, wedge them in their frame with small blocks of wood. This will hold them firm until they can be set in plaster. Make sure the position of the tiles is correct before the plaster sets, for mistakes are hard to rectify.

REGISTER GRATE 1. Elevation, 2. Section

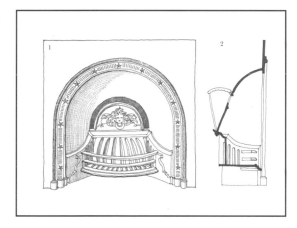

Mantelpieces

Mantelpieces were made of slate, marble, wood and cast iron (see p.146).

They are made up of sections which are assembled dry and held together in wooden frames. Blobs of quick-drying cement were often used to fix the pieces together.

The surfaces of antique marble mantelpieces will undoubtedly have deteriorated over the years. Sometimes they will have been given one, or several coats, of paint. This should be removed as carefully as possible with a weak solution of chemical paint stripper and a blunt stripping knife. Being porous, marble stains easily and stubborn stains can be removed with vinegar but this should not be left on the surface of the marble for longer than two minutes. Marble can be polished by rubbing on beeswax with a pad of 000 grade wire wool.

Some slate mantelpieces had imitation marble panels painted on them. Often these were surrounded by an incised border. If this kind of mantelpiece has been painted over it will be necessary to work very carefully indeed, stripping the paint a little at a time to see the effect on the surface below. When stripped, slate can be polished with a soft cloth and a beeswax polish.

Any missing pieces of marble or slate or any cracks can be repaired by using a hard, inert, resin-based filler of the type used to repair the bodywork of cars. When dry, the repair can be rubbed down to profile and carefully touched in with matt enamel paint mixed so that it resembles the color of the surrounding surface.

Cast-iron mantelpieces are often covered in many coats of paint, mainly because they are difficult to strip. The heat of a hot air stripper or a flame gun is diffused by the cast iron and the surface paintwork remains unaffected. The quickest and most effective method is to have cast iron shot-blasted. Firms specializing in this kind of work will insist on having the firechamber brought to them but some tool and equipment hire companies hire out shot-blasting equipment.

After a cast iron firechamber has been stripped back to the bare metal it can be polished by applying sparingly a black lead paste, or a non-lead based substitute, and buffing vigorously with a soft rag.

Plasterwork

Reproduction cornices, ceiling roses, pillars and moldings can be bought fairly cheaply from stores. However, many of these companies have a set of standard molds and they do not necessarily suit all Victorian houses. If at all possible, it is best to take a diagram or, better still, a remnant of the original plasterwork to a company that will produce a replica. This, of course, costs money. The cheaper option is to restore or patch up damaged plasterwork *in situ*.

CARE AND MAINTENANCE

Plaster moldings

Before attempting to clean or repair a large section of plaster molding, it is important to experiment first on a small area which is not vital. Most ceiling moldings are clogged with water-based latex or other coatings and these can quite literally hold the plaster together.

The most effective way of removing thick layers of paint from intricate moldings is to apply a layer of paint stripping paste over the top. Wear rubber gloves when doing this and be sure to work the paste into crevices and cracks. After spreading on the paste, cover it with polythene sheeting to prevent it from drying out and leave it for 24 hours.

Remove the stripper after it has had time to do its work with a blunt scraper and quantities of cold water. Various improvised tools, like a toothbrush and a spoon, are useful for getting the stripper out of deep or curved moldings. It is important to wear gloves and goggles when removing the stripper – it can burn skin and is particularly nasty if it gets into eyes.

Once the job is complete and all the paint has been washed out, the color of the underlying plaster should be an attractive creamy color.

Sash windows

A box-framed sash window has an upper and a lower sash each counterbalanced by two cast-iron weights. The weights run up and down inside the hollow box-sections of the frame when the sashes are opened and closed. The weights are supported by cords which run over pulleys at the top of the box frame. The sashes run in separate grooves and are divided by a parting bead. They are held in place by the edge of the frame on the outside and by staff beading on the inside. The staff beading should fit tightly around the frame and when closed the top rail of the lower sash and the bottom rail of the top sash should fit together to exclude drafts.

Attractive and practical though they are, sash windows are vulnerable to damage and misuse – rot, broken sash cords and layers of impenetrable paint can make them hard, if not impossible, to operate.

Rotten windows

Wet rot is the scourge of sash windows. It is likely to attack the base of the bottom sash rail and can quickly affect the frame itself. Flaking paint and soft wood indicate wet rot and although short-term remedies can be carried out, the only truly effective solution is to replace the damaged sections of wood. This is a task best left to a skilled carpenter who may be able to salvage the frame if not the affected sash. In extreme cases, the entire window and frame may have to be replaced.

There are two common reasons why wet rot latches on to sash windows. The first is that the paint covering may have cracked, letting in water and encouraging the fungus to develop. The second is a blocked drip groove on the underside of the sill (see pages 292-3). The purpose of the groove is to encourage rainwater to drain free of the sill and the wall beneath. If it gets blocked with dirt and cobwebs, water tends to run back to the wall and damp is the inevitable result.

Before repainting a window, it is imperative that all signs of wet rot have been eradicated, otherwise the problem will continue to spread. There is something of an art to repainting a sash window; it is only too easy to leave one or two surfaces uncoated and it is equally easy to allow wet paint surfaces to meet with the result that they stick together.

Broken sash cord

Sash cords tend to break either because they are old and have become rotten or because they have been painted over and have consequently become brittle. Replacing a broken cord is a fiddly business, especially if it involves the upper sash. The securing beadings have to be removed, followed by the sashes. Then the weights have to be lifted out from their pockets and new cords attached to them. Traditional hemp cords look marginally more at home in a Victorian house than nylon cords but the latter last almost indefinitely.

Security

An original Victorian sash window secured by a solitary ordinary latch is an invitation to burglars and it pays to secure all windows with special locks. The commonest type of secure sash bolt is an extremely hard steel screw that passes through the bottom sash into the top sash, one on each side, preventing the sashes from being opened. They are excellent value for the money.

Internal woodwork

If painted, paneling is easily scuffed and, although the simple remedy is to repaint it, a more satisfying solution can be to strip it back to bare wood. This is best done with a hot air stripper or with a chemical solvent. Both options require care – hot air strippers can scorch wood and chemicals can produce dangerous fumes.

Paneling that has buckled or "blown" from a wall may need special attention. Buckling usually indicates that the wood is damp and has expanded, so tackle the cause before attending to the paneling itself; if the paneling is on an outside wall, suspect damp rising from the ground or passing through the walls.

Paneling is usually fixed by nails driven into wooden plugs or battens embedded in the wall. Loose paneling usually means that the plugs or battens have worked free of the masonry. The only solution is to fit new wooden supports in the wall and to renail the boards in place.

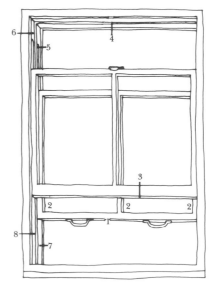

DOUBLE-HUNG SASH WINDOW Painting sequence

SUPPLIERS OF GOODS AND SERVICES

Despite the rapid proliferation of firms supplying original and reproduction Victorian fixtures, some materials and services can still be difficult to find. The yellow pages may not be enough if you are looking for someone to re-enamel a Victorian bath or make new tiles to match an old design, or for a specialist painter or carpenter.

The list that follows, compiled with the help of the *Old-House Journal's Restoration Directory*, does not include general building services, such as damp proofing and plumbing. Nor does it include every stripped-pine and fireplace shop, every junk shop and bric-à-brac emporium: readers will have their own favorite hunting grounds.

If you cannot find what you are looking for by contacting named suppliers, a number of organizations that may be able to help are listed on page 313.

ANTIQUES

Garden furniture, artwork, ornaments, lighting, tiles, wallpaper

GREAT GATSBYS
5070 Peachtree Ind. Blvd.
Atlanta, GA 30341
T: (800) 428-7297
F: (404) 457-7250
www.gatsbys.com

HELEN WILLIAMS TILES
12643 Hortense St.
Studio City, CA 91604
T: (818) 761-2756

RED BARON'S ANTIQUES
6450 Roswell Rd.
Atlanta, GA 30328
T: (404) 252-3770
F: (404) 257-0268
www.redbaronsantiques.com

SECONDHAND ROSE
138 Duane St.
New York, NY 10013
T: (212) 393-9002
F: (212) 393-9084
www.secondhandrose.com

SOUTHAMPTON ANTIQUES
172 College Hwy.
Rte. 10
Southampton, MA 01073
T: (413) 527-1022
F: (413) 527-6056
www.southamptonantiques.com

WOODEN NICKEL ANTIQUES
1400-1414 Central Pkwy.
Cincinnati, OH 45202
T: (513) 241-2985
F: (513) 412-5452
www.woodennickelantiques.net
Also sells salvage

YANKEE CRAFTSMAN
357 Commonwealth Rd.
Wayland, MA 01778
T: (508) 653-0031
F: (508) 650-4744
www.yankeecraftsman.com

ARCHITECTURAL MILLWORK

Straight, curved, monumental and spiral staircases, railings, balustrades, columns, entryways, gable ornaments and trim

ADAMS STAIR WORKS
1083 S. Corporate Cir.
Grayslake, IL 60030
T: (847) 223-1177
F: (847) 223-1188
www.adamsstair.com

AMERICAN WOOD COLUMN CORP.
913 Grand St.
Brooklyn, NY 11211
T: (718) 782-3163
F: (718) 387-9099
Also manufactures moldings

BREAKFAST WOODWORKS, INC.
135 Leetes Island Rd.
Guilford, CT 06437
T: (203) 458-8888
F: (203) 458-8889
www.breakfastwoodworks.com
Also does joinery

SYLVAN BRANDT LLC
651 East Main St.
Lititz, PA 17543
T: (717) 626-4520

F: (717) 626-5867
www.sylvanbrandt.com

CARPENTER AND SMITH
3301 Geneva Rd. Rte. 50
Burlington, WI 53105
T: (262) 537-2641
www.saveold.com
Also repairs horse-drawn vehicles

CHESTNUT WOODWORKING & ANTIQUE FLOORING
P.O. Box 204
W. Cornwall, CT 6796
T: (860) 672-4300
F: (860) 672-2111
www.chestnutwoodworking.com

COUNTRY ROAD ASSOCIATES, LTD.
63 Front St.
Millbrook, NY 12545
T: (845) 677-6041
F: (845) 677-6532
www.countryroadassociates.com

DAN DUSTIN, CUSTOM HAND-HEWING
1007 Penacook Rd.
Contoocook NH, 03229
T: (603) 746-5683
handhewing.bizland.com

JAMES R. DEAN, ARCHITECTURAL STAIRBUILDING & HANDRAILING
15 Delaware St.
Cooperstown, NY 13326
T/F: (607) 547-5863
www.jamesrdean.com

HOUSE OF ANTIQUE HARDWARE, INC.
39 N.E. Sandy Blvd.
BMP 106
Portland, OR 97214
T: (888) 223-2545
F: (503) 233-1312
www.houseofantiquehardware.com

MAD RIVER WOODWORKS
P.O. Box 1067
Blue Lake, CA 95525-1067
T: (707) 668-5671
F: (707) 668-5673
www.madriverwoodworks.com

MOHAMAD WOODTURNING CORP.
28 Meadow St., NY 11206
T: (718) 417-0025
F: (718) 417-0021
www.mohamadwoodturning.com

PAGLIACCO TURNING & MILLING
P.O. Box 229
Woodacre, CA 94973-0229
T: (415) 488-4333
F: (415) 488-9372
www.pagliacco.com

PRICE & VISSER MILLWORK
2536 Valencia St.
Bellingham, WA 98226
T: (360) 734-7700
F: (360) 734-7941
www.priceandvissermillwork.com

STAIR SPECIALIST, INC.
2257 W. Columbia Ave.
Battle Creek, MI 49015
T: (269) 964-2351
F: (269) 964-4824
www.stairspecialistinc.com

VINTAGE WOODWORKS
P.O. Box 30, Hwy. 34 S.
Quinlan, TX 75474-0039
T: (903) 356-2158
F: (903) 356-3023
www.vintagewoodworks.com

WINDHAM MILLWORK, INC.
684 Roosevelt Trail
Windham, ME 04062
T: (207) 892-3238
F: (207) 892-5905
www.windhammillwork.com

THE WOOD FACTORY
111 Railroad St.
Navasota, TX 77868
T: (936) 825-7233
F: (936) 825-1791

ARCHITECTURAL SALVAGE

Building materials, millwork, chimneypots, furniture, bathroom fixtures, lighting, hardware, stained glass

A.D.I. CORP.
5000 Nicholson Ct.
North Bethesda, MD 20895
T: (301) 486-6856
F: (301) 468-0562
Also sells antiques

ARCHITECTURAL ANTIQUITIES
Indian Point Lane
Harborside, ME 04642
T: (207) 326-4938
www.archantiquities.com

ARCHITECTURAL SALVAGE WAREHOUSE
53 Main St.

Burlington, VT 05401
T: (802) 658-5011
www.greatsalvage.com

AUTHENTIC WOOD FLOORS, INC.
P.O. Box 153
Glenrock, PA 17327
T: (800) 765-3966
F: (717) 428-0464
www.authenticwoodfloors.com

THE BATH WORKS, INC.
2646 Leah Circle
Columbia, TN 38401
T: (931) 381-5711
F: (931) 381-5712
www.thebathworks.com
Also sells reproduction bathtubs

FLORIDA VICTORIAN ARCHITECTURAL ANTIQUES
112 W. Georgia Ave.
Deland, FL 32720
T: (904) 734-9300
www.floridavictorian.com

GAVIN HISTORICAL BRICKS
2050 Glendale Rd.
Iowa City, IA 52245
T: (319) 354-5251
www.historicalbricks.com

GREAT AMERICAN SALVAGE CO.
14 Second Ave.
New York, NY 10003
T: (212) 505-0070

OFF THE WALL ARCHITECTURAL ANTIQUES
Lincoln Street near Fifth
P.O.Box 4561
Carmel, CA 93921
T: (831) 624-6165
www.imperialearth.com/OTW

OHMEGA SALVAGE
2407 San Pablo Ave.
Berkeley, CA 94702-2010
CASSIDY BROS. FORGE
Rte. 1, Rowley, MA 01969
T: (978) 948-7303
F: (978) 948-7629
www.cassidybros.com

SALVAGE ONE
1840 W. Hubbard
Chicago, IL 60622
T: (312) 733-0098
F: (312) 733-6829
www.salvageone.com

UNITED HOUSE WRECKING
535 Hope St.

Stamford, CT 06906-1300
T: (203) 348-5371
F: (203) 961-9472
www.unitedhousewrecking
.com

URBAN ARCHAEOLOGY
143 Franklin St.
New York, NY 10013
T: (212) 431-4646
F: (212) 343-9312
www.urbanarchaeology.com
*Also sells own-production
lighting, plumbing and
hardware*

CARPETS, CURTAINS AND UPHOLSTERY

*Roller blinds, curtain poles,
carpet rods, rugs, runners,
warps, furnishing fabrics*

ALAMEDA SHADE SHOP
914 Central Ave.
Alameda, CA 94501
T: (510) 522-0633
F: (510) 522-0651
www.shadeshop.com

BENTLEY BROS.
27095 Park Rd.
Louisville, KY 40219
T: (800) 824-4777
F: (502) 969-1702
www.bentleybrothers.com

J.R. BURROWS & CO.
P.O. Box 522
Rockland, MA 02370
T: (800) 347-1795
F: (781) 982-1636
www.burrows.com
Also sells wallpaper

CARTER CANOPIES
370 Honeycutt Rd.
Troutman, NC 28116
T: (800) 538-4071
F: (704) 528-6437
www.cartercanopies.com

DECORATIVE HARDWARE
STUDIO
P.O. Box 627
Chappaqua, NY 10514
T: (914) 238-5251
F: (914) 230-4880
www.decorative-hardware.com

FAMILY HEIRLOOM
WEAVERS
125 O'San Lne.
Red Lion, PA 17356
T: (717) 246-5787
www.familyheirloomweavers
.com

SCALAMANDRE
37-24 24th St.
Long Island City, NY 11101
T: (718) 361-8500
F: (718) 361-8311
www.scalamandre.com
Also sells wallcoverings

F. SCHUMACHER & CO.
The D&D Building

979 Third Ave.
Suite 832
New York, NY 10022
T: (212) 415-3900
F: (212) 415-3907
www.fschumacher.com
Also sells wallpaper

CONSERVATORIES AND GAZEBOS

*Custom-built and ready-made
arbors, conservatories, gazebos,
greenhouses, pavilions, pergolas,
orangeries and sunrooms*

AMDEGA MACHIN
CONSERVATORIES
P.O. Box 909
Front Royal, VA 22630
T: (800) 887-5648
F: (540) 636-2870
www.amdega.com

GLASS HOUSE LLC
50 Swedetown Rd.
Pomfret Center, CT 06259
T: (800) 222-3065
F: (860) 974-1665
www.glasshouseusa.com

GLASS HOUSES LTD.
506 Henry St., Suite 2
Brooklyn, NY 11231
T/F: (718) 596-9449
www.glass-houses.com

OAK LEAF
CONSERVATORIES
876 Davis Dr.
Atlanta, GA 30327
T: (800) 360-6283
F: (404) 250-6283
www.oakleafconservatories
.co.uk

PRIVATE GARDEN
GREENHOUSE SYSTEMS
36 Commercial Dr.
Hampden, MA 01036
T: (800) 421-4527
F: (413) 566-8806
www.private-garden.com

RENAISSANCE
CONSERVATORIES
132 Ashmore Dr.
Leola, PA 17540
T: (800) 882-4657
F: (717) 661-7727
www.renaissance
conservatories.com

TANGLEWOOD
CONSERVATORIES
15 Engerman Ave.
Denton, MD 21629
T: (800) 229-2925
F: (410) 479-4797
www.tanglewoodliving.com

VIXEN HILL
P.O. Box 389
Elverson, PA 19520
T: (800) 423-2766
F: (610) 286-2099
www.vixenhill.com
Also manufactures shutters

FIREPLACES, STOVES AND RADIATORS

*Hearths; chimneypieces,
restorations and inspections;
wood, gas and coal stoves;
kitchen ranges, parlor stoves;
metal and wooden grilles*

BARNSTABLE STOVE
SHOP
P.O. Box 472
W. Barnstable, MA 02668
T: (508) 326-9913
www.barnstablestove.com

THE CHIMNEY POT
SHOPPE
1915 Brush Run Rd.
Avella, PA 15312
T: (724) 345-3601
F: (724) 345-8243
www.chimneypot.com

GOOD TIME STOVE CO.
P.O. Box 306
Goshen, MA 01032-0306
T: (413) 268-3677
F: (413) 268-9284
www.goodtimestove.com

HOMESTEAD CHIMNEY
P.O. Box 5182
Clinton, NJ 08809
T: (973) 984-7668
www.homesteadchimney
.com

LEHMAN'S
P.O. Box 41
Kidron, OH 44636
T: (877) 438-5346
F: (800) 780-4975
www.lehmans.com
*Also sells kitchen accessories,
lighting, water pumps, garden
and farm tools*

REGGIO REGISTER CO.
31 Jytek Rd.
Leominster, MA 01453
T: (800) 880-3090
www.reggioregister.com

VERMONT CASTINGS
Consumer Call Centre
410 Admiral Blvd.
Mississauga, ON
L5T 2N6
T: 1-800-668-5323
F: 1-877-565-2929
www.vermontcastings.com

WOODSTOCK
SOAPSTONE CO.
66 Airpark Rd.
W. Lebanon, NH 03784
T: (800) 866-4344
F: (603) 298-5958
www.woodstove.com

WORTHINGTON STOVE &
HEARTH
222 N. Main St.
St Charles, MO 63301
T: (314) 947-3165
F: (947) 947-1730
www.worthingtonstove.com

FLOOR, WALL AND CEILING FINISHES

*Wallpaper, silkscreen, wall fills,
murals, friezes, stenciling,
paint; painted, molded, ceramic,
embossed, encaustic, mosaic, flat
and plain tiles; decorative pressed-
metal ceiling and wall panels*

AMERICAN OLEAN TILE
CO.
5105 Campus Dr.
Plymouth Meeting, PA
19462
T: (215) 247-8988

AMERICAN
RESTORATION TILE
11416 Otter Creek S. Rd.
Mabelvale, AR 72103
T: (501) 455-1000
F: (501) 455-1004
www.restorationtile.com

BRADBURY & BRADBURY
WALLPAPERS
P.O. Box 155
Benicia, CA 94510
T: (707) 746-1900
F: (707) 745-9417
www.bradbury.com

CHELSEA DECORATIVE
METAL CO.
8212 Braewick Dr.
Houston, TX 77074
T: (713) 721-9200
F: (713) 776-8661
www.thetinman.com

CLASSIC CEILINGS
902 E. Commonwealth Ave.
Fullerton, CA 92831
T: (800) 992-8700
www.classicceilings.com

DESIGNS IN TILE
P.O. Box 358
Mount Shasta, CA 96067
T: (530) 926-2629
F: (530) 926-6467
www.designsintile.com

EPOCH DESIGNS
P.O. Box 4033
Elwyn, PA 19063
T: (610) 565-9180
www.epochdesigns.com

EVERGREENE PAINTING
STUDIOS, INC.
450 W. 31st St., 7th Fl.
New York, NY 10001-4608
T: (212) 244-2800
F: (212) 244-6204
www.evergreene.com

FIREBIRD
335 Snyder Ave.
Berkeley Heights, NJ 07922
T: (908) 464-4613
F: (908) 464-4615
www.firebirdtiles.com

JOHN CANNING & CO.,
LTD.
125 Commerce Ct. #5

Cheshire, CT 06410
T: (203) 272-9868
F: (203) 272-9879
www.canning-studios.com
*Also sells ornamental moldings
and architectural millwork*

LYNNE RUTTER MURALS
AND DECORATIVE
PAINTING
629 Wisconsin St.
San Francisco, CA 94107
T: (415) 282-8820
www.lynnerutter.com

M.J. MAY BUILDING
RESTORATION
141 W. State St.
Burlington, WI 53105
T: (262) 763-8822
F: (262) 763-1882
www.mjmayrestoration.com
*Also supplies an extensive
range of ornamental moldings
and architectural millwork*

STARBUCK GOLDNER TILE
315 W. Fourth St.
Bethlehem, PA 18015-1503
T: (610) 866-6321
F: (610) 866-7701
www.starbucktile.com

TERRA DESIGNS
214 E. Blackwell St. Rear
Dover, NJ 07801
T: (973) 328-1135
F: (973) 328-3624

TILE SOURCE, INC.
4 Indigo Run Dr. #4021
Hilton Head Island,
SC 29926
T: (843) 689-9151
F: (843) 689-9161
www.tile-source.com

VICTORIAN
COLLECTIBLES LTD
845 E. Glenbrook Rd.
Milwaukee, WI 53217
T: (800) 783-3829
F: (414) 352-7290
www.victorianwallpaper.com

GARDENS, FENCING AND EXTERIOR ACCESSORIES

*Benches, wrought-iron fencing and
gates, fountains, gazebos, lampposts,
finials, statues, urns, vases*

ARCHITECTURAL IRON
COMPANY, INC.
104 Ironwood Ct.
P.O. Box 126
Milford, PA 18337-0126
T: (800) 442-4766
F: (570) 296-4766
www.architecturaliron.com

CANTERA ESPECIAL
15332 Antioch St., #343
Pacific Palisades, CA 90272
T: (800) 564-8608
F: (818) 907-0343
www.cantera-especial.com

CASSIDY BROS. FORGE
Rte. 1
Rowley, MA 01969
T: (978) 948-7303
F: (978) 948-7629
www.cassidybros.com

COPPER-INC.COM
P.O. Box 244
Dickinson, TX 77539
T: (888) 499-1962
F: (888) 499-1963
www.copper-inc.com

CUSTOM HOME
ACCESSORIES, INC.
9245 Beatty Dr.
Sacramento, CA 95826
T: (800) 265-0041
F: (916) 362-0410
www.mailboxes.info

ENCHANTED FOREST
IMPORTS, INC.
P.O. Box 266
Land O' Lakes, WI 54540
T: (715) 547-8000
F: (715) 547-8001
www.enchantedforest
imports.com

FLORENTINE
CRAFTSMEN, INC.
46-24 28th St.
Long Island City, NY 11101
T: (800) 577-1188
F: (718) 937-9858
www.florentinecraftsmen
.com

GLADDING, MCBEAN
601 7th St.
Lincoln, CA 95648-1828
T: (916) 776-1133
F: (916) 645-1723
www.gladdingmcbean.com
*Also manufactures terra cotta
roofing and decorative paving tiles*

HADDONSTONE, LTD.
201 Heller Pl.
Bellmawr, NJ 08031
T: (856) 931-7011
F: (856) 931-0040
www.haddonstone.com

KENNETH LYNCH &
SONS, LTD.
P.O. Box 488
84 Danbury Rd.
Wilton, CT 06897
T: (203) 762-8363
F: (203) 762-2999
www.klynchandsons.com

ROBINSON IRON CORP.
1856 Robinson Rd.
Alexander City, AL 35010
T: (256) 329-8486
www.robinsoniron.com

GLASS

*Stained, etched, leaded, beveled,
engraved, wheel-cut and faceted
glass; doors, windows, skylights,
lamps, transoms, sidelights, panels,
vases, ornaments; restoration*

ANDERSON GLASS ARTS
548 Tremont St.
Boston, MA 02116
T: (617) 357-5166
F: (617) 350-6209
www.jimandersonstained
glass.com

ART GLASS UNLIMITED, INC.
412 N. Euclid Ave.
St. Louis, MO 63108
T: (314) 361-0474
www.artglassunlimited.com

FERGUSON'S CUT
GLASS WORKS
5890 E. Harbor Rd.
Marblehead, OH 43440
T: (419) 734-0800
www.fergusongallery.com

GOLDEN AGE
GLASSWORKS
338 Bellvale Lakes Rd.
Warwick, NY 10990
T: (579) 729-8687
www.goldenageglassworks.com

THE JUDSON STUDIOS
200 South Ave. 66
Los Angeles, CA 90042
T: (800) 445-8376
F: (323) 255-8529
www.judsonstudios.com

LIGHT IMPRESSIONS
GLASSCRAFTERS
P.O. Box 4562
Portland, ME 04112
T: (207) 883-9144
www.lightimpressionsglass
crafters.com

TOMAS TISCH
499 Van Brunt, #6B
Brooklyn, NY 11231
T/F: (718) 643-9028
www.antart.net

HARDWARE

*Brass, porcelain and iron
window latches, cupboard
and drawer pulls, hinges, feet,
casters, door knockers, handles
and stops, kick plates, locks,
escutcheons, rosettes, levers,
rails and railing parts; hooks
and dishes; clock hardware.*

18TH CENTURY
HARDWARE CO.
131 E. Third St.
Derry, PA 15627
T: (724) 694-2708
F: (724) 694-9587

AL BAR WILMETTE
PLATERS
127 Green Bay Rd.
Wilmette, IL 60091
T: (866) 823-8404
F: (847) 251-0281
www.albarwilmette.com

BALDWIN HARDWARE
CORP.
841 E. Wyomissing Blvd.

Reading, PA 19611
T: (800) 566-1986
F: (610) 796-4601
www.baldwinhardware.com

BALL & BALL
463 W. Lincoln Hwy.
Exton, PA 19341
T: (610) 363-7330
F: (610) 363-7639
www.ballandball-us.com
Also sells fireplace accessories

BONA DECORATIVE
HARDWARE
3073 Madison Rd.
Oakley, OH 45209
T: (513) 321-7877
F: (513) 321-7879
www.bonahardware.com

E. R. BUTLER & CO.
38 Charles St.
Boston, MA 02114
T: (617) 722-0230
F: (617) 722-0250
www.erbutler.com

GERBER HINGE CO.
21034 Osborne St.
Canoga Park, CA 91304
T: (800) 643-7237
F: (818) 717-5016
www.gerber-hinge.com

KAYNE & SON CUSTOM
HARDWARE, INC.
100 Daniel Ridge Rd.
Candler, NC 28778
T: (828) 667-8868
F: (828) 665-8303
www.customforgedhard
ware.com
Also sells fireplace accessories

KIRKPATRICK LTD.
155 Lynn Cove Lane
Mooresville, NC 28117
T: (704) 658-1016
F: (704) 998-3558
www.kirkpatrick.co.uk

G. KRUG & SON
415 W. Saratoga St.
Baltimore, MD 21201
T: (410) 752-3166
F: (410) 685-6091
www.gkrugandson.com

NOTTING HILL
DECORATIVE
HARDWARE
P.O. Box 1376
Kathryn, WI 53147
T: (262) 248-8890
F: (262) 248-7876
www.nottinghill-usa.com

OLD & ELEGANT
DISTRIBUTING
10203 Main St. Lane
Bellevue, WA 98004
T: (425) 455-4660
F: (425) 455-0203
www.oldandelegant.com

OMNIA INDUSTRIES
5 Cliffside Dr.

P.O. Box 330
Cedar Grove, NJ 07009
T: (937) 239-7272
F: (937) 239-5960
www.omniaindustries.com

PATTEN DESIGN
15561 Product Lane, #D-5
Huntington Beach, CA
92649
T: (714) 894-0131
F: (714) 894-0031
www.pattendesign.com

P. E. GUERIN, INC.
23 Jane St.
New York, NY 10014
T: (212) 243-5270
F: (212) 727-2290
www.peguerin.com

WILLIAMSBURG
BLACKSMITHS
26 Williams St.
Williamsburg, MA 01096
T: (800) 248-1776
F: (413) 268-9317
www.williamsburgblack
smith.com

JOINERY

*Wooden screens and doors, panels,
windows, blinds and shutters,
custom-built cabinets, tables,
chairs, mantels, shelves and feet*

ALEXANDRIA WOOD
JOINERY
Plumer Hill Rd.
Alexandria, NH 03222
T: (603) 744-8243

BEECH RIVER MILL
30 Rte. 16B
Centre Ossipee, NH 03814
T: (603) 539-2636
F: (603) 539-1384
www.beechrivermill.com

BERGERSON CEDAR
WINDOWS, INC.
P.O. Box 184
Hammond, OR 97121
T: (800) 240-4365
F: (503) 861-0316
www.bergersonwindow.com

COPPA WOODWORKING
1231 Paraiso Ave.
San Pedro, CA 90731
T: (310) 548-4142
F: (310) 548-6740
www.coppawoodworking
.com

DISTRESSEDCABINET.COM
P.O. Box 33
Dickinson, TX 77539
T: (888) 849-1252
F: (888) 849-1253
www.distressedcabinet.com

DRUMS SASH & DOOR CO.
392 W. Butler Dr.
Drums, PA 18222
T: (570) 788-1145
F: (570) 788-3007

HISTORIC DOORS
P.O. Box 139
Kempton, PA 19529
T: (610) 756-6187
F: (610) 756-6171
www.historicdoors.com

MARION H. CAMPBELL,
CABINETMAKER
39 Wall St.
Bethlehem, PA 18018-6012
T: (610) 837-6604
F: (610) 837-7775
*Also manufactures moldings
and architectural millwork*

MAURER & SHEPHERD,
JOYNERS
122 Naubuc Ave.
Glastonbury, CT 06033
T: (860) 633-2383
Also produces custom millwork

PINECREST, INC.
2118 Blaisdell Ave.
Minneapolis,
MN 55404-2490
T: (612) 871-7071
F: (612) 871-8956
www.pinecrestinc.com
*Also manufactures stamped
metal wall and ceiling panels*

THE SHUTTER DEPOT
437 LaGrange St.
Greenville, GA 30222
T: (706) 672-1214
F: (706) 672-1122
www.shutterdepot.com

STARKE MILLWORK INC.
671 Bangor Rd.
Nazareth, PA 18064
T: (610) 759-1753
F: (610) 746-4708
www.starkemillwork.com
Also manufactures moldings

WOOD WINDOW
WORKSHOP
839 Broad St.
Utica, NY 113501
T: (800) 724-3081
F: (315) 733-0933
www.woodwindowworkshop.com

KITCHENS AND
BATHROOMS

*Ceramic and cast-iron sinks and
basins; footed, slipper, bateau
and Saracen bathtubs; showers,
toilets, plumbing, bathroom
hardware and accessories*

A-BALL PLUMBING
SUPPLY
1703 W. Burnside St.
Portland, OR 97209
T: (800) 228-0134
F: (503) 228-0030
www.a-ball.com

BATHROOM
MACHINERIES
495 Main St.
Murphys, CA 95247
T: (800) 255-4426

F: (209) 728-2320
www.deabath.com

CLAWFOOT SUPPLY
2700 Crescent Springs Pike
Erlanger, KY 41017
T: (877) 682-4192
www.clawfootsupply.com

GEORGE TAYLOR
SPECIALTIES
76 Franklin St.
New York, NY 10013-3444
T: (212) 226-5369
F: (212) 274-9487
Also rebuilds antique plumbing

MAC THE ANTIQUE
PLUMBER
6325 Elvas Ave.
Sacramento, CA 95819
T: (800) 916-2284
F: (916) 454-4150
www.antiqueplumber.com

THE SINK FACTORY
2140 San Pablo Ave.
Berkeley, CA 94702
T: (510) 540-8193
F: (510) 540-8212
www.sinkfactory.com

SUNRISE SPECIALTY
930-98th Ave.
Oakland, CA 94603-2306
T: (800) 444-4280
F: (510) 729-7270
www.sunrisespecialty.com

LIGHT FITTINGS

*Chandeliers, crystal parts and
trimmings, wall sconces,
ceiling fans, oil lamps and
lanterns, pendant fixtures,
shades and finials,
candleholders*

BEVOLO GAS &
ELECTRIC LIGHTS
521 Conti St.
New Orleans, LA 70130
T: (504) 522-9485
F: (504) 522-5563
www.bevolo.com

BRASS LIGHT
GALLERY, INC.
131 S. First Street
Milwaukee, WI 53204
T: (800) 243-9595
F: (800) 505-9404
www.brasslight.com

JEFFERSON ART
LIGHTING, INC.
10640 W. Ellsworth Rd.
Ann Arbor, MI 48103
T: (734) 428-7260
www.jeffersonartlighting.com
*Also supplies ornamental
moldings*

SPECTRUM HOME
FURNISHINGS, INC.
P.O. Box 306
Staten Island, NY 10312
T: (800) 616-7576

www.spectrumhome3.com
Also sells rugs and furniture

ST. LOUIS ANTIQUE
LIGHTING CO.
801 North Skinker Blvd.
St. Louis, MO 63130
T: (314) 863-1414
F: (314) 863-6702

STEVEN HANDELMAN
STUDIOS
716 N. Milpas St.
Santa Barbara, CA 93103
T: (805) 962-5119
F: (805) 966-9529
www.stevenhandelman
studios.com
*Also sells fireplace grilles and
accessories*

STUDIO STEEL
159 New Milford Tpke.
New Preston, CT 06777
T: (860) 868-7305
F: (860) 868-7306
www.studiosteel.com

THOMAS LIGHTING
10350 Ormsby Park Pl.
Suite 601
Louisville, KY 40223
T: (502) 420-9600
www.thomaslighting.com

VICTORIAN LIGHTING
WORKS, INC.
251 S. Pennsylvania Ave.
Centre Hall, PA 16828
T: (814) 364-9577
www.vlworks.com

WILLIAM SPENCER, INC.
118 Creek Rd.
Mt. Laurel, NJ 08054-2084
T: (856) 235-1830
www.williamspencerinc.com
Also sells furniture

METAL STAIRCASES

*For wooden staircases, see
Architectural Millwork*

DEANGELIS IRON
WORK, INC.
P.O. Box 350
305 Depot St.
South Easton, MA 02375
T: (800) 676-4766
F: (508) 238-7757
www.deangelisiron.com
*Also manufactures fencing
and gates*

FINE ARCHITECTURAL
METALSMITHS
P.O. Box 30
Chester, NY 10918
T: (845) 651-7550
F: (845) 651-7857
www.iceforge.com
*Also manufactures fencing
and gates*

STEWART IRON WORKS
CO.
P.O. Box 2612

Covington, KY 41012-2612
T: (606) 431-1985
F: (606) 431-2035
www.stewartironworks.com

**ORNAMENTAL
MOLDINGS**

*Plaster, metal, stone and wood
sculpting, casting, capitals,
corbels, medallions, domes
and niches*

ARCHICAST
2527 Broad Ave.
Memphis, TN 38112
T/F: (901) 323-8717
www.archicast.com

CAS DESIGN CENTER
12201 Currency Ct.
Forney, TX 75126
T: (800) 662-1221
F: (972) 552-9054
www.casdesign.com

CUMBERLAND
WOODCRAFT CO., INC.
P.O. Drawer 609
Carlisle, PA 17013-0609
T: (800) 367-1884
F: (717) 243-6502
www.cumberlandwoodcraft
.com
*Also manufactures
architectural millwork and
period wallpaper*

DECORATORS SUPPLY
CORP.
3610-12 S. Morgan St.
Chicago, IL 60609
T: (773) 847-6300
F: (773) 847-6357
www.decoratorssupply.com

DRIWOOD MOULDING CO.
P.O. Box 1729
Florence, SC 29503
T: (843) 669-2478
F: (843) 669-4874
www.driwood.com
*Also manufacture millwork
and joinery*

FELBER ORNAMENTAL
& PLASTERING CORP.
P.O. Box 57
1000 W. Washington St.
Norristown, PA 19404
T: (800) 392-6896
F: (610) 275-6636
www.felber.net

FRANK J. MANGIONE, INC.
21 John St.
Saugerties, NY 12477
T/F: (845) 247-9248

DIMITRIOS KLITSAS
378 North Rd.
Hampden, MA 01036
T: (413) 566-5301
F: (413) 566-5307
www.klitsas.com

W.F. NORMAN CORP.
P.O. Box 323, 214 N. Cedar

Nevada, MO 64772
T: (800) 641-4038
F: (417) 667-2708
www.wfnorman.com
*Also manufactures stamped
metal roofing and ceiling panels*

J.P. WEAVER CO.
941 Air Way
Glendale, CA 91201
T: (818) 500-1740
F: (818) 500-1798
www.jpweaver.com

WHITE RIVER
HARDWOODS
1197 Happy Hollow Rd.
Fayetteville, AR 72701
T: (800) 558-0119
www.mouldings.com

WORLD OF MOULDING
3041 S. Main St.
Santa Ana, CA 92707
T: (800) 336-5011
www.womoc.com

ROOFING

*Shingles, slates, tiles and
ornaments; restoration*

BOSTON VALLEY TERRA
COTTA
6860 South Abbott Rd.
Orchard Park, NY 14127
T: (716) 649-7490
F: (716) 649-7688
www.bostonvalley.com

THE CEDAR GUILD
51579 Gates Bridge E.
Gates, OR 97346-9611
T: (503) 897-2541
www.cedar-guild.com

THE NEW ENGLAND
SLATE CO.
1385 Rte. 7
Pittsford, VT 05763
T: (888) NE-SLATE
F: (802) 247-0089
www.neslate.com

ORNAMETALS, LLC
1812 Grant St. S.E.
Decatur, AL 35601
T: (256) 350-7410
F: (256) 309-5921
www.ornametals.com

PENN BIG BED SLATE CO.
P.O. Box 184,
8450 Brown St.
Slatington, PA 18080
T: (610) 767-4601
F: (610) 767-9525
www.pennbigbedslate.com
*Also supplies slate for
fireplaces, floors, etc.*

SHAKERTOWN
P.O. Box 400
1200 Kerron St.
Winlock, WA 98596
T: (800) 426-8970
F: (360) 785-3076
www.shakertown.com

**STRUCTURAL
DISMANTLING,
REMODELING AND
RESTORATION**

*Alteration services, floor
plans, historical exterior plans,
moving, repairs*

AUTHENTIC HISTORICAL
DESIGNS LLC
3908 N. State St.
Jackson, MS 39206
T: (800) 426-5628
F: (601) 981-8185
www.historicaldesigns.com

CHESTNUT OAK CO.
3810 Old Mountain Rd.
West Suffield, CT 06093-2125
T: (860) 668-0382
www.chestnutoakcompany
.com

EARLY NEW ENGLAND
RESTORATIONS
32 Taugwonk Rd.,
Unit A12
Stonington, CT 06359
T: (860) 599-4393
F: (860) 535-1628
www.werestoreoldhomes
.com
Also sells salvage

LEEDS CLARK
300 N. Third St.
Midlothian, TX 76065
T: (972) 775-3843
F: (972) 723-8856
www.leedsclark.com

WOODEN FLOORING

CRAFTSMAN LUMBER
CO.
P.O. Box 222
436 Main St.
Groton, MA 01450
T: (978) 448-5621
F: (978) 448-2754
www.craftsmanlumber.com

LIVING ELEMENTS, L.P.
2046 County Rd. 115
Burnet, TX 78611
T: (512) 756-0702
F: (512) 756-0154
www.livingelements.com
*Also produces kitchen
countertops*

MOUNTAIN LUMBER
CO. INC.
6812 Spring Hill Rd.
Ruckersville, VA 22968-
3641
T: (800) 445-2671
F: (434) 985-4105
www.mountainlumber.com

RELIANCE SPECIALTY
BUILDING PRODUCTS
P.O. Box 28163
Spokane, WA 99228
T: (800) 697-4705
F: (509) 466-9300
www.reliancesbp.com

MUSEUMS AND ASSOCIATIONS

THE 1890 HOUSE
MUSEUM
37 Tompkins St.
Cortland, NY 13045
T/F: (607) 756-7551
www.1890house.org

ARTIST-BLACKSMITHS
ASSOCIATION OF
NORTH AMERICA
P.O. Box 3425
Knoxville, TN
37927-3425
T: (865) 546-7733
F: (865) 215-9964
www.abana.org

ARTISTIC LICENSE
P.O. Box 881841
San Francisco, CA 94188
T: (510) 534-7632
www.artisticlicense.org

BILTMORE ESTATE
1 Approach Rd.
Asheville, NC 28803
T: (800) 624-1575
www.biltmore.com

CAMPBELL HOUSE
1508 Locust St.
St. Louis, MO 63103
T: (314) 421-0325
www.campbellhouse
museum.org

CAMRON-STANFORD
HOUSE
1418 Lakeside Dr.
Oakland, CA 94612
T: (510) 444-1876
www.cshouse.org

CENTER FOR
TAPESTRY ARTS
167 Spring St.
New York, NY 10012
T: (212) 431-7500

CHATEAU-SUR-MER
424 Bellevue Ave.
Newport, RI 02840
T: (401) 847-1000
www.newportmansions.org

CLAYTON HOUSE
514 N. Sixth St.
Fort Smith, AR 72901
T: (479) 783-3000
www.fortsmith.org

CRAMER-KENYON
HERITAGE HOUSE
509 Pine St.
Yankton, SD 57078
T: (605) 665-7470
www.vpa.org/
museumssd.html

EBENEZER MAXWELL
MANSION
200 W. Tulpehocken St.
Philadelphia, PA 19144
T: (215) 438-1861
www.philadelphia.city
search.com/profile/
8987687

ECKHART HOUSE
810 Main St.
Wheeling, WV 26003
T: (888) 700-0118
www.eckharthouse.com

EMLEN PHYSICK ESTATE
Mid-Atlantic Centre
for Arts
P.O. Box
1048 Washington St.
Cape May, NJ 08204
T: (609) 884-5404
F: (609) 884-2006
www.capemaymac.org

FREDERICK DOUGLASS
HOME
1411 W. St. S.E.
Washington, DC 20020
T: (202) 426-5961
www.nps.gov/frdo

THE GLASS ART
SOCIETY
3131 Western Ave.,
Ste. 414
Seattle, WA 98121
T: (206) 382-1305
F: (206) 382-2630
www.glassart.org

GLESSNER HOUSE
1800 S. Prairie Ave.
Chicago, IL 60616
T: (312) 326-1480
F: (312) 326-1397
www.glessnerhouse.org

HANDWEAVERS GUILD
OF AMERICA, INC.
1255 Buford Hwy., Ste. 211
Suwanee, GA 30024
T: (678) 730-0010
F: (678) 730-0836
www.weavespindye.org

HARRIET BEECHER
STOWE HOUSE
77 Forest St.
Hartford, CT 06105
T: (860) 522-9258
F: (860) 522-9259
www.harrietbeecherstowe
center.org

HENRY MORRISON
FLAGLER MUSEUM
P.O. Box 969

1 Whitehall Way
Palm Beach, FL 33480
T: (561) 655-2833
F: (561) 655-2826
www.flaglermuseum.us

HIGH MUSEUM
OF ART
1280 Peachtree St. N.E.
Atlanta, GA 30309
T: (404) 733-4400
F: (404) 733-4502
www.high.org

HISTORIC ADAMS
HOUSE
22 Van Buren St.
Deadwood, SD 57732
T: (605) 578-3724
www.adamsmuseum
andhouse.org

HUDSON RIVER
MUSEUM
511 Warburton Ave.
Yonkers, NY 10701
T: (914) 963-4550
F: (914) 963-8558
www.hrm.org

HUNTER HOUSE
VICTORIAN
MUSEUM
240 W. Freemason St.
Norfolk, VA 23510
T: (757) 623-9814
www.hunterhousemuseum
.org

JAMES WHITCOMB
RILEY HOUSE
528 Lockerbie St.
Indianapolis, IN 46202
T: (317) 631-5885
james-whitcomb-riley-
house.visit-
indianapolis.com

LAWNFIELD
8095 Mentor Ave.
Mentor, OH 44060
T: (440) 255-8722
F: (440) 255-8545
www.wrhs.org/lawnfield

THE MARK TWAIN
HOUSE
351 Farmington Ave.
Hartford, CT 06105
T: (860) 247-0998
www.marktwainhouse.org

STRONG NATIONAL
MUSEUM OF PLAY
1 Manhattan Sq.
Rochester, NY 14607
T: (716) 263-2700
www.strongmuseum.org

NATIONAL ORNAMENTAL
& MISCELLANEOUS
METALS ASSOCIATION
1535 Pennsylvania Ave.
McDonough, GA 30253
T: (888) 516-8585
F: (770) 288-2006
www.nomma.org

NATIONAL PARK
SERVICE
HEADQUARTERS
1849 C Street N.W.
Washington, DC 20240
T: (202) 208-6843
www.nps.gov

THE NATIONAL TRUST
FOR HISTORIC
PRESERVATION
1785 Massachusetts
Ave. N.W.
Washington D.C. 20036
T: (020) 588-6000
F: (020) 588-6038
www.nationaltrust.org

NEWARK MUSEUM
49 Washington St.
Newark, NJ 07102-3176
T: (973) 596-6550
www.newarkmuseum.org

OLANA
P.O. Box 199
Hudson, NY 12534
T: (518) 828-1872
F: (518) 828-1793
www.olana.org

OLD-HOUSE JOURNAL
1000 Potomac St. N.W.
Suite 102
Washington, DC 20007
T: (202) 339-0744
www.oldhousejournal.com

PABST MANSION
2000 W. Wisconsin Ave.
Milwaukee, WI 53233
T: (414) 931-0808
F: (414) 931-1005
www.pabstmansion.com

PARK-MCCULLOUGH
HOUSE
P.O. Box 338
1 Park St.
N. Bennington, VT 05257
T: (802) 442-5441
www.parkmccullough.org

THE RENGSTORFF
HOUSE
3070 N. Shoreline Blvd.
Mountain View, CA 94043
T: (650) 903-6392
www.r-house.org

SHADOWS-ON-THE-TECHE
317 E. Main St.
New Iberia, LA 70560
T: (337) 369-6446
www.shadowsontheteche.org

SHAKER VILLAGE
3501 Lexington Rd.
Harrodsburg, KY 40330
T: (800) 734-5611
www.shakervillageky.org

THE SOCIETY
OF ARTS AND
CRAFTS
175 Newbury St.
Boston, MA 02116
T: (617) 266-1810
F: (617) 266-5654
www.societyofcrafts.org

SONNENBERG
GARDENS AND
MANSION
151 Charlotte St.
Canandaigua, NY 14424
T: (585) 394-4922
F: (585) 394-2192
www.sonnenberg.org

THE VICTORIA
MANSION
109 Danforth St.
Portland, ME 04101
T: (207) 772-4841

THE VICTORIAN
SOCIETY IN AMERICA
205 S. Camac St.
Philadelphia, PA 19107
T: (215) 545-8340
F: (215) 545-8379
www.victoriansociety.org

VILLA MONTEZUMA
MUSEUM
1925 K St.
(20th and K St.)
San Diego, CA 92012
T: (619) 239-2211
www.sandiegohistory.org

THE WADSWORTH
ATHENEUM
600 Main St.
Hartford, CT 06103
T: (860) 278-2670
F: (860) 527-0803
www.wadsworthatheneum
.org

WOODWORKING
ASSOCIATION OF
NORTH AMERICA
P.O. Box 478
Depot Rd.
Tamworth, NH 03886
T/F: (603) 323-7500

PICTURE CREDITS

Sources for the photographs and illustrations in this book are listed from the top of the left-hand column to the bottom of the right-hand column on each double page.

Many of the photographs were specially commissioned. They were shot on location by Ken Kirkwood, Robin McCartney, Derry Moore, James Mortimer, George Ong and Peter Woloszynski.

For reasons of space the names of the above photographers have been shortened to initials, as follows:
KK = Ken Kirkwood
RMcC = Robin McCartney
DM = Derry Moore
JM = James Mortimer
GO = George Ong and
PW = Peter Woloszynski.

Front Cover/Back Cover - JM. Back Flap - JM. Endpapers - Sheldrake Press, courtesy of The House Of Commons. 1/5 - JM. 6/7 - RMcC. 8/13 - All by JM. 14/15 - Christopher Wood Gallery, London & The Bridgeman Art Library. 16/17 - Jon Bouchier; Alain Le Garsmeur/Impact Photos; RMcC; Hulton-Deutsch Collection; Edifice/Lewis.18/19 - Ray Joyce/Weldon Trannies; Campbell Smith & Co. 20/21 - Vernon Gibberd; Architectural Association/Cannon Parsons; George Wright; Alain Le Garsmeur/Impact Photos; Mayotte Magnus. 22/23 - Andrew Lawson; Angelo Hornak; Timothy Woodcock Photolibrary; Mayotte Magnus; Charles McKean. 24/25 - Architectural Association/Valerie Bennett; Ray Joyce/Weldon Trannies; Andrew Lawson; John Bethell; Osborne House/Bridgeman Art Library; Timothy Woodcock. 26/27 - KK; KK. 28/29 - Robert Estall Photo Library; Sheldrake Press; Sheldrake Press. 30/33 - All artwork by Ann Winterbotham. 34/35 - Architectural Association/Colin Penn; The Design Archive, Arthur Sanderson & Sons Ltd; Mary Evans Picture Library; West Surrey College Of Art & Design; Watts & Co; Woodmansterne Picture Library. 36/37 - Mary Evans Picture Library; Geoff Morgan; Studio Magazine; Architectural Association/Barry Capper. 38/39 - S.& O. Mathews Photography; Topham; Topham; Aldus Archives; Topham. 40/41 - Topham; Richard Bryant/Arcaid; Woodmansterne Picture Library; National Trust; Edifice/Darley. 42/43 - Robin Guild. 44/45 - Ray Joyce/Weldon Trannies; Andrew Lawson; S.& O. Mathews Photography. 46/47 - Jane Lewis/Robert Estall Photo Library; Edifice/Lewis; Michael Boys Syndication; Andrew Lawson. 48/53 - cut-away house drawings by Nigel Husband RIBA. 54/55 - Jon Bouchier. 56/57 - Angelo Hornak; Ray Joyce/Weldon Trannies; Jerry Harpur; The Garden Picture Library/G.Rogers; The Garden Picture Library/R.Sutherland. 58/59 - Robert Estall Photo Library; Jerry Harpur; Andrew Lawson; RMcC; Andrew Lawson; Robert Estall Photo Library; Robert Estall Photo Library; Robert Estall Photo Library. 60/61 - Edifice/Lewis; Edifice/Darley; Ray Joyce/Weldon Trannies. 62/63 - Jon Bouchier; Edifice/Lewis; Edifice/Lewis; Edifice/Lewis; George Wright; S.& O. Mathews Photography; Ann Kelly/Elizabeth Whiting Agency. 64/65 - Andrew Lawson; Ray Joyce/Weldon Trannies; Jon Bouchier; Edifice/Darley; Robert Estall Photo Library; Edifice/Darley; Jessica Strang; Edifice/Lewis. 66/67 - Robert Estall Photo Library; Robert Estall Photo Library; Andrew Lawson; Robert Estall Photo Library; Andrew Lawson. 68/69 - Robert Estall Photo Library; Peter Aaron/Esto; Robert Estall Photo Library; Robert Estall Photo Library; Ray Joyce/Weldon Trannies; Ray Joyce/Weldon Trannies; Andrew Lawson; Robert Estall Photo Library. 70/71 - Nigel Husband RIBA and Stephen Carpenter RIBA. 72/73 - Robert Estall Photo Library; Robert Estall Photo Library; Robert Estall Photo Library. 74/75 - Andrew Lawson; Edifice/Lewis; Richard Bryant/Arcaid; Edifice/ Lewis; Robert Estall Photo Library. 76/77 - Edifice/Lewis; Edifice/Lewis; Jon Bouchier; Timothy Woodcock Photolibrary. 78/79 - Lucinda Lambton/Arcaid; Robert Estall Photo Library; Edifice/Lewis; Robert Estall Photo Library; S.& O. Mathews Photography; George Wright; Robert Estall Photo Library; Robert Estall Photo Library; Sonia Halliday Photographs/Else Tricket; Robert Estall Photo Library. 80/81 - Nigel Husband RIBA and Stephen Carpenter RIBA. 82/83 - Gary Pownall. 84/85 - Dornsite Collection of The Victorian Society in America at the Athenaeum of Philadelphia; The Athenaeum of Philadelphia Collection; The Athenaeum of Philadelphia Collection. 86/87 - Edifice/Lewis; Michael Boys Syndication; Gary Pownall; Edifice/Lewis. 88/89 - Michael Boys Syndication; Edifice/ Lewis; Edifice/Lewis; Spike Powell/Elizabeth Whiting Agency; Robert Estall Photo Library; Robert Estall Photo Library; Robert Estall Photo Library; Robert Estall Photo Library. 90/91 - Ray Joyce/Weldon Trannies; Andrew Lawson. 92/93 - Nigel Husband RIBA and Stephen Carpenter RIBA; Edifice/Lewis; Linda Burgess/Insight Picture Library; Robert Estall Photo Library; Edifice Lewis; Andrew Lawson. 94/95 - Ray Joyce/Weldon Trannies. 96/97 - Robert Estall Photo Library; S.& O. Mathews Photography; Andrew Lawson. 98/99 - Robert Estall Photo Library; Robert Estall Photo Library; Linda Burgess/Insight Picture Library; Lucinda Lambton/Arcaid; Robert Estall Photo Library; Jon Bouchier; KK. 100/101 - Nigel Husband RIBA and Stephen Carpenter RIBA 102/103 -Lucinda Lambton/Arcaid. 104/105 -Woodmansterne Picture Library; Christine Hanscomb; Richard Bryant/Arcaid. 106/107 - The Royal Incorporation of Architects in Scotland. 114/115 - Lucinda Lambton/Arcaid; Peter Aaron/Esto. 116/117 - Ray Joyce/Weldon Trannies; RMcC; RMcC. 118/119 - KK; Architectural Association/Ethel Hurwicz; KK; Michael Boys Syndication. 120/121 - DM; PW. 122/123 - Nigel Husband RIBA and Stephen Carpenter RIBA. 124/125 - RMcC; Lucinda Lambton/Arcaid. 126/127 - Ianthe Ruthven; KK; RMcC; KK; RMcC. 128/129 - Nigel Husband RIBA and Stephen Carpenter RIBA. 130/131 - Richard Bryant/Arcaid. 132/133 - KK. 134/135 - The National Trust; Woodmansterne Picture Library; KK. 136/137 - Nigel Husband RIBA and Stephen Carpenter RIBA. 138/139 - DM; Michael Dunne/Elizabeth Whiting Agency. 140/141 - DM; PW; Rodney Hyett/Elizabeth Whiting Agency. 142/143 - DM; PW. 144/145 - Nigel Husband RIBA and Stephen Carpenter RIBA. 146/147 - Christine Hanscomb; Ken Kirkwood; Christine Hanscomb. 148/149 - Townsends, London; Richard Bryant/Arcaid. 150/151 - RMcC; RMcC; DM; Jessica Strang; Woodmansterne Picture Library, Mary Evans Picture Library. 152/153 - Nigel Husband RIBA and Stephen Carpenter RIBA. 154/155 - DM. 156/157 - Christine Hanscomb; Robert Estall Photo Library; Robert Estall Photo Library; Robert Estall Photo Library; Robert Estall Photo Library; Robert Estall Photo Library; Robert Estall Photo Library; Robert Estall Photo Library; Robert Estall Photo Library; Robert Estall Photo Library; Robert Estall Photo Library; Robert Estall Photo Library. 158/159 - Victoria & Albert Museum, London & The Bridgeman Art Library London; Aldus Archives; Ceramic Tile Design, London; Fine Art Society Catalogue and The Bridgeman Art Library; Woodmansterne Picture Library; E.T. Archive; private collection, The Bridgeman Art Library; Mary Evans Picture Library. 160/161 - RMcC. 162/163 - Charles Parsons, courtesy Susie Bower, Glasscapes; Ray Joyce/Weldon Trannies; Ray Joyce/Weldon Trannies; C.M.Swash; Ray Joyce/Weldon Trannies; Sonia Halliday Photographs; Pamla Toler/Impact Photos; Woodmansterne Picture Library. 164/165 - Sonia Halliday Photographs; Robin McCartney. 166/167 - KK; GO. 168/169 - KK; The Design Council; by courtesy of the board of Trustees of The Victorian & Albert Museum, London; National Trust/ J.Gibson; The Design Council; Christopher Wray's Lighting Emporium, London; Christopher Wray's Lighting Emporium, London; The End Of The Day Lighting Company; Christopher Wray's Lighting Emporium, London; Christopher Wray's Lighting Emporium, London; Christopher Wray's Lighting Emporium, London. 170/171 - Nigel Husband RIBA and Stephen Carpenter RIBA. 172/173 - KK; Ray Joyce/Weldon Trannies; Ray Joyce/Weldon Trannies; Lucinda Lambton/Arcaid. 174/175 - Nigel Husband RIBA and Stephen Carpenter RIBA. 176/177 - Harrogate Art Gallery/Robert Harding Picture Library; Aldus Archives. 178/179 - George Wright. 180/181 - All artwork by Ann Winterbotham. 182/183 - GO; Christine Hanscomb; JM; Christine Hanscomb. 184/185 - All by KK. 186/187 - all courtesy of Leonard Pardon, Principal of the Pardon Schools, London and New York. 188/189 - private collection, Bridgeman Art Library; by courtesy of the board of Trustees of The Victoria & Albert Museum, London; The Victoria & Albert Museum, London, and The Bridgeman Art Library. 190/191 - The Design Archive, Arthur Sanderson & Sons Ltd; Sheldrake Press, courtesy of The House of Commons; Sheldrake Press, courtesy of The House of Commons; Sheldrake Press, courtesy of The House of Commons; Sheldrake Press, courtesy of The House of Commons; The Design Archive, Arthur Sanderson & Sons Ltd; Watts & Co; E.T. Archive; Watts & Co; The Victoria & Albert Museum, London, and The Bridgeman Art Library; The Design Archive, Arthur Sanderson & Sons Ltd; Watts & Co; RD 125 Anaglypta Original. 192/193 - The Victoria & Albert Museum, London and The Bridgeman Art Library; by courtesy of the board of Trustees of The Victoria & Albert Museum; William Morris Gallery, London and The Bridgeman Art Library; Lenoble by Charles Hammond; Palmyra by Charles Hammond; Osborne and Little Botanica Collection; The Victoria & Albert Museum and The Bridgeman Art Library; Osborne and Little Botanica Collection. 194/195 - E.T. Archive; Victoria & Albert Museum, London and the Bridgeman Art Library. 196/197 - private collection, The Bridgeman Art Library; National Trust/L & M Gayton. 198/199 - GO. 200/201 - JM; Mary Evans Picture Library; KK; KK. 202/203 - Nigel Husband RIBA and Stephen Carpenter RIBA. 204/205 - JM; all the others courtesy of Bernard Thorp, (Paris, London), Custom Weaving and Printing. 206/207 - Nigel Husband RIBA and Stephen Carpenter RIBA. 208/209 - GO. 210/211 - Spike Powell/Elizabeth Whiting Agency; JM; KK. 212/213 - KK; Jon Bouchier/Elizabeth Whiting Agency. 214/215 - JM; JM. 216/217 - GO; PW; KK. 218/219 - Lucinda Lambton/Arcaid; KK. 220/221 - Michael Boys Syndication; GO. 222/223 - Lucinda Lambton/Arcaid; Smithsonian Institution (National Museum of History and Technology), Washington; The Design Council. 224/225 - JM; JM; Woodmansterne Picture Library. 226/227 - National Trust/J.Bethell. 228/229 - Michael Nicholson/Elizabeth Whiting Agency; Michael Boys Syndication; National Trust. 230/231 - National Trust; PW. 232/233 - Spike Powell/Elizabeth Whiting Agency; JM. 234/235 - Ianthe Ruthven; Automobile Association Photo Library; DM; KK. 236/237 - Ianthe Ruthven; Smallbone; PW; JM. 238/239 - Michael Nicholson/Elizabeth Whiting Agency; KK; GO; KK; Smallbone. 240/241 - Rodney Hyett/Elizabeth Whiting Agency; Sheldrake Press; PW; Tim Street-Porter/Elizabeth Whiting Agency. 242/243 - KK; Pipe Dreams. 244/245 - Rodney Hyett/Elizabeth Whiting Agency; Michael Boys Syndication; Michael Dunne/Elizabeth Whiting Agency; GO; B.C. Sanitan; Traditional Bathroom Warehouses, London. 246/247 - KK; PW; PW; Michael Boys Syndication; KK. 248/249 - Rodney Hyett/Elizabeth Whiting Agency; Michael Boys Syndication. 250/251 - Michael Nicholson/Elizabeth Whiting Agency; Peter Aaron/Esto; Traditional Bathroom Warehouses, London; Nigel Husband RIBA and Stephen Carpenter RIBA; KK. 252/253 - DM. 254/255 - Mary Evans Picture Library; DM. 256/257 - KK. 258/259 - Woodmansterne Picture Library; DM; PW. 260/261 - JM; Richard Bryant/Arcaid; Michael Boys Syndication; KK. 262/263 - DM; DM. 264/265 - JM. 266/267 - Nigel Husband RIBA and Stephen Carpenter RIBA. 268/269 - Jerry Harpur. 270/271 - Ray Joyce/Weldon Trannies; Lucinda Lambton/Arcaid; Photograph Courtesy of Fine Art Photographic Library. 272/273 - Neil Holmes; Neil Holmes; Jerry Harpur; KK. 274/275 - Paul Miles; The Garden Picture Library/G.Bouchet; Linda Burgess/Insight Picture Library; The Garden Picture Library/B.Carter. 276/277 - Jerry Harpur; George Wright; Andrew Lawson; Pamla Toler/Impact Photos. 278/279 - KK; Town & Country Conservatories. 280/281 - Linda Burgess/Insight Picture Library; George Wright; Ray Joyce/Weldon Trannies. 282/283 - Linda Burgess/Insight Picture Library; George Wright; Lucinda Lambton/Arcaid. 284/285 - George Wright; Jerry Harpur; Jerry Harpur; National Trust/P.Lacey; Linda Burgess/Insight Picture Library; Edifice/Lewis. 286/287 - George Wright; Eric Crichton Photos; Linda Burgess/Insight Picture Library; S.& O. Mathews Photography; Eric Crichton Photos; Linda Burgess/Insidght Picture Library; Linda Burgess/Insight Picture Library; Eric Crichton Photos; Linda Burgess/Insight Picture Library; Linda Burgess/Insight Picture Library. 290/307 - All artwork by Sime/Baillie Lane/Architecture Environment

Ann Winterbotham. 182/183 - GO; Christine Hanscomb; JM; Christine Hanscomb. 184/185 - All by KK. 186/187 - all courtesy of Leonard Pardon, Principal of the Pardon Schools, London and New York. 188/189 - private collection, Bridgeman Art Library; by courtesy of the board of Trustees of The Victoria & Albert Museum, London; The Victoria & Albert Museum, London, and The Bridgeman Art Library. 190/191 - The Design Archive, Arthur Sanderson & Sons Ltd; Sheldrake Press, courtesy of The House of Commons; Sheldrake Press, courtesy of The House of Commons; Sheldrake Press, courtesy of The House of Commons; Sheldrake Press, courtesy of The House of Commons; The Design Archive, Arthur Sanderson & Sons Ltd; Watts & Co; E.T. Archive; Watts & Co; The Victoria & Albert Museum, London, and The Bridgeman Art Library; The Design Archive, Arthur Sanderson & Sons Ltd; Watts & Co; RD 125 Anaglypta Original. 192/193 - The Victoria & Albert Museum, London and The Bridgeman Art Library; by courtesy of the board of Trustees of The Victoria & Albert Museum; William Morris Gallery, London and The Bridgeman Art Library; Lenoble by Charles Hammond; Palmyra by Charles Hammond; Osborne and Little Botanica Collection; The Victoria & Albert Museum and The Bridgeman Art Library; Osborne and Little Botanica Collection. 194/195 - E.T. Archive; Victoria & Albert Museum, London and the Bridgeman Art Library. 196/197 - private collection, The Bridgeman Art Library; National Trust/L & M Gayton. 198/199 - GO. 200/201 - JM; Mary Evans Picture Library; KK; KK. 202/203 - Nigel Husband RIBA and Stephen Carpenter RIBA. 204/205 - JM; all the others courtesy of Bernard Thorp, (Paris, London), Custom Weaving and Printing. 206/207 - Nigel Husband RIBA and Stephen Carpenter RIBA. 208/209 - GO. 210/211 - Spike Powell/Elizabeth Whiting Agency; JM; KK. 212/213 - KK; Jon Bouchier/Elizabeth Whiting Agency. 214/215 - JM; JM. 216/217 - GO; PW; KK. 218/219 - Lucinda Lambton/Arcaid; KK. 220/221 - Michael Boys Syndication; GO. 222/223 - Lucinda Lambton/Arcaid; Smithsonian Institution (National Museum of History and Technology), Washington; The Design Council. 224/225 - JM; JM; Woodmansterne Picture Library. 226/227 - National Trust/J.Bethell. 228/229 - Michael Nicholson/Elizabeth Whiting Agency; Michael Boys Syndication; National Trust. 230/231 - National Trust; PW. 232/233 - Spike Powell/Elizabeth Whiting Agency; JM. 234/235 - Ianthe Ruthven; Automobile Association Photo Library; DM; KK. 236/237 - Ianthe Ruthven; Smallbone; PW; JM. 238/239 - Michael Nicholson/Elizabeth Whiting Agency; KK; GO; KK; Smallbone. 240/241 - Rodney Hyett/Elizabeth Whiting Agency; Sheldrake Press; PW; Tim Street-Porter/Elizabeth Whiting Agency. 242/243 - KK; Pipe Dreams. 244/245 - Rodney Hyett/Elizabeth Whiting Agency; Michael Boys Syndication; Michael Dunne/Elizabeth Whiting Agency; GO; B.C. Sanitan; Traditional Bathroom Warehouses, London. 246/247 - KK; PW; PW; Michael Boys Syndication; KK. 248/249 - Rodney Hyett/Elizabeth Whiting Agency; Michael Boys Syndication. 250/251 - Michael Nicholson/Elizabeth Whiting Agency; Peter Aaron/Esto; Traditional Bathroom Warehouses, London; Nigel Husband RIBA and Stephen Carpenter RIBA; KK. 252/253 - DM. 254/255 - Mary Evans Picture Library; DM. 256/257 - KK. 258/259 - Woodmansterne Picture Library; DM; PW. 260/261 - JM; Richard Bryant/Arcaid; Michael Boys Syndication; KK. 262/263 - DM; DM. 264/265 - JM. 266/267 - Nigel Husband RIBA and Stephen Carpenter RIBA. 268/269 - Jerry Harpur. 270/271 - Ray Joyce/Weldon Trannies; Lucinda Lambton/Arcaid; Photograph Courtesy of Fine Art Photographic Library. 272/273 - Neil Holmes; Neil Holmes; Jerry Harpur; KK. 274/275 - Paul Miles; The Garden Picture Library/G.Bouchet; Linda Burgess/Insight Picture Library; The Garden Picture Library/B.Carter. 276/277 - Jerry Harpur; George Wright; Andrew Lawson; Pamla Toler/Impact Photos. 278/279 - KK; Town & Country Conservatories. 280/281 - Linda Burgess/Insight Picture Library; George Wright; Ray Joyce/Weldon Trannies. 282/283 - Linda Burgess/Insight Picture Library; George Wright; Lucinda Lambton/Arcaid. 284/285 - George Wright; Jerry Harpur; Jerry Harpur; National Trust/P.Lacey; Linda Burgess/Insight Picture Library; Edifice/Lewis. 286/287 - George Wright; Eric Crichton Photos; Linda Burgess/Insight Picture Library; S.& O. Mathews Photography; Eric Crichton Photos; Linda Burgess/Insidght Picture Library; Linda Burgess/Insight Picture Library; Eric Crichton Photos; Linda Burgess/Insight Picture Library; Linda Burgess/Insight Picture Library. 290/307 - All artwork by Sime/Baillie Lane/Architecture Environment.

BIBLIOGRAPHY

William T. Comstock: *Victorian Domestic Architectural Plans and Details: 734 Scale Drawings of Doorways, Windows, Staircases, Moldings, Cornices, and Other Elements*, Dover Publications (New York & London) 1987.

Randolph Delehanty: *In the Victorian Style*, Chronicle Books (San Francisco) 1991.

Charles Eastlake: *Hints on Household Taste* (London) 1868.

Janet Foster: *The Queen Anne House: America's Victorian Vernacular*, Abrams (New York) 2006.

Katherine C. Grier: *Culture and Comfort: Parlor Making and Middle Class Identity*, Smithsonian Institution Press (Washington DC & London) 1997.

Henry Russell Hitchcock: *American Architectural Books*, Da Capo Press (New York) 1976.

John Claudius Loudon: *An Encyclopedia of Cottage, Farm, and Villa Architecture and Furniture* (London) 1833.

Virginia and Lee McAlester: *A Field Guide to American Houses*, Knopf (New York) 1984.

Hermann Muthesius: *Das Englische Haus* (Berlin) 1904.

Ellen M. Plante: Victorian Home: *The Grandeur and Comfort of the Victorian Era, in Households Past and Present*, Michael Friedman Publishing Group, Inc. (New York) 1995.

Vincent Scully: *Shingle Style and the Stick Style*, Yale University Press (New Haven) 1971.

Gail Caskey Winkler and Roger W. Moss: *Victorian Interior Decoration, American Interiors 1830-1900*, Henry Holt & Co. (New York) 1986.

INDEX

A C K N O W L E D G E M E N T S

The authors, contributors and editors have relied heavily on the help, goodwill and enthusiasm of a large number of people. We are enormously grateful to them all for their support. In particular we would like to thank:

Elizabeth Aslin, Joanna Banham, Mrs Chris Base, Sarah Bevan, Kit Boddington, Roger and Sandy Boulanger, John Brandon-Jones, Asa Briggs, Angela Burgin, Alexandra Carlier, Elaine Clifton, Julia Courtney, Bob Crayford, Kathryn Cureton, Penny David, Fenella Dick, Caroline Eardley, Brent Elliott, Ray Evans, Mrs David Fenwick, John Fidler, Fergus Fleming, Jennifer Freeman, Charlotte Gere, Barbara Gold, Christophe Gollut, Ian Gow, Ian Grant, John Griffiths, John Hardy, Hugh Harris, Vicky Hayworth, Ian Headley, Bridget Heal, Chris Hesford, Stephen Hoare, Gabrielle Hopkins, Jane Howell, Sinclair Johnston, Charyn Jones, Bernard Kaukas, Todd Longstaff-Gowan, Debbi Loth, Mr and Mrs A. Lyle, Francis Machin, Richard Man, David and Sue Milton, Barbara Morris, Mr and Mrs Trevor Nunn, Mimi O'Connell, Stanley Paine, Ruth Prentice, Paul Robinson, David Rodgers, Alistair Service, David Seaton, Liz Sheriff, Professor Jack Simmons, Keith Sugden, Nicole Swengley, Jasmine Taylor, Robert Thorne, Susanne Togna, Clive Wainwright, Mr and Mrs Bernard Weatherill, Sally Weatherill, Antony Wells-Cole, Robert and Josyane Young.

TYPES OF ENTRANCES & BOUNDARIES

RECESSED OPENING

FRAMED DOOR

SIMPLE CANOPY

BRACKETED CANOPY

CORBELLED DECORATIVE CANOPY

WOODEN CANOPY

WOODEN PORCH

GLAZED PORCH

COLUMNED PORCH

TRELLIS PORCH

CLASSICAL PORCH

'GOTHIC WOODEN PORCH

BAY WINDOW & PORCH

METALWORK VERANDAH PORCH

WOODEN PORCH (AMERICAN)

ARTS & CRAFTS PORCH